The Rise of
the Trading State

THE RISE OF THE TRADING STATE

Commerce and Conquest in the Modern World

RICHARD ROSECRANCE

Basic Books, Inc., Publishers   New York

Table 1, *Income Distribution of Developing Nations,* reprinted by permission of Yale University Press from Simon Kuznets, *Modern Economic Growth* (New Haven: Yale University Press, 1966).

Table 2, *Battle-inflicted Deaths,* reprinted by permission of J. David Singer from J. David Singer and Melvin Small, *The Wages of War* (New York: John Wiley & Sons, 1972).

Table 6, *Exports of Goods and Services,* reprinted by permission of the United Nations from *The United Nations Yearbook of National Accounts Statistics, 1980.* Copyright © 1980 by the United Nations.

Germany and United Kingdom Foreign Investment table reprinted by permission of Cambridge University Press from David Landes, "Technological Change and Development in Western Europe 1750–1914," vol. 6 of the *Cambridge Economic History of Europe* (Cambridge: Cambridge University Press, 1965).

Library of Congress Cataloging-in-Publication Data

Rosecrance, Richard N.
  The rise of the trading state.

  Bibliographic references: p. 240
  Includes index.
    1. Commerce—History—20th century. 2. World
politics—1945-   . 3. Munitions—Economic
aspects—History—20th century. I. Title.
HF1007.R549 1985   382'.09'04   85–47558
ISBN 0-465-07035-3

Civibus Orbis Terrarum

Jane, Jill, Gail, Rich, Tom, and Anne

CONTENTS

PART IV
FUTURE WORLDS

PREFACE

Nineteen eighty-four has passed. There is a breathing space in world politics. Some will see this as only an interlude between episodes of chaos and warfare that must occur in the future as they have before. This philosophy holds that another major conflict, perhaps a nuclear war, will occur. Despite such beliefs, the main thesis of this book is that a new "trading world" of international relations offers the possibility of escaping such a vicious cycle and finding new patterns of cooperation among nation-states. Indeed, it suggests that the benefit of trade and cooperation today greatly exceeds that of military competition and territorial aggrandizement. States, as Japan has shown, can do better through a strategy of economic development based on trade than they are likely to do through military intervention in the affairs of other nations.

This does not mean that nations will lay down their arms, beat swords into ploughshares, or abandon traditional arenas of military competition and rivalry. Nor should they precipitately do so: a tolerable balance in world military politics is necessary to permit a trading system to function. But what is interesting and different about the world of international relations since 1945 is that a peaceful trading strategy is enjoying much greater efficacy than ever before. Through mechanisms of industrial-technological development and international trade, nations can transform their positions in international politics, and they can do so while other states also benefit from the enhanced trade and growth that economic cooperation makes possible. International "openness," low tariffs, efficient means of transport, and abundant markets offer incentives to many nations that have only to find a niche in the structure of world commerce to win new rewards. The returns, as Japan, Korea, Taiwan, Hong Kong, the Association of Southeast Asian Nations (Singapore, Malaysia, Thailand, Philippines, Indonesia, and Brunei), Brazil, Mexico, China, India, and others have demonstrated, can be incredibly high. Small European nations, like Switzerland, Belgium, Holland, Austria, Denmark, Norway, and Sweden, have also grown dynamically as their foreign trade has risen as a fraction of the gross national product. The vigor of such growth resembles that of late medieval and early modern city-states which, like Venice, Genoa, the Dutch Republic, and the members of the Hanseatic League, were dependent on trade for food, raw materials, and markets and yet prospered in consequence of that dependence.

From the sixteenth to the mid-nineteenth century there were few states that gained their livelihood strictly through trade. Then Great Britain began a new experiment with an open trading system, a system fueled by industrialization and new and cheaper means of transport, which held the promise of peacefully trans-forming the position of one country after another. That experiment, despite its initial success, did not catch on, and it was not until the end of the Second World War that the world as a whole could seek to benefit from international trade, for only then did worldwide tariffs begin to decline and to stay down. Moreover, it was not until after 1945 that the threat of an all-out military conflict (including the use of nuclear and thermonuclear bombs) became catastrophic, and such wars as did occur took on a more limited character. The risks of trying to take new territory through military invasion mounted while the alternative of development through economic processes and trade heralded new rewards for a peaceful strategy. The shift toward an international trading world gained momentum and adherents while raising important questions about the traditional military and territorial orientation of Western and industrial states.

This shift, or partial shift (for the dominant orientation of the international system still remains military-political and territorial in character), has largely escaped notice in the study of international politics. Even though states have traded extensively with one another (with and without restrictions) since before the sixteenth century, the theory of international relations has largely proceeded as if trading was unimportant. Boundaries, territory, sovereignty, independence, and military power have remained the key concepts.

Preface

The notion of the state as a sovereign unit, dependent in the final analysis only on itself, has largely captured intellectual fashion. But today, no state can aspire to the degree of independence that such concepts have entailed. Even the United States and the USSR are dependent on other nations, and most of all on each other, for their continued existence. The theory of international exchange and trade gives a basis for mutual cooperation and mutual benefit, and it applies to the essence of what states do day by day. When noticed, trading is dismissed as "low politics," pejoratively contrasting it with the "high politics" of sovereignty, national interest, power, and military force. However, it is possible for relationships among states to be entirely transformed or even reversed by the low politics of trade. Through trade Japan has become the third industrial nation in the world, and it will soon become the second nation, surpassing Soviet Russia. It may in time exceed the United States of America.

Many have misunderstood the differences between Japan and America, believing that Japan is simply a youthful, smaller edition of the United States, a still not fully developed major power with political and economic interests that have yet to be defined on a world stage. Sooner or later, many feel, Japan too will become a world power with commensurate political and military interests. This is a misconception of the Japanese role in world affairs and a mistaken assimilation of a trading state to the military-political realm. Even if, at some distant future time, Japan increased her defense expenditure to 2 percent of gross national product, she would not follow the United States and Soviet strategy in international politics or try to become the world's leading naval or military power. As a trading state it would not be in her interest to dominate the world, control the sea lanes to the Persian Gulf, or guarantee military access to markets in Europe or the western hemisphere. She depends upon open trading and commercial routes to produce entry for her goods. It is not the American model that Japan will ultimately follow. Rather, it is the Japanese model that America may ultimately follow.

It is thus important to consider how states advance themselves and to bring the trading strategy into a regular and durable place in the theory of international politics. The work that follows is in four parts. An introductory section shows the presence of the two worlds in the contemporary international politics of the Yom Kippur War and the Oil Crisis of 1973 (chapter 1), explores their different characteristics (chapter 2), and observes how international theory has neglected such dualistic approaches (chapter 3). Part II discusses past worlds in two chapters. One highlights the preexisting fluidity of world and local relationships, a fluidity that hardened into the growing preponderance of the military-political and territorial world (chapter 4), and the second describes the triumph and defeat of that system between 1914 and 1945 (chapter 5). Part III records the conflicting deductions from the Second World War in the period after 1945. Chapter 6 explains the stimulus provided to the military-political world, chapter 7 to the trading world. Chapter 8 seeks to draw a contemporary trial balance between them. But present trends may not depict the future, and part IV grapples with the problem of future worlds, discussing both retrograde and positive tendencies. Chapter 9 considers the intensification of one or more features of the Westphalian system, chapter 10 the conditions and policies in countries least likely to join the trading system: the United States, the USSR, and the nationalist states of the Third World. Future worlds could be more beneficient, however, and chapter 11 outlines international and domestic states of affairs that might follow in a new, trading environment. The appendix depicts the two opposed worlds in game theoretic terms and can be omitted by the general reader.

I have benefited greatly from the critical ideas of others in the research for this work. In the early stages, Jeff Hughes and Sally Barbour were of great assistance; later Susan Brewer and Herman Schwartz lent me aid. Peter Katzenstein and Tom Ilgen read and commented on the book in at least two different drafts, and Roger Haydon, John Mueller, and Harold Jacobson helped enormously with the penultimate version. I drew some leading ideas from Alastair Buchan and Sam Huntington, though they have been reshaped beyond recognition. Isaac Kramnick, Walter Pintner, and Dan Baugh offered needed historical perspectives, while Donald Lamm and Alan Alexandroff argued persuasively with every point. I did not agree with the theses of Joe Grieco and Darryl Roberts, but I learned a great deal from both of them. Matt

Preface

Evangelista, Deone Terrio, and Ben Miller enriched my understanding of the Soviet Union, Matasaka Kosaka of Japan, and Chongwhi Kim, Sung-Joo Han, Wiwat Mungkandi, and Thanat Khoman of the emergent trading nations in the Far East. With discretion, competence, but increasing exasperation, Nancy Sokol produced three, Emma Gibson one, and Mary Schuler two versions of the manuscript. Steve Rock and Bill Kinsel considered the work in seminar and made useful suggestions. Martin Kessler showed me how the book might be made better. The Ford Foundation provided a year's leave at just the right time and the Rockefeller Foundation offered summer support at both Aspen and the Villa Serbelloni. The Society for the Humanities at Cornell provided needed facilities. Barbara Rosecrance took time from her professional responsibilities to help with numberless problems. My children, to whom the study is dedicated, endured my preoccupations with good humor and encouragement. My greatest debt is to Edward Whiting Fox, who read virtually every word I wrote in the past five years. His insights have been enormously significant in shaping the final work.

RICHARD ROSECRANCE
Ithaca, New York

PART I

INTRODUCTION

1

Crises: The Yom Kippur War (1973), the Oil Crisis (1973–80)

The Yom Kippur War, 1973

In the evening of October 24, 1973, the crisis brought on by the Egyptian and Syrian attack on Israel eighteen days earlier was coming to a head. Egyptian forces had crossed the Suez Canal and seized a part of Sinai. Syrian troops had broken over the Golan frontier and moved down toward the Jordan Valley. Israel, summoning all its resources and with an airlift of supplies from America, repulsed the Syrian offensive, and on October 16, drove a wedge between the Egyptian Second and Third Armies. Under Brigadier General Arik Sharon, Israeli units crossed the Canal and penetrated Egyptian lines, slowly cutting off supply routes for the encircled Third Army and for the Egyptian city of Suez. By 11:00 A.M. Washington time on October 23, the process was complete. Israel now had only to tighten the noose to strangle the large Egyptian force. "My God," erupted Secretary of State Kissinger, "the Russians will think I have double-crossed them. And in their shoes, who wouldn't?"[1]

The Soviet Union would not tolerate a final Egyptian defeat. Her Arab allies had proved their military abilities in the early successful days of fighting with Israel; they could not be allowed to be humiliated. Israel's reputation for invincibility should instead be tarnished. To save Egypt, however, meant Israel had to be forced to halt its operations. A cease-fire, to take effect at 1:00 A.M., October 24, had been agreed to by Egypt, Syria, and Israel, but that cease-fire, like others before it, did not hold. Tel Aviv claimed that Egypt was trying to break out of its encirclement, but in the course of repelling the Arab attack Israel managed to occupy the Egyptian naval base at Suez. Leonid Brezhnev, the Russian leader, had proposed a United States–Soviet guarantee of a settlement and imposition of withdrawal on Israel, but the United States would not agree to such a one-sided scheme. As the cease-fire broke down, Russia faced two stark possibilities. She could threaten Washington in order to make Secretary of State Kissinger and President Nixon put a rein on Israel, or threaten direct Soviet military intervention in Egypt.

As early as October 21 the Russians had alerted seven airborne divisions capable of intervening in the Middle East. East German forces had been placed at a higher stage of readiness. Soviet ships in the Mediterranean had been increased to eighty-five and a Soviet flotilla of twelve ships was moving toward Alexandria. Radioactivity was detected on a Soviet ship proceeding to Alexandria. It was assumed that there were nuclear warheads on board. Meanwhile, Egypt's President Anwar Sadat had been persuaded by the Russians that the United States might accept a joint military observer force to be sent to Cairo, and he had formally made such a proposal at the United Nations. Brezhnev then tried to force the issue. In an urgent message to Nixon at 9:35 P.M. on October 24, he proposed sending Soviet and American military contingents to Egypt to insure implementation of the cease-fire, and he continued: "I will say it straight that if you find it impossible to act jointly with us in this matter, we should be faced with the necessity urgently to consider the question of taking appropriate steps unilaterally.[2]"

Kissinger found the proposal "unthinkable." It would allow

Soviet troops into the Middle East, where they might remain for years; it would place the Arabs in thrall to Moscow, their "defender," and would terminate the new and budding American relationship with Sadat. Israel would receive a crushing setback. The Americans could not accept Soviet intervention, but how were they to prevent it? First they had to make sure Israel was not snuffing out the Egyptian Third Army. Next they had to convince the USSR that intervention was a risky course. For a brief time, the fate of international peace lay in the hands of two small allies of the superpowers: Israel and Egypt. If Sadat did not withdraw his proposal for the observer force or if Israel continued to squeeze the Third Army, Russia might send troops. America could not stand aside, and a major conflict loomed.

Kissinger called in Simcha Dinitz, the Israeli ambassador in Washington. Israel was told in no uncertain terms to stop its military operations, otherwise Tel Aviv risked American "dissociation" from the U.S.–Israeli relationship.[3] A message had already been sent from Nixon to Sadat emphasizing that while the United States would agree to American military attachés as ground observers of a cease-fire, it would not accept the Soviet proposal for American and Russian troops. This stand had been made clear as well at the United Nations in New York. If Israel complied, the next hurdle was to get Sadat to withdraw his proposal. Early in the morning of October 25, Sadat cabled Nixon that he was no longer insisting on a U.S.-Soviet force but rather on an international force composed of contingents from small nations. This would remove the sanction of either the host country or the United Nations for a Soviet airlift of troops to Egypt.

Even before the reply to Brezhnev's threat was dispatched to Moscow at 5:30 A.M., October 25, a special meeting of the United States' National Security Council (minus Nixon and the vice-President) had decided on a worldwide alert of United States forces, raising their readiness to Defense Condition III (DefCon 3), in military parlance the stage just prior to that in which an attack is believed imminent: B–52 bombers were returned from Guam; the aircraft carrier *Franklin Delano Roosevelt*, then off the Italian coast, was ordered to move swiftly toward Egypt; the 82nd Airborne Division was put on full alert for deployment abroad.

The reply to Brezhnev stressed that the United States would accept Soviet and American noncombatant personnel as part of a United Nations supervisory force but would "in no event accept unilateral action." The ball was now in Moscow's court.

First at the United Nations and then in a reply from Brezhnev, Russia indicated that she would not intervene. A small group of Soviet "representatives"—seventy in number—would be sent to Egypt to observe the cease-fire, but otherwise Moscow was prepared to accept a United Nations force composed of troops from small nations. Even then the danger was not entirely over—the Soviets were also on alert status and the Russian flotilla was approaching Egypt because the Third Army's fate still hung in the balance. It was not until Saturday, October 28, at 6:20 A.M. that Israel accepted a convoy to give food, water, and medical supplies to the Third Army, but only in return for an Egyptian agreement to direct Israeli-Egyptian talks. The Soviet force heading toward Egypt halted and dispersed.

The crisis of October 24–28, 1973, underlined the ever-present danger of war among nation-states, units that must always be concerned with the territorial and military balance existing between them. Since any large territorial gain by any one state will give it more power than the others, military expansion must be resisted. A power capable of winning hegemony can impose its will on other nations and perhaps even determine their domestic systems. In Western and world history attempts at hegemony—by Spain, France, and Germany—had been checked by countercoalitions or, in the extreme case, by war against the imperial aspirant. It was not surprising that the threat of war increased dramatically in the waning hours of October 24, 1973—territorial plums of the greatest weight were suspended over the parties, ready to fall on one side or the other.

Why have nations been so concerned with territory? First, and most importantly, because nations are themselves territorial organizations. Unchecked expansion by one state will impinge upon the territory controlled by others. Second, power, an objective of state policy, was historically defined in territorial terms. The state with the greatest land mass would have the largest population, the greatest stock of natural resources, and presumably as well the greatest wealth. These resources could be tapped by taxation, and the national monarchies who formulated these notions could organize the finances of their realm and use them to create military power. In the past, leaders, such as Charles V, Louis XIV, Frederick the Great, Napoleon, sought greater territory and larger domains for revenue and power. As long as waging war was relatively uncomplicated, one battle would take place after another. Great kings made war, for only war could gain empire and new territories.

In the age of mercantilism—an era in which power and wealth combined—statesmen and stateswomen (for who dares to slight Elizabeth I or Catherine the Great) sought not only territory but also a monopoly of markets of particular goods highly valued in Europe, gold, silver, spices, sugar, indigo, tobacco. Who controlled local production and sales also determined the market in Europe and obtained a monopoly return. Initially, Venice and Genoa vied for dominance of the spice trade from the twelfth to the fourteenth centuries, a struggle that was interrupted by Portuguese navigators, sailors, and soldiers who temporarily established control of the Indies at their source. Later Holland ousted Portugal in the East Indies, and England and France took her place in India. By the seventeenth century, Spain could no longer hold her position in the Caribbean and the New World as Holland, England, and France disputed her monopoly, first by capturing her bullion fleets, then by seizing sugar islands as well as parts of the North American mainland. In the eighteenth century Britain won victory practically everywhere, though Holland was left with the Dutch East Indies, France with her sugar islands in the Caribbean, and Spain with a reduced position in North and South America. As William Pitt the Elder pointed out, "commerce had been made to flourish by war"[4]—English monopolies of colonial produce won her great dividends in trade with the Continent. Her near monopoly of overseas empire and tropical products produced a great flow of continuing revenue that supported British military and naval exploits around the world. From either standpoint—territorial or economic—military force could be used to conquer territories or commodity-producing areas that would contribute greater revenue and power in Europe. With a monopoly on goods or territories, one nation or kingdom could forge ahead of others.

Thus we have one basic means by which nations have made their way in the world—by increasing their territories and maintaining them against other states. Sometimes, less cultured or civilized nations have by this means upset ruling empires or centers of civilization. In the past the barbarian invasions disrupted Rome; Attila the Hun and his followers intruded upon Mediterranean civilization; Genghis Khan and his military nomads ranged into Eastern Europe; Islam and the Turks dynamically transformed the culture of the Mediterranean and Southern Europe. In fact, it was not until the relatively recent period that highly developed economic centers could hold their own against military and agrarian peoples. The waging of war and the seizure of territory have been relatively easy tasks for most of Western history. It is not surprising that when territorial states began to take shape in the aftermath of the Reformation, they were organized for the purpose both of waging and of resisting war, and the seventeenth century became the most warlike of epochs. Kings and statesmen could most rapidly enhance their positions through territorial combat.

Associated with the drive for territory is an allied system of international relations which we will here call the "military-political or territorial" system. The more nations choose to conquer territory, the more dominant the allied system of international politics will be. Because territorial expansion has been the dominant mode of national policy since 1648 and the Peace of Westphalia, it is not surprising that the military-political and territorial system has been the prevailing system of international relations since then. In this system, war and the threat of war are the omnipresent features of interstate relationships, and states fear a decisive territorial setback or even extinction. This has not been an idle concern, if one considers that 95 percent of the state-units which existed in Europe in the year 1500 have now been obliterated, subdivided, or combined into other countries.

Whatever else a nation-state does, therefore, it must be concerned with the territorial balance in international politics and no small part of its energies will be absorbed by defense. But defense and territory are not the only concerns of states, nor is territorial expansion the only means by which nations hope to improve their fortunes. If war provides one means of national advancement, peace offers another.

The Oil Crisis, 1973–1980

Probably more important in the long-term than the battles of the fourth Arab-Israeli war was the oil crisis and embargo of 1973–74. While the war was being fought, the Organization of Petroleum Exporting Countries (OPEC) announced on October 16, 1973, its first unilateral increase of 70 percent, bringing the cost of a barrel of oil to $5.12. At the end of the year it had been raised to $11.65 (a further 128 percent increase), and by 1980 had risen to almost $40.00 a barrel, about twenty times the price in early 1970. In addition, the Arabs announced oil production cutbacks and on October 20, embargoed all oil exports to the United States and The Netherlands, the two countries closest to Israel.

These decisions stimulated different responses in America and abroad. Most European allies and Japan quickly made it clear that they sympathized with the Arab cause and distanced themselves from the United States. Nixon in response announced "Project Independence" on November 7, which committed the United States to free itself from the need to import oil by 1980. This difficult goal was to be accomplished by conservation and the development of alternative sources of energy. The objective was not achieved, of course, for the United States imported roughly the same 36 to 37 percent of its oil needs in 1980 as it had in 1973. No evolution would allow it to return to the nearly self-sufficient 8.1 percent level of 1947.

There were four ways in which the oil crisis might have been overcome. The first was through the traditional method used by the United States in the Middle East crises of 1956 and 1967. In response to an oil embargo, the United States could simply increase its domestic production of oil, allocating stockpiles to its allies. The

United States had had the leverage to do this in previous years because excess domestic capacity more than provided for national requirements, leaving a surplus to be exported abroad, if need arose. In 1956, the United States imported 11 percent of its oil but had a reserve domestic production capacity that could provide for an additional 25 percent of its needs. In 1967, while oil imports had risen to 19 percent of its oil consumption, the United States possessed a similar ability to expand its production by 25 percent, more than replacing imported oil. By 1973, however, the low price of oil and past domestic production had eroded United States reserves. It now imported 35 percent of its needs and could increase production only by an additional 10 percent.[5] When the Arabs embargoed oil shipments to the United States, there was no way for the country to increase domestic production to cover the shortfall. If a solution was to be found, it depended upon reallocating production abroad. As it turned out, the embargo caused no difficulty or shortage in America, because the oil companies simply re-routed production, sending Arab production to compliant European states and Japan, and non-Arab production to the United States and Holland. This measure solved the supply problem, but it did nothing to alleviate the high price. Extra United States production would not be sufficient to create a glut in the world marketplace and thus force a drop in the OPEC price.

A second method of coping with the crisis was to form a cartel of buyers of oil, principally the United States, Europe, and Japan, together with a few developing countries. If all could agree to buy oil at a fixed low price, OPEC would not be able to sell abroad on its terms and would have to reduce the price. Since it was the formation of the producers' cartel (OPEC) which had forced up the price of oil, many thought that only a consumers' cartel could offset its bargaining leverage and bring the price down. Despite American attempts to organize such a consumers' group in 1973 and 1974, the other nations preferred to play an independent role. France, Germany, and Japan negotiated separate oil contracts with individual Arab countries, guaranteeing access to Middle Eastern oil over the long term. They would not cooperate with the United States. When the American-sponsored International Energy Agency was finally set up in 1974, it became an information gathering agency which could allocate supplies of oil only in a crisis and had no monopoly bargaining power.

A third means of overcoming the oil crisis and reducing the real price of oil was through military intervention. This was considered at the end of 1974 and the beginning of 1975 when Secretary of State Kissinger hinted intervention if "actual strangulation of the West" was threatened. Some concluded that the Persian Gulf fields should be seized by United States marines or units of a Rapid Deployment Force. Occupation of such thinly populated areas was possible. The question, however, was whether production could be started up and maintained in the face of determined sabotage by Arab resistance groups, including the Palestine Liberation Organization. Would pipelines be cut or harbors mined? Would oil tankers have free passage through the Gulf? These uncertainties could not be resolved over the long period that would be required to break the Arab embargo and reduce the price of petroleum.

The final and ultimately successful means of overcoming the crisis came through diplomacy and the mechanism of the world market. After the success of the Israeli-Egyptian shuttle negotiations producing a withdrawal of forces on the Sinai front, the very beginning of talks on the Golan with Syria and Israel led the Arabs to end the oil embargo on March 18, 1974.[6] This had no impact on oil prices or supply and therefore did not change the OPEC bargaining position. That awaited complex developments in the world market for oil and for industrial products. In 1973–74, it was generally believed that the market for oil was inelastic, that demand would not decline greatly with an increase in the oil price. If it did not, the Arabs would gain an incredible premium, and a huge surplus of funds. It was estimated that as much as $600 billion might flow to Arab producers over a ten-year period. They would never be able to spend that much importing goods from the industrial and oil-consuming countries; hence, huge Arab surpluses would build up—funds that could have no economic use in the Arab states themselves. The flow of funds from importing countries to OPEC was partly offset when about half the surplus was used to buy Western imports and another large portion was invested in the world financial market, largely in the form of short-term deposits in Western banks. The banks and international financial agencies could then lend funds to the consuming countries, enabling them to finance their oil purchases. At the same time consumers became unwilling or unable to pay the high price. Even in the traditionally energy-extravagant United States, the amount of energy needed to produce one dollar of the gross national product declined 25 percent from 1973 to 1983. The average gas consumption of American-made automobiles almost doubled in the same period to reach 24.6 miles per gallon. Most of the leading industrial corporations instituted energy-conservation programs. The demand for oil dropped.

Between 1973 and 1979 industrial prices in the developed world increased more than oil prices. In the wake of the oil crisis and the ensuing inflation, many governments resorted to freely fluctuating exchange rates for their currencies. No longer under the discipline of gold flows, they could experiment with domestic economic expansion, convinced that their currency values would not get out of line or their trade balance deteriorate. The result was further inflation of wages, prices, and industrial products. This had two effects on the Arab oil countries. First, it meant that they had to pay a great deal more to buy industrial goods, using up the oil surplus that they were beginning to accumulate. Second, as inflation advanced in the West and Japan, industrial entrepreneurs hesitated to invest, uncertain of their long-run return. Western economies ground to a halt and unemployment mounted. For a decade after 1973, the industrialized world grew at only 2 percent per year, and the number of jobless workers doubled. As a result, Arab investments in the developed countries were threatened by declines in Western profits and wages. Too high oil prices temporarily forced the industrial world into economic stagnation in which it would buy little Middle Eastern oil. The oil price increase, with the exception of the sudden rise of 1979–80, halted and reversed. Even the Iran–Iraq war did not lead to a new jump in prices. Oil consumption of the advanced industrial countries fell by seven million barrels a day between 1979 and 1982. In addition new oil production outside of OPEC increased, and OPEC production declined by twelve million barrels a day. Oil came into surplus, and the price fell back to $28 per barrel by 1983. The oil countries, which also suffered from the worldwide inflation, found they did not have a sufficient export surplus to meet their needs in food and industrial imports. In 1982, eight Middle Eastern producers faced a deficit of $23 to $26 billion. Even Ayatollah Ruhollah Khomeini's Iran had to increase its oil production to finance imports and its war with Iraq.

The strange outcome was that the oil and energy crisis abated. The Arabs saw reason for increasing production while holding down the price, but the collapse in international demand for oil was so great, that the price could not be maintained. Consumers emerged in a much better position. The developing countries, which had borrowed to cover oil and industrial imports found high interest rates imperilling their financial solvency in the first half of the 1980s. Paradoxically, there was then too little Arab money and too small an oil surplus to cover their borrowing needs.

The oil crisis underscored another means of dealing with conflict among nation-states. Instead of defending or fighting over territorial claims, nations found a way to reach a compromise through an international flow of funds, domestic economic adjustments, and world trade. The imbalance in payments threatened by the huge Arab oil surpluses in 1973–74 was reversed by the first years of the 1980s. Despite Kissinger's threats, force was not used to assure Western access to oil, and overarching cooperation was the ruling principle between industrial and oil-producing regions of the world. Each benefited from the exchange, and consuming countries did not have to adopt policies of national self-sufficiency, reducing income and employment to the point where energy needs could be met on a national basis. Each side, instead, relied upon the other for the products it required.

Territorial gain is not the only means of advancing a nation's interest, and, in the nuclear age, wars of territorial expansion are not only dangerous, they are costly and threatening to both sides. Much more tenable is a policy of economic development and progress sustained by the medium of international trade. If national policies of economic growth depend upon an expanding world market, one country can hardly expect to rely primarily upon territorial aggression and aggrandizement. To attack one's best customers is to undermine the commercial faith and reciprocity in which exchange takes place. Thus, while the territorial and military-political means to national improvement causes inevitable conflict with other nations, the trading method is consistent with international cooperation. No other country's territory is attacked; the benefits that one nation gains from trade can also be realized by others.

If this is true, and two means of national advancement do indeed exist, why is it that Western and world history is mainly a narrative of territorial and military expansion, of unending war, to the detriment of the world's economic and trading system? Louis XIV and Napoleon would easily understand the present concern with territorial frontiers and the military balance, to the degree that one is hard put to explain what has changed in the past three hundred years.

The answer is that states have not until recently had to depend upon one another for the necessities of daily existence. In the past, trade was a tactical endeavor, a method used between wars, and one that could easily be sacrificed when military determinants so decreed. The great outpouring of trade between nations in the latter half of the nineteenth century did not prevent the First World War; it could be stanched as countries resorted to military means to acquire the territory or empire that would make them independent of others. No national leader would sacrifice territory to gain trade, unless the trade constituted a monopoly. Leaders aimed to have all needed resources in their own hands and did not wish to rely upon others.

As long as a state could get bigger and bigger, there was no incentive to regard trade with others as a strategic requirement, and for most of European history since the Renaissance, state-units appeared to be growing larger. The five hundred or so units in Europe in 1500 were consolidated into about twenty-five by the year 1900.[7] If this process continued, statesmen and peoples could look forward to the creation of a few huge states like those in Orwell's *1984* which together controlled the globe. The process of imperialism in the late nineteenth century forwarded this conception: ultimately a few empires would become so enormous that they would not have to depend upon anyone else. Thus, the failure of the imperialist drive and the rapid decolonization of recent years have meant a change of direction in world politics. Since 1900, and especially after 1945, the number of nation-states has greatly increased, even more swiftly than the number belonging to the United Nations organization. Between 170 and 180 states exist, and the number is growing. If contemporary nationalist and ethnic separatist movements succeed, some states in Europe, Africa, Asia, and Oceania may be further subdivided into new independent states or autonomous regions. These small and even weak states will scarcely be self-reliant; increasingly they will come to depend on others for economic and even military necessities, trading or sharing responsibilities with other nations. The age of the independent, self-sufficient state will be at an end. Among such states, the method of international development sustained by trade and exchange will begin to take precedence over the traditional method of territorial expansion and war.

This would not necessarily affect the policies of the greatest powers. Indeed, the trend in world politics since the 1920s and 1930s has been for the number of world powers to decline and their size to increase. The five European great powers before 1914, with Austria subtracted, yielded to seven (including the United States, Japan, and Italy) after World War I. It was only in World War II that the two superpowers, the United States and the USSR, emerged to dwarf their erstwhile competitors. In the 1920s and 1930s, both the United States and the Soviet Union remained isolated from general world politics; both believed that they could subsist on their own resources. Both came to understand, however, that the defeat of Hitler and Nazi Germany required a combined military effort of the greatest magnitude. Nonetheless, with the development of the atomic and thermonuclear bomb, the intercontinental missile, and large conventional defense capabilities, some military leaders of both countries have been led to believe that they could virtually stand on their own. No other power could defeat them. No doubt they have occasionally come to think that assisted by their allies they could stave off attack and perhaps even make territorial gains at the enemy superpower's expense. The territorial and military-political system thus retains supporters among the greatest powers, and there is no ineluctable tendency that will turn them into "trading states," partisans of the international commercial system.

Two Worlds of International Relations

Since 1945, the world has been poised between two fundamentally different modes of organizing international relations: a territorial system which hearkens back to the world of Louis XIV and which is presided over by the USSR and to some extent the United States, and an oceanic or trading system that is the legacy of British policy of the 1850s and which is today organized around the Atlantic and Pacific basins. The territorial system is composed of states that view power in terms of land mass: the more territory the more power. In theory such countries wish to acquire enough land to emancipate themselves from dependence on other nation-states, gaining the resources, raw materials, and markets to be self-sufficient and self-reliant. The oceanic or trading system, in contrast, is based on states which recognize that self-sufficiency is an illusion. Assuming trade is relatively free and open, they do not need to conquer new territory to develop their economies and to provide the essentials of a consumer existence. Japan and the European states, particularly West Germany, reside at the center of this system. Today West Germany and Japan use international trade to acquire the very raw materials and oil that they aimed to conquer by military force in the 1930s. They have prospered in peaceful consequence.

The United States takes an ambivalent stance in world politics. While it is not yet ready to abandon the territorial postulates of continental development, manifest destiny, and a century of largely internal exploitation of its resources and markets, since 1945, America has moved evermore into a system of world interdependence, accepting increased trade, investment, and economic specialization. It has, while not entirely rejecting past conceptions of Fortress America, participated more and more in the oceanic and trading system and has come to acknowledge the need to import energy, minerals, and advanced products from other societies. It has slowly moved toward greater reliance on its trading partners, on the oil countries, Western Europe, and Japan. In the end it is possible that the United States will increasingly shift toward the growing group of trading nations in the Atlantic and Pacific basins. China may do so as well. If the Soviet Union would modify its past territorial orientations and adopt reliable policies of exchange and trade with other nations, the prospects for peace in the last years of the twentieth century would be greatly enhanced.

The Balance Between Trade and Territory

No nation entirely neglects its territorial defense and stakes its livelihood solely on trade. Even the smallest and weakest states, the ones with the least chance of providing a defense on their own, still devote money to protection of their territory. Of the European countries only Iceland spends nothing on military defense and limits its efforts to protect itself to a coast guard. Nations at all times and places have had to decide to emphasize one method or the other. The first choice is expressed in regard to a single other state: should one's attitude and policy toward that state be governed by military-political (and territorial) or trading incentives? The second choice is toward the world at large: should one's overall policy toward other states be characterized by territorial or trading orientations? What balance should be drawn between them? The usual choice in Western and world history has been for the greatest states, the ones that could afford the risk of military expansion, to emphasize territory while others relied on exchange and trade and an association with larger states to provide for their needs. But smaller states were not only trading nations; from time to time thay had to fashion a balance of power against an aggressive great power. To do this they had to ally together to defend a military and territorial position. In the seventeenth century, Louis XIV of

France had no single powerful rival; only a coalition of lesser states could limit his expansive designs.

In fact, trading orientations were frequently chosen by states that no longer had the possibility of overturning the territorial balance. After 1713, Holland gave up her great power ambitions and concentrated upon trade in the Baltic region, as did Sweden and Denmark. The only instance of the greatest nation in world politics adopting a trading stance is that of mid–19th-century Great Britain, which from the 1840s to the 1870s elected to abjure territorial ambitions in Europe or outside and to concentrate upon the development of her industry and trade with other nations. The successors to her leadership, Germany, and later the United States, did not follow a trading course. And England herself, in the latter part of the nineteenth century returned to a position stressing territorial defense against the German naval threat.

One of the difficulties facing the trading system throughout history is its inability to gain universal adherence so long as important and powerful states are still primarily devoted to the territorial system. Unchecked gains by territorial nations would lead even the most conspicuous protagonists of trade to reconsider their position and, ultimately, to renew their territorial defenses. Thus the territorial system could always nibble away at the fringes of the trading system and sometimes overturn it entirely as it did during World War I.

Trade and the Balance of Power

The trading system's ability to endure depended in part on the operation of the balance of power—a means of restraining the great powers from seeking too large territorial gains. War or the threat of war was the traditional method of checking aggressors, and in the territorial system, war had to take place periodically to prevent the single greatest power from establishing a hegemonic system in which the leader might not only regulate the policies of lesser states but also determine their domestic forms of government.

The balance of power thus effected did not guarantee an uninterrupted success of peaceful economic growth and commercial exchange, for wars were occasionally required to maintain the balance. During peacetime, however, commerce was given its head, and nations turned to trade as a mode of national progress.

This system lasted so long as the waging of war was limited in its effects. In the eighteenth century war had a ritual character and, in contrast to the early seventeenth century, did not disrupt civilian life. Wars of maneuver and position were seldom decisive, and peace terms often restored the status quo that existed before the war. On the continent of Europe various coalitions were organized to restrain aggressive powers, and fighting was a tolerable, if not enjoyable, pursuit. In the nineteenth century the conquest of territory became easier with the development of new offensive capabilities, but with some exceptions, even losers in war did not emerge much worse off. Thus there was still a considerable incentive to engage in both offensive and defensive combat. One great power could seek to overturn and others to maintain a balance of power. This system lasted until the First World War, which proved that fighting no longer had a rational purpose. The consequences of trying to maintain a balance through war were as destructive as those of not opposing an aggressive power. The unlimited means of war were disproportionate to rational and limited ends.

As the balance of power system came to have largely destructive effects, the costs of fighting increased and the benefits declined. Many believed that the World War of 1914 to 1918 would be the last military conflict on a major scale. No longer would states be willing to risk great casualties for territorial purposes; no longer would states have to use force to stop an aggressor. From both standpoints the strategy of improving the national position through territorial gains in battle had seemed to reach a dead end.

If it had, the trading system might have dominated after 1918, and all the evils of the period from 1918 to 1945 avoided. But if the maintainers of the balance were not willing to fight— because fighting was too costly—aggressors seeking to expand at the expense of weak states would find no one in their way. Appeasement, a rational policy deduction from World War I, would thereby contribute to the causation of World War II. Thus it was not until after 1945 that large-scale territorial expansion began to evolve as too costly—too dangerous and too uncertain as a general strategy of national advancement. As that lesson gradually dawned, a trading strategy and the development of the international trading system could begin to substitute peacefully for the military-political and territorial system. When such a time arrived, one would have reached the "Japanese period" in world politics, a period in which nations thought not in terms of mastery of the three dimensions of height, width, and breadth of territory and space but of the fourth dimension: persistence over time. But which country would be most successful in peacefully competing for trade at the beginning of the twenty-first century?

Two Crises and Two Worlds of International Relations

The Yom Kippur War and the oil crisis, both in 1973, illustrate the different means that nations use to advance their interests in world politics. Where territory is disputed and nations continually fear an attack, the military-political world governs relations among states. In Arab-Israeli politics even the most marginal gains and losses of territory might be decisive. Accordingly war and counter-war have been the methods of survival and national gain. Trade plays virtually no role in Arab-Israeli relations; and it cannot do so until territorial and political issues have been settled. Waging war must be seen as a futile gesture before trading cooperation can possibly emerge between the parties. United States–Soviet relations have also failed to reach a plateau of stability. The United States has not finally accepted Soviet hegemony in Eastern Europe or in Afghanistan; the Russians have not stopped assisting guerrilla movements in Central America. In addition, Moscow does not wish to be excluded from the Middle East. In Africa and Asia superpower rivalries remain acute, and the issue is largely territorial. Who will control or influence which region of the world?

In regard to other countries, however, United States policy is largely determined by issues of exchange and trade. No longer does America think in terms of fighting Western nations or Japan. In defense and trade, there is mutual exchange and a sharing of responsibilities. For a time in 1973–74 it seemed as if the oil crisis could become a territorial crisis, with military force the final arbiter. But economic and trading means were found that reduced the pressure of higher oil prices and recycled the Arab surplus. Ultimately oil prices declined as the demand for oil decreased. Nor did Arab states seek to put maximum pressure on Western and industrial economies: they did not seek to throw the world into recession and cooperated in holding prices down and supplies up. Third World countries contracted great debts in the recycling process, and high interest rates complicated their problems of repayment. Even here, however, a combination of refinancing of loans and a rescheduling of payments together with a possible cap on interest charges offered hope for a purely economic and commercial solution of the problem. Military force certainly provided no answer.

2

The Worlds of International Relations: The Military-Political World, the Trading World

The choice between territorial and trading means to national advancement has always lain before states. Most often, however, nations have selected a point between extremes though nearer the territorial end. In the early years of the modern period in the sixteenth and seventeenth centuries, that point was close to the territorial and military pole; at mid-nineteenth century it briefly moved toward the trading pole. In World Wars I and II the military and territorial orientation was chosen once again. Only after 1945 did a group of trading nations emerge in world politics. Over time this group has grown and its success, at least in economic terms, has been greater than that of either the United States or the Soviet Union. Before we look at the hybrid forms that have been attempted, it may be desirable to sketch the polar or pure types: the military-political and the trading worlds.

The Worlds of International Relations

The Military-Political World

In a military-political world nations are ranged in terms of power and territory from the greatest to the weakest. States in such a world are homogeneous in form; that is, they do not have differentiated objectives or perform a variety of functions.[1] They all seek the same territorial objectives and each, at least among the major powers, strives to be the leading power in the system. None of the contenders wishes to depend upon any other for any vital function, from the provision of defense to economic resources. Such a world might be stable in the sense of avoiding war if one single state achieved hegemony over the others.

If one power attained total mastery, the other members of the system would finally cease resisting because no advantage could be gained. Instead, they could compete for favors from the hegemonic overlord, who would reward them from his seemingly inexhaustible political and military surplus.[2] Recognizing that opposition served no purpose, the members would return allegiance and support. Historically, only the Roman Empire attained such mastery in the Western tradition: Charlemagne, Louis XIV, Napoleon, and Hitler never achieved it. Since the decline of the Roman Empire in the third to the fifth century A.D., contending feudal or state units have been the order of the day, and anarchy has been the principle of interstate relations.

The military-political world involves a continual recourse to war because the units within it compete for primacy. None is content to accept the hegemony of one of their number if it can be prevented; each is afraid that the dominance of one power will undermine its domestic autonomy and perhaps its very existence. Hence the balance of power becomes a means of resistance to threatened hegemony. The means of constructing a balance ultimately involves a resort to force to discipline an ambitious pretender. Warfare may be stabilizing if it succeeds in restraining challenge, but it cannot be acceptable if the destruction it causes more than outweighs the evil it seeks to prevent. In addition, since every state in a political-military order seeks to be self-sufficient, each strives to grow larger in order to achieve full independence. This drive itself is a cause of war.

The Trading World

In contrast, the trading world is not composed of states ranked in order of their power and territory, all seeking preponderance. Instead, it is composed of nations differentiated in terms of function. Each may seek to improve its position, but because nations supply different services and products, in defense as well as economics, they come to depend upon each other.[3] While some will be stronger than others, their functions give them a kind of equality of status. They may specialize in terms of particular defense functions: conventional or nuclear forces. They may offer raw materials or primary products to the international trading system as opposed to manufactured goods. Within the category of manufacturers, there may be intra-industry specialization in terms of technology. Certain industrial countries may concentrate, like Switzerland and Italy, on producing goods of very high quality and craftsmanship. Others, like Korea or Taiwan, may produce shoes, watches, textiles, steel, or ships on an efficient low-cost basis. Trading states will also normally form alliances as a precaution against sudden intrusion by military-political nations.

While trading states try to improve their position and their own domestic allocation of resources, they do so within a context of accepted interdependence. They recognize that the attempt to provide every service and fulfill every function of statehood on an independent and autonomous basis is extremely inefficient, and they prefer a situation which provides for specialization and division of labor among nations. One nation's attempt to improve its own access to products and resources, therefore, does not conflict with another state's attempt to do the same. The incentive to wage war is absent in such a system for war disrupts trade and the interdependence on which trade is based. Trading states recognize that they can do better through internal economic development sustained by a worldwide market for their goods and services than by trying to conquer and assimilate large tracts of land.

In general terms, the competition for power emerges in social relations wherever needs are provided for independently and without reciprocity and where resources are limited. If needs do not have to be met independently, a reciprocal division of labor may give rise to stable cooperation. If resources are in unlimited supply, self-sufficient persons or nations may gain all they need without encroaching on the wants of others. Hence in a bountiful state of nature, primitive people could have an idyllic existence free from competition and conflict. Alternatively, in a social order characterized by a degree of scarcity, conflict could still be limited by interdependence, exchange, and sharing. But where scarcity and the urge to full independence exist, government and law are needed to restrain a competition over power leading to social conflict.

In international society where government does not exist, nations will have power conflicts unless they can work out a system of interdependence to satisfy their needs. Only the reciprocal exchange and division of labor represented by the trading world can prevent conflict in such an anarchic environment. Industrial and population growth strengthen interdependence and make it harder to achieve national objectives autonomously. When technology was rudimentary and population sparse, states had little contact with one another and did not generally get in each other's way. With the commercial and industrial revolutions, however, they were brought into closer proximity. As the Industrial Revolution demanded energy resources—great quantities of food, coal, iron, water power, and petroleum—the number of states which could be fully independent declined. Those which sought complete autonomy and even autarky had to conquer the lands which contained the materials they needed. The military-political and territorial system, then, required more war. Only a shift in direction toward an interdependent trading system, giving up autonomy in return for greater access to world resources and markets, could produce greater cooperation among nations.

The trading system does not require large, self-sufficient units. As the national objective is exchange and trade with other states, trading countries do not need large territories and populations. Like Singapore and Hong Kong, they may be small countries, little more than cities, which manufacture the raw materials of other nations into finished commodities, gaining a high return in foreign trade.

Military technology also influences the trend toward one system or the other. One theory of historical development charts an increase in the size of the state as developments in military technology make smaller predecessors vulnerable to attack. Thus the medieval castle became vulnerable to gunpowder loaded in the siege gun. Large territorial states achieved a hard-shell character for a time, but even they become permeable when economic blockade, airpower, and the intercontinental missile allowed one country to strike at the very heart of another's population.[4] Now the largest territorial state is no longer immune to attack and depends upon its opponent's decisions. Such trends make the goals of the military-political and territorial system harder and harder to achieve.

Shifts in domestic cohesion also affect the choice between trading and military-political worlds. The ramshackle feudal monarchies were hardly integrated enough to fight purposeful and continuous war against each other. They did not enjoy the loyalty of their citizens and were hard pressed to find the finances for military campaigns. As greater resources were tapped by the new administrative systems of the centralizing monarchies emerging from the Reformation, the conquest of adjacent territories became easier. Sixteenth-century Spain and eighteenth-century England proved that states with relatively efficient administrative structures could create large navies and conquer empires. The French Revolution and the Napoleonic reforms lent even greater authority to the revolutionary leader or his imperial successor. With greater discipline existing in citizen armies, soldiers fighting for their country would be more effective than the hired mercenaries of eighteenth-century monarchies. New vistas of territorial expansion beckoned. Finally, in the late nineteenth and first half of the twentieth centuries, further increases in nationalism and support for the policies of the government produced the final gusher of massive violence in World Wars I and II. The greater the obedience of an unquestioning citizenry, the more acceptable were the demands of the military-political and territorial world.

Conversely, the trading system depended on setting free the productive and trading energies of peoples and merchants who, without guidance and direction from the administrative capital of the state, would find markets for their goods overseas.[5] Governments had to loosen control of their populace in order to generate the opportunities required to establish the trading system. They had to revoke mercantilist requirements and controls, abolish monopolies and chartered companies to enlist the efforts of capitalists and bring forth the necessary investment to finance productive enterprise. In certain cases trading cities with a wide range of independence grew up inside territorial states. They served the economic and financial interests of merchants and investors in other countries as well as their own. The nineteenth-century age of laissez faire in which government moved out of domestic economic activity fostered their aims better than the old official sponsorship and control. By liberating groups engaged in commerce on the high seas, governments in fact created classes of persons who were not exclusively loyal to the national state but catered to a wider constituency. In the American Civil War, New York merchants and financiers were close to the trading cities of the Confederacy and were initially tempted to secede as well.[6] In the late nineteenth century, Hamburg traders were closer to their English markets and suppliers than they were to the administrative and imperial center in Berlin. The development of such trading relations stimulated the revival of connections like those uniting the trading city-states of the Renaissance. Free from imperial supervision and control these early-modern city-states banded together, as in the Hanseatic League, to further mutual relations, protection, and trade, enforcing contracts between them. In the nineteenth century although no such formal organization was established, the connections of centers of commerce were much the same. They transcended exclusive loyalties to a single political jurisdiction.

To sum up: military-political and territorial states are homogeneous competing countries. Each seeks to secure hegemony or at a minimum to gain independence and self-sufficiency from foreign control. They do not generally cooperate except when the balance of power requires opposition to a hegemonic aspirant. In the territorial system in the past, wars were continually fought to safeguard independence and prevent preponderance by any single power. Trading states, in contrast, are interdependent nations which accept equality of status on the basis of differentiation of function. Their objectives—to improve national welfare and the allocation of resources through internal development and trade— do not require preventing other states from achieving similar goals. As long as states were generally out of contact with one another and the waging of war was relatively easy, the military-political and territorial world would predominate over the trading world. When interdependence grew with large populations, industrialization, and need for resources, the military-political world faced greater difficulties. Rulers in that tradition sought to compensate by drawing more support from their people for imperial policies and war, but this solution only went so far.

Hybrid Possibilities

Despite the contradictory requirements of military-political and trading systems, states have sometimes tried to live in both worlds. The great hegemonic pretenders—Philip II of Spain, Louis XIV, the Sun King of France; and Napoleon—aimed to govern Europe. Spain used her monopoly on the gold and silver production of the mines in Mexico and Peru to build unexampled military strength in the sixteenth century. Spain's objective was to conquer new lands in Italy, Portugal, the Low Countries, France, and England, reducing the rest of Europe to subjection. But the effort involved in campaigns of such magnitude ruined her economy. Even Spain's conquest of gold had a double-edged effect. The great imports of bullion inflated Spanish domestic prices and made her goods less attractive in world markets. By 1640, the Spanish challenge had been defeated and she neared the brink of internal collapse.

In the late seventeenth century, Louis XIV wanted to dominate the states of Europe, overseas trade, and also found an empire. But his offensive policy was costlier than the Dutch fortifications which resisted it. His naval forces were no match for England or Holland, and on land his armies were checked by Austria, the German states, Holland, and England. Jean Baptiste Colbert, Louis's great finance minister, had tried to fashion a French alternative to Amsterdam's control of world trade, but he failed miserably. French culture permeated continental Europe, but the French King's territorial expansion was defeated at home and abroad.

A century later, Napoleon conquered a great deal more territory in Europe than his royal predecessors, hoping after 1805 that by concentrating upon one objective he could establish a lasting empire. Recognizing that he could not compete with British trade in the Atlantic and Pacific, he gave up colonies overseas. Instead, through the Continental System, he sought to exclude British goods and develop a self-sufficient commerce within Europe itself. The Continent ultimately rebelled against this system; and Britain was able to sell as well as to buy from Europe. Russian and German armies defeated Napoleon at Leipzig (1813) and finally with English help at Waterloo (1815).

Thus none of the historic hegemonic pretenders actually achieved his goal. Only Great Britain came close to establishing a lesser version of such a system, but she did so by avoiding commitments in Europe itself.[7] In the mid-eighteenth century she gave economic help to Prussia but otherwise abjured a role on the Continent. Against Napoleon she contributed small forces which alone never would have turned the French tide. Her success is gaining an empire overseas was partly due to her avoidance of a military role in Europe. But Britain never established hegemony over other European states, the only powers who could be real military rivals. Instead, she kept out of their way. Thus, the attempt to maximize both trading and military-political possibilities has failed throughout history, and, since Rome, hegemony has never been won by any state.

The Choice Between Military-Political and Trading Worlds

If states cannot realistically expect to succeed at both ends of the spectrum, to be both fully developed military-political and trading countries, it is nevertheless possible to combine traits from the two systems in different ways. No nation entirely dispenses with police or military authority. Each has armed officials who can arrest evil-doers, whether they are domestic or foreign. Equally, even the most territorially oriented governments of all time, those of Nazi Germany and interwar Japan, engaged in international trade. Germany needed food, iron ore, and petroleum; Japan a variety of materials, including rubber, tin, iron ore, and oil. German and Japanese manufactures were sent abroad to pay for these goods so that the two countries could build a stockpile for war. If most states were to rely exclusively on trading methods, the few that specialized in military and territorial expansion would make great gains at the formers' expense. If most nations were to have no defense, the cost of war for others would be low and the incentive to engage in it high. Thus every state procures some defense and participates in some trade.

The difference between states is that some rely primarily on military force and only incidentally engage in trade; others make their livelihood in trade and use defense only against the most remote contingencies. For the first, trade is an economic palliative between the territorial wars that truly determine a nation's fate; for the second, trade and internal development are primary and defense a tactical measure to reduce another state's temptation to strike. Each country has to determine where it will place its emphasis in policy terms, which method it will primarily seek to use.

There is a third possibility: that nations will rely on internal economic development without resorting to trade *or* to military force. They could then remain isolated and nonparticipants in broader international politics. With the growth of interdependence among states, this alternative ultimately reduces to one of the two other choices. Once an industrial machine has been built, to what use will it be put? At the end of the nineteenth century, Imperial Germany began to rearm for the coming conflict to decide the final distribution of colonies and resources in world politics. Taking a different course, mid-Victorian England used her industrial prowess to further her trade and sought neither empire nor territory on the Continent.

In the twentieth century most developed nations have industrial capacities that are too large to be sustained entirely by the home market. Unless they can sell overseas—to other industrial countries and to states with a less developed manufacturing plant— they cannot expect to maintain employment and growth. The excess capacity must be disposed of in some way—either through arms production or through sales of manufactured goods to other nations. When they make such a choice, they elect one of the two major competing worlds.

What decides the choice they will make? What balance will the future generations choose between trading and territorial worlds? That depends upon the cost and benefit of waging war on the one hand and engaging in trade on the other. The greater the restraints on trade and the fewer its likely benefits, the more willing nations have been to seek to improve their position through military force. The higher the cost of war and the more uncertain its benefits, the more nations have sought trade as a livelihood.

THE RISE OF INTERDEPENDENCE

The first point to bear in mind in assessing the respective costs and benefits of war and trade is that international interdependence is growing. Modern technology, transportation, communication, and international sources of energy bring nations into greater contact. They cannot avoid interaction and are required to deal with one another. This could be a force for either peace or war: as an irritant, it could stimulate the desire to escape from foreign influences; as a basic fact, it could overcome naïve or reckless responses to growing association with the outside world. As nations increasingly depend on products, funds, and even security contributed by other states, it becomes harder to solve national problems by military means. Unless they can conquer several large and well-endowed continents, most nations cannot emancipate themselves from external restraints. Further increases in interdependence will probably have the effect of raising the costs of war and diminishing the barriers to trade.

The cost and benefit of using force is related to two additional factors: how easy it is to conquer territory and to govern it once it has been taken. The ease of conquest involves not only the ability to seize or destroy an opponent's land or troops but also the damage that occurs to one's homeland in the process. There is little profit in winning lands abroad if the home country is devastated as a result. Thus military technology must make possible successful attacks that leave both the aggressor and the defender relatively intact. If the newly acquired lands are permanently destroyed or rendered a radioactive wasteland, they contribute little or nothing. Moreover, the aggressor must be able to organize and govern the new territories, possibly against the will of the inhabitants. Each of these requirements is complicated and difficult to meet.

Military technology is a volatile factor which has varied greatly from epoch to epoch. Broadly speaking, technology has greatly increased the ability to destroy real estate at a distance, but it has not necessarily offered protection of real property at home. A "Star Wars" defense against intercontinental missiles might theoretically do this, but it would be so costly that it could be frustrated by less expensive improvements in an opponent's offensive force. An aggressor considering an attack could not hope to emerge unscathed. In purely conventional war—on the armored battlefield, for example—technology tends to make destruction of fighting units easier and cheaper. An aggressor then might fail to make much headway against a well-prepared and alerted defense. Destruction of an aggressor's second echelon forces could open up terrain for the counterattack. If destruction rates for tanks and aircraft are very high, the edge will either go to the side with the greatest stockpiles or to the side with cheaper or more elusive means of destruction. But gaining ascendancy in battle is only one part of the problem: it will still be necessary to ensure that the territory gained is worth the price paid in acquiring and governing it. An additional deterrent is the possible destruction of home territory.

In 1940, the strategy of the blitzkrieg, or "lightning war," allowed Germany to cut through the French lines at an unexpected place in the Ardennes and then to surround the forces engaged to the West and in Belgium. Israel used such techniques in 1967 and attempted them at the close of the 1973 war with Egypt and Syria. In Central Europe, terrain and population would make such attacks much more difficult, and Soviet tanks would be vulnerable to "precision guided munitions" ("smart" bombs) in the hands of the defenders.[8] Nor could the Soviets be sure that there would be no use of nuclear weapons in defense or retaliation. In open terrain, conventional war can usually be risked only where the other side does not have and cannot obtain air superiority. Otherwise gains on the ground would be canceled by air attacks on offensive formations.[9]

The uncertainty of results in war is not the only reason for a rise in the costs of using force since, say, the 1870s. The expense of engaging in a conventional arms race (not to mention a major nuclear arms race) is another. Procurement costs are rising at about 3 to 5 percent per year *above* the rate of inflation.[10] The countries which commit themselves to conventional wars or arms races, thus, usually pledge themselves to spending an increasing fraction of their national product on arms. They certainly do so if they seek to maintain a fixed margin of superiority over an opponent. Only the largest powers or states can afford this expense over a long period, and even the superpowers cannot do so if it means that they will ultimately be economically outpaced by other states.

The disincentives to engaging in war—it is likely to be expensive, destructive, and perhaps ultimately futile—do not prevent wars from taking place, however. Various incentives exist which, from the standpoint of particular regimes, may still make war worthwhile. First, ideological conflicts, like those between the Arabs and Israel, Communist and noncommunist nations, India and Pakistan, may still produce wars between protagonists even though the cost is high and benefit low. Unstable nationalistic regimes have sometimes resorted to war to create a greater social cement among their own peoples. Differences in internal political forms have contributed to the division between nations.

Even after a state has supposedly won a war, it must consider its relations with other states and the defeated people: it must face the "dilemma of the victor's inheritance." Will a Pyrrhic victory so weaken an aggressor that it falls victim to one of the powers on the sidelines? All through the war and at its end, the attacker must be able to deter the powers that have not yet committed themselves. (In 1854–56 Russia lost the Crimean War, in part because she did not dare to remove forces from the frontier with Austria.) Deterring Russia from nuclear attack on China in the late 1980s is the thought that she could not be certain of eliminating all Chinese retaliatory capabilities and of avoiding all danger of weakening herself vis à vis the United States.

Even presuming that the target of invasion remains intact and that the homeland of the aggressor is spared, the attacker must still consider the problem of ruling the new territory. Eighteenth-century military technology made it difficult to conquer territory in Europe. Once won, however, new territories could easily be amalgamated with old ones. Nationalism had not yet arisen to make foreign rule impracticable. In the nineteenth and twentieth centuries it was relatively easier to take new land (except in the First World War) but more difficult to rule it once acquired. Such rule succeeds only where repressive or totalitarian domestic systems are forced upon the conquered peoples. Even unremitting authoritarianism may not last in the long term against resurgent nationalism—the problem that the Soviet Union confronts in Eastern Europe and Afghanistan.

Mobilized, urban, and literate populations participate in politics in a way that rural, semiliterate peasants do not. In Afghanistan, however, even peasants and rural dwellers have been mobilized to defend themselves against the ideological and military invader. Imperialism and indirect rule were successful strategies for European imperialists in Africa and the Far East in the nineteenth century, but they have been much less useful in dealing with mobilized populations since the end of colonialism in the 1950s and 1960s. The issue, of course, is not merely whether a metropolitan power can remain in alien colonial territory, given opposition from the local population. It is whether that territory can be organized in such a way as to add to the power base of the metropole. Great Britain defeated the Boers in Southern Africa but had shortly to concede independence to them. The Soviet Union may be able to persist in Afghanistan, but that riven and embittered country will never add to Soviet power; it will only detract from it. Where there are ethnic differences, within and between states, an outside party faces an intractable problem in trying to reshape national orientations or direct the use of resources.

These considerations should be set against the Soviet successes in Eastern Europe since 1944 and the Nazi administration of much of Europe during World War II. Historically and traditionally, Eastern European populations have been hostile to Russia. Only in Bulgaria is there a population that might support friendly ties to Russia on the basis of free elections. In Poland, Czechoslovakia, Hungary, Rumania, and Yugoslavia, indigenous political tendencies have been generally anti-Russian and anti-Soviet in character. Thus, the control of anti-Soviet sentiment in Eastern Europe since World War II represents the considerable success of Soviet propaganda and military occupation. Furthermore, until very recently, Moscow has been able to use the satellite countries as a base for its power, extracting food, raw materials, and hard currency from them over the past forty years. With some of the Eastern European countries in debt and the Soviet Union as their major guarantor, however, it appears that the USSR is now a major contributor to (rather than a beneficiary of) the economy of the Soviet bloc. In the mid-1980s a dependent Poland was not an addition to Soviet power and in wartime it would be a substantial liability.

Nazi Germany's rule of the occupied territories during World War II also showed ambivalent and contrasting facets. On the one hand, Germany's captured territories furnished over three million laborers to German factories and mines.[11] Taxes were collected in a normal manner in occupied Europe, and the Germans forced Frenchmen to pay them at the rate of the last independent French war budget in 1940. Except in Yugoslavia, the Resistance was small and largely ineffective. Industries continued to function, food was grown, and sabotage irregular. But the Nazis had one particular factor in their favor, the hatred of Bolshevism on the part of the European Right. Collaboration was facilitated by some common ideological dispositions.

In the same manner the Soviet Union might hope that communist movements in several European countries would support their rule of Western and Central Europe should they decide to move West. But much more than the Nazis, they would face domestic movements of opposition, for even Euro-communism is largely national and not pro-Soviet in orientation. It is therefore unclear how much support an aggressor could count on from the local population.

The Soviet Union moved into Eastern Europe in 1944 when ideological views of many colorations had been discredited and people were yearning for peace. The USSR benefited from the great disorganization wrought by the war and Nazi misrule. In contrast if Russia tried to occupy West Germany in the next twenty years she would face a much greater pan-German nationalism than had existed after the war. Successful Soviet aggression in Central Europe would bring about the unification of the two German states. A new communist country of eighty million people endowed with German technical and economic efficiency would not be easy to govern from a somewhat backward capital like Moscow. Even if it could be maintained in the Communist fold, a united Germany would become a premier Communist state, rivaling the Soviet Union itself. It would therefore perhaps be better for Russia to remain content with the refractory empire it already controls and not to seek new administrative responsibilities that it could not fully discharge. For it is important to recognize that up to now Moscow has had little difficulty ruling present-day East Germany, an artificial creation which has no legitimacy and would not exist but for Russian armies on the border with the West. A united Germany, in contrast, would represent a historical and legitimate nation-state with particular national interests. This consideration must raise grave uncertainties to the planners in Moscow.

It would be premature to conclude that aggression is no longer possible in Europe because of problems of governance that an invasion would present. Highly developed economies are much more dependent upon social cooperation and obedience to the rulers of the state than are primitive or transitional economic systems. Armed resistance in Yugoslavia in 1943–44 and in Afghanistan in the 1980s did not disrupt the delicate mechanism of a well-established industrial division of labor because it did not exist in either case. The livelihood of the population was not greatly disturbed by the Resistance in a way that it would be in northern Europe, if guerrilla war were to be fought against Soviet invaders. Thus the rise of mobilized populations, the spread of guerrilla insurgency, and the growing consciousness of ethnic nationalism would make future conquest more difficult than it was in the nineteenth century or even in World War II. This would, however, not necessarily rule it out.

The conditions of the balance of power also affect the willingness of states to wage war and the benefit which they expect to derive. Cabinet wars of maneuver and position were the accepted practice in the eighteenth century, and there was little disadvantage in waging them. While rulers might be bankrupted, their citizens were not usually worse off and the destructiveness of such wars (except perhaps in Prussia) was tolerable by ruler and ruled alike. But the balance of power system collapsed after World War I. Costs could no longer be kept low enough so that states would be prepared to wage war rather than submit to an aggressor power. The antecedent system rested on the presumption that equilibrium was more important than peace, disequilibrium more noxious than the most disastrous war.

After 1918, there were two completely opposite possible conclusions: that war could not occur again and that no one, even the most aggressive state, would dare to risk it; or that most states would not risk war to ensure a balance, but the ones which did could make signal gains. Thus the partisans of peace became more numerous at precisely the time that the partisans of challenge also grew stronger. The result was the appeasement which led directly to 1939 and to the Second World War. If war is to be avoided, its cost must be high and outcome sufficiently uncertain to deter aggressors, but it must not be so high as to prevent others from even considering the need to stop an expansive power. Deterrence only works if the incentive to respond is greater than the incentive to initiate. In Europe today it is not fully certain that this condition is met.[12]

A further factor which influences the choice of war is its impact upon social cohesion at home. If war does not cost too much, benefits can conceivably be gained in greater social support, which in turn might further reduce costs. As war became more total—both in destructiveness and in impact on populations—it could not be carried on unless rulers had strong support at home. It is perhaps not surprising that as the military-political world reached its height in the 1930s, internal political systems became their most solidaristic and repressive. Fascism and National Socialism (and to some degree Russian Stalinism) were means of gearing up the population for war. But the equation worked the other way as well. If war increased social support at home then regimes under fire might use military expansion and adherence to the military-political world as a means of solving their domestic problems. Opponents could not carry on their campaigns against the government in a context of nationalistic war preparations.

But in the twentieth century some wars have led to greater domestic opposition and discontent. The greater the sacrifices involved in war, the harder it is to get populations to make them or to serve in the army. If war reduced social support, this would be a considerable disincentive to waging it and to the choice of a military-political system.

Thus the costs of war increase with its destructiveness, social impact, and financial exactions. The benefits of war decline if the coveted territory is either destroyed or cannot be organized to produce revenue and resources for the aggressor nation. Benefits may still be sufficiently high to produce war, however, if ideological differences between states or peoples are of overriding importance. The benefits of peace must surely be seen by all Lebanese factions, but that does not necessarily lead them to compromise or to avoid military strife. The Arab-Israeli dispute should have been settled long ago, but the ideological differences between camps have provoked war after war. It is not yet clear that the costs of the military-political system outweigh its benefits for individual nation-states.

The Cost and Benefit of Trade

If every factor favoring the military-political and territorial system is itself an augury against the trading system, the reverse is also true. The greater the attractiveness of the trading system, the less likely the military-political world is to be chosen by nations. Trade cannot operate in face of heavy restrictions. Tariffs, exchange controls, quotas, restraints (voluntary or involuntary), and competitive devaluation of currencies are instruments which limit the amount of trade among nations. In a network of such restraints, key nations will find they do not have sufficient access to the raw materials and markets that they need and will likely abjure the trading system in favor of the territorial alternative. Economic conditions will also influence the choice in that prosperity is a much greater inducement to trade than recession or depression. Typically nations remove restraints on trade and investment when economic conditions are favorable and reinstitute them when depression dampens economic activity and leaders come to feel that they must have guaranteed access to markets in their own countries. Tariffs and restrictions are then raised to keep the goods of other countries out. The net result is further to reduce world trade and world production, making everyone worse off. In the 1880s and again in the 1930s, the world opted for restraints on trade and accentuated the depression then in progress.

A trading system may also exact a certain social or governmental cost. Since opening one's trading and financial centers to foreigners gives them an access and a role in the economic outcome in one's own country, it is not a step lightly taken. The home population may find that income and employment are partly determined by international economic forces over which they have no control. The operations of the multinational corporation and movements of funds from country to country are thus in one sense a derogation from democracy, for democratic electorates no longer have the means of controlling their own fates.[13] At the same time, they are scarcely consistent with extremely repressive regimes which refuse to allow their policies to be affected by external influences.

In one sense the trading world works best when there is a "mediative state," a state which is the intermediary between internal and international pressures—reshaping international forces to make them more hospitable to domestic needs, but at the same time building understanding at home for the intransigent international factors which cannot be altered. Such governments would bargain and balance between their own populations on the one hand and foreign governments on the other. Unless mutual adjustment is possible, international economic conflict will follow. Adjustment in turn requires a relatively high level of popular understanding of the situation in which the nation finds itself and of the fallacy of one-sided attempts to change it. Limited government may not be the natural outcome of democratic political institutions, but governments of limited powers are fostered by international pressures which may be gradually depriving all nations of economic and, to some degree, military sovereignty.

Questions therefore arise whether certain regimes are flexible enough to move toward the trading world or to participate reliably in it. Can, for example, the USSR adjust its internal institutions sufficiently to respond to economic changes on an international basis? Would this undermine the monopoly of the Communist party in Russia's governing apparatus? These questions have not yet been answered because in Russia at least they have not been addressed. But it is clear that internal democracy is not the minimum requirement for adherence to a trading system. Authoritarian regimes in many Third World and developing nations have made the transition to a trading world. It is nevertheless true that the more dependent a state becomes on foreign trade, the more its institutions have to be adjusted to accommodate the change. The full force of international competition is a powerful solvent for some kinds of domestic rigidity.[14]

The amount of interdependence also conditions the choice between military-political and trading worlds. If nations have in the past been dependent upon one another, the attempt suddenly to install independence or self-sufficiency works only if populations will accept a more modest level of economic performance. If the economy is already operating at moderate to low levels of capacity, self-sufficiency at those levels can be more easily achieved. Prosperity, on the other hand, brings in vast quantities of goods from overseas which consumers begin to want and expect, and they are less content to sacrifice them and go to a lower level of consumption just because self-sufficiency may be desired by political leaders. Conversely, high inflation or unemployment will discredit the trading system and focus attention on alternatives, including recourse to a military-political and territorial system. Thus, in the broadest sense the costs and benefits which accrue under the two world systems will determine the point between them that nations select. That point is not foredestined, and it may change with time. The notions of sovereignty and independence which come down to us from the Westphalia settlement in 1648 are no more axiomatic than the exchange and trade that David Hume and Adam Smith commended to nations in the eighteenth century.

Social Learning

One reason why no single theory of international politics has ever been adequate is that nations modify their behavior in face of experience and theory. If statesmen believe that the balance of power must determine their policies, then they will act in such a way as to validate the theory. If they believe that past power-balancing has been disastrous, they will act against the theory.

Since 1919, there has been no single valid theory of international politics because leaders and statesmen have been acting on different and contrasting theories of international politics. Some have concluded that the international economy only works when there is a single hegemonic lender of last resort which provides a market for the goods of countries in trouble.[15] Such approaches do not take into account the changes that financiers have made since the 1930s—when the theory supposedly operated and accentuated the Great Depression and international conflict. Since present-day economists and finance ministers do not want to repeat the disastrous experience of the interwar period, they act together to prevent it even when no single hegemonic power—like the United States or Great Britain—is strong enough to hold the system together. International cooperation increases to provide the needed extra funds and market potential.

Equally, the Westphalian conceptions that each separate nation should be sovereign and independent—while they continue to have relevance and application in the field of international law—are disastrous if taken literally by statesmen or their publics. For nations to act as if they were totally sovereign means that they should each strive to control the whole world—a totally malign and anachronistic notion. Yet it is one which still has too many adherents. How leaders act is partly determined by the theories and past experience that they bring with them. The growth of interdependence has no necessary connection with any particular type of international behavior. Statesmen can reject the restraints that growing interdependent connections place upon them or they can use and build upon them. The same factual situation can elicit different national responses, as the experience of Britain and Germany in the nineteenth century shows. The same could be true of the United States and the Soviet Union today.

The phenomenon of social learning attests to the strength and vitality of concepts formed on the basis of national experience of hundreds of years. It is also true that social learning will partly determine the acceptance of the trading or the military-political world in the years to come. Great Britain was a leading power in the mid-nineteenth century when she decided to follow a preponderantly trading role in world politics. Germany was emerging into a leading position when she decided against the trading vocation and in favor of a military one. After defeat in World War I, German leaders in the 1930s decided to repeat the military experiment. After defeat in World War II, Japanese leaders of the 1950s decided to try an entirely different tack in world politics. The Soviet Union's military success in World War II has confirmed a primarily territorial and military orientation in her policy. Despite enjoying a similar (indeed an even greater) success, the United States moved toward the trading alternative in the 1970s while still retaining many past military and territorial orientations.

What states do is ultimately determined by the theories they hold and the national experience they have endured. But the conception of the trading alternative—with its costs and benefits—will influence the choice that states make.

Conclusion

The choice that nations make between placing primary emphasis on the trading or on the military-political system of world politics is influenced by a host of other factors. If war is easy to wage and win, the assimilation of territory relatively simple, then states will generally be inclined to use forceful methods in international relations. If war is costly, difficult, and uncertain; if new territories cannot be assimilated and governed; if trading strategies hold out the prospects of rapid new growth, the latter will likely be selected as the primary means of national advancement. War has become much more complicated, costly, and destructive in the twentieth century, but this does not mean that states will not resort to it. That depends on ideological dispositions as well as doctrinal fashions. If states, like some in the Third World today, place nationalism and state independence at the top of the list of priorities, they may engage in actions that cannot strictly be defended on the basis of narrow cost and benefit considerations. What states do is influenced by what they believe they must or ought to do, and that in turn is the product of social learning, a factor which continues to determine much in international politics.

Nations aim to improve their position in world politics. There are two general means of improvement: one through the acquisition of new territory; the other through economic development and trade. There are fateful consequences involved in choosing one primary means over the other. In an open economy greater production and trade by one nation does not prevent another from achieving similar goals. The forceful seizure of additional territory by one nation, however, diminishes the possibilities of others.

3

Theories in Search of Reality

Most theories of international politics have offered one model of the subject: a single set of mandates according to which nations continue to behave today as they did in the past. These monistic approaches have helped to explain individual facets of international relations, but they have not succeeded in making comprehensible the full variety of international experience. If an author pushes his theory too far, hoping to cover each possibly deviant case, the theory often ends up as a truism—a statement about the meanings of words not about the nature of reality. Thus one can justly ask whether a dualistic approach—offering two models of the subject— might not be better. But an answer to this question depends upon an investigation of the theories that are presently in vogue.

Realism

The first and perhaps oldest theory, dating at least from Thucydides, claims that power rivalries cause war. Realistic theories emphasize the factor of conflict among states. Nations cannot all improve their power positions, for "power" is a relative term.

They cannot all conquer geographic space, because there is only so much space. International relations then becomes a game where the sum of all players' positions is a constant. At the extreme there may even be a zero-sum game among international participants.[1] Realistic approaches stress that states aim to achieve sovereign independence, seeking ultimately to depend only on themselves. Their goal is self-help.[2] They pursue similar goals and use similar means and constitute in fact "like units." The only difference between them in theoretical terms is their degree of success in achieving power and position: some are weaker and some stronger. The sole common interests which unite such power-oriented states are defense against a superior power and resistance to hegemony. For limited purposes, states may band together in alliances or wartime coalitions, but their joint interests are limited to preventing another power from becoming too strong. Ideological conflicts do not enter into this account except to exacerbate power rivalries. Ideological solidarity, however, does not produce a lasting accommodation among states.[3] Even if Great Britain had emerged as the world's second power in 1945, there would have been the same rivalry and the same ensuing Cold War as occurred between the United States and the Soviet Union.

In one version of the realist account, changes in power directly affect the stability of the system. A power relationship determined at a prior period may be undermined if a rising state transforms its position through industrialization. Then the balance of political responsibilities and rewards in the system will no longer correspond to power realities, and the new challenger will seek a redistribution of the spoils, usually through war.[4] This view appears to assume that if power relations were entirely static, there would be less reason for military conflict. One possible explanation for this is that if nations agree on what the distribution of power is and if that distribution remains unchanged, there is little reason to use force. Weaker powers defer to the requests of the stronger without fighting. When industrialization increases one nation's power, however, it may be tempted to rival with a prior champion, whose power has declined. The older power does not agree that it should give way, and fighting occurs because of a dispute "in the measurement of power."[5] In this view war is periodically required to bring respective national estimates into accord with one another. Then peace will prevail until further changes cause further disputes.

In the realist catechism, conflict will take place even where there are common interests and a game of increasing-sum in international relations.[6] Frequently, two parties can benefit from cooperating with one another, as in establishing free trade between them, but each can benefit more by defecting from free trade and levying a tariff on the other's goods. As a result, both defect and achieve a rational (that is, an equilibrium) outcome that assigns smaller rewards (lower trade) than each would have achieved under mutual cooperation (free trade). Neither can resist trying to take advantage of the other's cooperative play, and at the same time neither wants to become the "sucker" (that is, the player who cooperates, by removing tariffs while the other defects, by keeping tariffs). In technical terms this game is known as the Prisoner's Dilemma.[7] The only way, so it is said, that both parties can reach a stable strategy of cooperation is to make agreements which can be enforced, and since in international relations there is no law above the parties and no enforcement mechanism, mutual defection will be the typical result. Conflict will persist even though the game is increasing-sum in character.

Also problematic is the Assurance Game, where the mutually cooperative payoff is the highest available to the parties, but neither can be assured that the other will choose it: if one chooses it and the other does not, the former gets the sucker's payoff. There must be coordination beforehand to achieve the mutually desirable result.[8]

The solution to the Assurance Game is prior coordination—like driving on the right or flying West at odd altitudes. For the Prisoner's Dilemma, one needs something more: some way of ensuring that the parties abide by their agreements. In small face-to-face groups or in repetitive play where the two parties know that they will encounter each other again, cooperative bargains can sometimes be worked out. But even this depends on one party following a tit-for-tat strategy, so that his partner will realize that he cannot reap untoward benefits by playing Defect on every turn.[9] But in international relations groups are not always small, leaders rotate in and out of power, and repetitive play in regard to a specific issue may be minimal. Such conditions, then, cannot always be met. In more practical and historical terms, realists can point to the fact that experience with the catastrophic outcome of World War I resulting from mutual choice of defection strategies did not prevent World War II (also a defection outcome). Higher tariffs after 1880—which reduced the growth of international trade and hurt all nations—did not prevent high tariffs after 1930. According to realist theories, conflict remains as the typical outcome in international politics and that conflict will periodically lead to war.

A special subcase of realist theories deals with the balance of power. According to this version, states act to produce a balance of power among their number, resisting those who seek to build up their power to a position of dominance.[10] In this analysis, states first seek to ally against the potential hegemonic power, but if alliances do not restrain him, they remain prepared to go to war. To be effective, the balance of power strategy requires that the dire consequences of an imbalance in power must more than outweigh the dangerous results of a war. Maintaining a balance of power in fact can be a strong deterrent to war on the part of the strongest power, for it cannot hope to win. Many disciples of realism have held that a firm balance of power is the best guarantee of peace.

Yet there is something left out of the realist lexicon. It does not seem to the external observer that all states are in an equal condition of conflict with one another. Perhaps the superpowers are, but lesser states have found means of allying with one another over the long term, without engaging in shifts to take into account the latest changes in the international equilibrium of power. Some states have established such a high degree of reciprocity, similarity in values, institutions, and economic transactions, that war between them has for practical purposes been ruled out.[11] The United States and Canada, Norway and Sweden, the Benelux countries, and perhaps most of the countries of the European Economic Community have established such close and reciprocal relations, such a sharing of responsibilities and benefits that they can assume that their relations will remain peaceful. For them, there is no chronic power struggle, no conflicts that are likely to end in war. Canada does not ensure the sanctity of its southern boundary with the United States by buttressing it with either a conventional defense or a nuclear retaliatory capability. She sees no need for such precautions even though she could surely take them. The Franco-German frontier is no longer fortified, though it was from 1871 to 1945. The Mexican-American frontier is so far from being manned that many cross it illegally every day. An improvement in Canadian economic performance does not disturb the United States because the two powers are not jostling for primacy in political or military terms. In contrast, Soviet economic, as well as military, gains would be attended to in the West and would probably call for some form of counteraction in the United States, Europe, or Japan. At the very least, it seems true that all states do not exist in a constant-sum relation with one another, where the gains of one are likely to be losses for the remaining powers. Rather, the states of the world are parceled into categories, and only some of the actions of some of the powers are a threat to a particular nation's security. For the rest, relations are determined on another basis, and the power struggle recedes into the background. Relatively permanent islands of peace have been created that it would take an earthquake or a tidal wave to disturb.[12]

Nor is it true that all states seek to depend only on themselves—to move to a condition of sovereign autarchy in international relations. Many nations, and Japan first among them, have accepted almost complete dependence on the resources and markets provided by the rest of the world. No longer is there any disposition to try to conquer militarily the lands, resources, and markets that Japan thinks it might need. Instead, she relies on the oceanic trading system for her sustenance and growth. Other countries in Western Europe and Eastern Asia have experienced and accepted a similar degree of interdependence with the rest of the world. This process has hastened a modest differentiation of function in international politics. As countries become accustomed to their role as trading partners, they in effect specialize to serve this role even better. We now have agricultural and industrial producers, oil and raw material producers in world economics and politics. Some areas provide capital for the others; some offer fertile grounds for investment. Some supply industrial or agricultural commodities and engage in "visible" trade; others provide services in information, communication, transportation, finance, and shipping and specialize in "invisibles." And the functions that nations perform are changing all the time, as smokestack industries shift to the South and East and erstwhile manufacturing countries become foreign investors. The entire apparatus of international trading—one of the most important activities in which nations engage—is testimony to the degree to which nations are *unalike.*

This does not mean that there are not elementary similarities in how nation-states look at the world. Each seeks to ensure its own persistence, cultural and political. But this does not mean that it fights each time its autonomy is impinged upon. President Eduard Beneš of Czechoslovakia decided in September 1938 that it was better to concede to Hitler and cede the Sudetenland than to fight and be defeated. An eventual renaissance of Czech culture was deemed more important than maintaining the autonomy of the political state in the short run. His successor, Alexander Dubcek, reached the same conclusion when menaced by Soviet armies in 1968. Thus, the fact that states are alike in certain respects does not impute a particular and singular view of the world to them. It does not foredestine military calculations and an ever-present readiness to assert sovereignty and autonomy. The ultimate problem with realist theories is that they are too unidimensional to capture the full variety of national policies. Theories that focus primarily on conflict neglect features of complementarity and cooperation; those that stress states are like units omit the important and growing ways in which they are becoming differentiated and unalike. Neither is suited to describe the entire international spectrum.

Marxism-Leninism

If realistic approaches are too limited, too attuned to structural and power dimensions, perhaps Marxism-Leninism with its stress upon economic factors could remedy the situation and provide a valid but univocal theory. Two versions of such approaches exist. According to the first, the Leninist school, there is inexorable conflict among capitalist states which results from imperialism and the "uneven development of capitalism."[13] Domestically, according to Lenin, capitalist enterprise faces underconsumption and overproduction because the working class is not paid well enough to buy the products of its labor. Continual depressions require capitalists to seek new markets for the goods that they cannot sell at home and to invest their surplus capital abroad. Imperialism is the result with the political state drawn in to serve the interests of the capitalist class. As outside markets and realms for capitalist investment are divided up, imperialists clash in the struggle for colonies. In addition, Lenin claimed that the law of uneven development among capitalist states would bring recurrent war. Capitalist alliances and divisions of the international spoils are made at one point in time; but since capitalism develops unevenly, the emergent strongest states at the end of a period of growth do not yet possess the spoils—the allies, empire, markets, and prestige—that are commensurate with their new economic power. Wars then occur to bring the political position into accord with the economic position of nations. World War I was one such conflict, and Lenin forecast others.

The Leninist interpretation of imperialism, however, runs into the shoals of economic history: the same economic forces—industrialization and modernization in the metropole—have led to contradictory results in the external world. In the period between 1850 and 1870, there were depressions and uneven development in European history, but there was little imperialism. Countries did not acquire large tracts of land overseas. Equally in the period 1945 to 1980 there were recessions and uneven economic development among capitalist states, and yet, while surplus capital was invested overseas, there was no formal establishment of imperial control of new colonial areas. In fact, the period after World War II was the most rigorous and unremitting epoch of decolonization in modern history. Far from fighting over the division of colonial spoils, the capitalist nations withdrew from overseas involvements and began instead to engage in peaceful competition for the trade of developing nations and energy producers. The general prevalence of free trade or low trade barriers facilitated economic access to needed markets and raw materials.

War also did not occur with a regularity corresponding to the predictions of the law of uneven development of capitalism. World War I may be regarded as a war in which Germany, the newly powerful challenger, sought to extract gains and tribute from Great Britain, the established naval and imperial power. But new nations did not always challenge. Britain, which moved to the forefront of European powers in the 1830s and 1840s, did not do so. The United States, which was as strong as Germany and Britain together in 1910, did not fight a war to gain imperial spoils and generally remained on the sidelines. Russia, which passed England and Germany in the 1930s, strove to remain out of the Second World War and was embroiled only because of the German attack of June, 1941. Japan, which has an industrial plant superior to every West European country and is now excelling the Soviet Union in gross national product, did not feel obliged to challenge any of her rivals militarily as she transcended them industrially. Clearly the uneven development of capitalism only brings war under certain restricted conditions.[14]

In contrast to the Leninist theory, the second version of Marxism contends that capitalists of the First World conspire together to impose a condition of dependency on the less developed nations of the Third World. According to this view, the decline of political and military control of erstwhile colonial areas after 1945 does not change the nature of the imperial relationship which now becomes structural, that is, economic and technological in character.[15] The capitalist North, acting as a cohesive center of world politics, gets richer while the largely agrarian South, the periphery, gets poorer. Because the South does not have access to technology of its own, there are few spin-offs in education, transport, communications, and research and development that will allow Third World nations to grow independently on a long-term basis. The capitalist North coöpts retrograde elites of the South to serve its purposes and to enrich these elites but at the expense of their own populations. Divisions in the Third World country increase until a revolution occurs to throw the handmaidens of the industrial North out of power. Only then can indigenous development begin to take place on an equalitarian basis. In the absence of revolution, this second account stresses that even if development occurs in the Third World state, it is dependent development in which formal increases in gross national product and per capita income do not benefit the mass of the population. The dependency involved is then not economic subservience to the center nations but local adoption of a means of development that deprives workers and peasants of their rightful rewards. Brazil, so it is argued, is a case of such dependent development.[16]

The major problem with these arguments is that if imperialism is to be defined in a specific way, they do not appear to be true. We know that important members of the erstwhile periphery, like China, have moved to influence, power, and complete independence. China was revolutionized in the process but now has become the world's sixth ranking industrial country. Other nations have also transformed their positions. Brazil and India now vie with Canada for the ninth position in world gross national product. They are no longer the tributaries of others. Today many of the previous colonial areas of world politics are developing rapidly, more swiftly than their previous overlords, and they are likely to continue to do so. Internally, present-day Third World nations suffer more inequality in the distribution of income than did developing nations in the nineteenth century, but the difference between them is not as great as some might think.

Nineteenth-century Great Britain and 1930s Sweden did not have quite as much disparity in income before taxes as contemporary Brazil, but they had more than Argentina, India, and Mexico have today. Yet no one regarded British or Swedish development as dependent. It was taken for granted in the nineteenth century that the developmental process was one in which the income pyramid temporarily narrowed at the top, at least until income taxes were applied to equalize the differences. It will then be said that many contemporary Third World governments are authoritarian and will not apply such remedies. But nineteenth-century Japan and Germany—to say nothing of Russia and the Austro-Hungarian Empire—were also authoritarian, having a small class of landowners and wealthy capitalists controlling politics. But this political deficiency did not lead contemporary

TABLE 1

Income Distribution of Developing Nations
(19th- and 20th-centuries)

| Country | Date | Percentage of Income Earned | |
		Lowest 60 Percent	Highest 20 Percent
Prussia	1875	34	48
Saxony	1880	27	56
United Kingdom	1880	—	58
Denmark	1908	31	55
Prussia	1913	33	50
Germany	1913	32	50
United States	1929	26	54 (before taxes)
Sweden	1930	19	59 (before taxes)
Sweden	1935	23	54 (after taxes)
Argentina	1979	28.2	50.3
Brazil	1979	16.4	66.6
Egypt	1979	29.5	47.0
India	1979	31.5	48.9
Mexico	1979	23.5	54.4
Venezuela	1979	23.2	54.0

NOTE: Michael P. Todaro, *Economic Development in the Third World*, 2nd ed. (New York: Longman, 1981), p. 128 and Simon Kuznets, *Modern Economic Growth* (New Haven: Yale University Press, 1966), pp. 208–11.

observers to castigate German development as dependent.[17] Nor should it today.

It was true that many of the late developers of the nineteenth century received capital investments from the early pioneers of economic growth, with Great Britain and France facilitating American, Russian, Canadian, Australian, and Asian industrial development. But no one believed that foreign capital would produce an indefinite dependence upon the original lender. If that were to be true then present-day North America would have to be regarded as a left-over dependency of the United Kingdom, which it most assuredly is not. It may be, as Marxists assert, that international capitalism holds the whole world in thrall, but if that is so, it hardly explains the amount of competition among individual nations of capitalist persuasion. Modern-day dependency theory has not yet elaborated the point at which the prior colony is at last able to sever the controlling supports of the mother country and emerge on its own. But that point has already been reached for many erstwhile dependent countries. If final economic independence has not been achieved in all cases, this is partly tribute to the overarching interdependence of the world economy as a whole and not to the dominance of the previous metropole.

In certain respects the dependency analysis is directly contrary to another strand of economic analysis, and one which cannot be dismissed lightly: that capitalism has the tendency to move funds from areas of less to greater return. Thus the previous success of Great Britain and then the United States was moderated by foreign investment in new areas, outside of Europe and North America. Investment takes place where the returns are likely to be highest. After a time investment outlets are saturated in the metropole, and funds shift overseas where lower labor costs and perhaps new mineral resources favor a cheaper method of production. Goods produced overseas are then reimported into the original innovator where they have the effect of undercutting domestic prices and causing unemployment. Just as British development was slowed in the later nineteenth century by investment overseas[18] so capitalism's tendency is to exploit neglected opportunities and to develop the rest of the world, sometimes to the discomfort of its earlier centers in Europe or the United States.

There are thus two accounts of present-day relations between developed and developing countries. According to the first, the capitalist world acts as a concerted entity to advantage itself against the countries of the Southern Hemisphere. According to the second, individual capitalist states compete with one another for returns, and foreign investment gradually shifts to production, markets, and raw materials in the developing countries, leading to greater unemployment and perhaps economic stagnation in the North. Marxists bewail the plight of the Third World while neo-mercantilists deplore the unemployment in erstwhile industrial countries. At the very least, the dependency theory neglects many of the gains that the Third World has achieved in recent years.

The two versions of Marxism have separate virtues, but they are largely in opposition. If Leninism holds, there should be continual war and conflict among capitalist states as their growth proceeds; if the dependency analysis is correct, the tension should be entirely between First and Third worlds. Neither succeeds in conveying the reciprocity and mutual benefit that trading relations between states can often create, and each minimizes the complexity of world economic relationships.

Hegemonic Stability

An offshoot of the realist approach is the theory of hegemonic stability, which strives to explain the occasional but temporary success of trading relations among states. In two forms, it contends that states can only cooperate economically with one another when a hegemonic power holds the ring, economically or militarily. According to this view, in the nineteenth century, Great Britain was the hegemonic leader of world politics, and under her aegis a burgeoning financial and trading system could be created. Britain had the world's largest market and disposed of the greatest pool of funds. She policed the seas and guaranteed free access to the commerce of all nations. As long as the British market was open and British funds available to tide over any power in balance of payments difficulty, no country would have to put on tariffs or to ration its supply of foreign exchange. When Britain was no longer the premier industrial and trading country or could not afford to lend abroad in large amounts, other countries would be forced to control their trade and their exchanges, seeking to limit their imports to the amount they could export. Then depression would follow and international trade would decline.

In the 1920s and 1930s the theory contends that the Great Depression worsened and international trade collapsed largely because there was no single hegemonic leader in charge. Britain was then too weak to support the international trading system, and the United States was not yet ready to take on such responsibilities.[19] The problem that this theory raises in the late twentieth century is how to regulate the international trading system in the aftermath of U.S. economic and financial hegemony. In the 1960s and 1970s America showed that she could no longer carry the burden of the system alone and did not have sufficient funds to serve as a single lender of last resort in the system. Political factors and considerable domestic unemployment have made it impossible for her to offer a market of last resort to the goods of all other nations. Thus, according to the theory, other states are tempted to put on tariffs and move to economic closure because they cannot risk a deterioration in their balance of payments.

Another version of the theory stressed the crucial political function which military hegemony performs for the rest of the members of the international system.[20] If one country is fully in charge, no one worries about the possibility of war, and investors, consumers, and capitalists can make decisions based on the assumption of continuing peace. When the military surplus of a hegemonic nation begins to run out, however, as America's did in the Vietnam War, stable peace would no longer be the long-term prospect. Once again, entrepreneurs and investors would be unable to take the long-range decisions on which continued economic progress rests. Thus from either standpoint—military or economic— the decline of hegemony would threaten past economic and trading gains and raise the specter of economic chaos and depression. Since the decline of British hegemony was associated with economic and military breakdown at the end of the nineteenth century, so the decline of United States hegemony foretells another period of economic conflict and perhaps war in the late 1980s and 1990s.

The hegemonic stability theory conflicts with the balance of power theory in most of its aspects. According to the latter, only a balance in economic and military power will safeguard the interests of the members of the system. According to the former, a balance will undermine the prospects for peaceful economic progress among states. However, Great Britain did not achieve hegemony militarily in the nineteenth century, and she remained vulnerable to a pooling of the navies of her adversaries until the early twentieth century. It was not the force of British arms that imposed peace on the Continent and allowed investors to make their long-run economic decisions. There was in fact no British hegemony.

Economically, Britain did retain her financial and trading advantage down to the First World War, but she had already been matched by German industrial progress in 1890. Yet even in the period in which British strength was relatively waning (1900–13) the international, financial, and trading system remained fragile but intact. It was destroyed by World War I, but that was not due to a depression or a financial crisis brought on by British incapacity.

The hegemonic stability theory appears to explain the results of the 1930s, and it makes apocalyptic forecasts of the trend of events in the 1990s. It does not explain why there has not *already* been a marked decline in international economic cooperation or why it has proved possible to mobilize capital to help countries in financial trouble well after the onset of decline in American economic and military power. Certain financial and economic indicators place the first inklings of American decline as early as 1963, and yet the international trading system has not collapsed in the face of protectionist demands and the international financial system is even more open and capital more mobile than it was in the 1950s. Somehow multilateral sources of funds have been mobilized to cover shortfalls in the positions of international debtors—Mexico, Brazil, and Argentina—with the International Monetary Fund sharing the lead with the United States. Cooperation of the leading industrial nations and lending agencies has here supplanted the past primacy of the American capital market.[21] Nor has the somewhat greater American military weakness led investors to halt their long-term operations or to fear for future returns. Countries like Japan, France, and Germany continue to make long-run economic plans. The curbing of inflation in many countries has been more responsible for the resurgence of long-term investment than any change in the worldwide military balance.

This is not to disparage the hegemonic stability theory's contention that economic activities depend in some degree on power relations within the international system. Indeed, we have already argued that hegemony is a theoretical means of establishing stability in a military-political system. It has not been a desirable or useful means because hegemony has been impossible to achieve in the past seventeen hundred years of the Western tradition. In any event and whatever its benefits in terms of imposing general peace, the members of the system will always resist it. It makes individual states subject to the dictates of one single Leviathan. Well short of this, some would argue that having one power stronger than others—though not in a position of hegemony—may also be useful in facilitating the important functions of trading, investment, and international economic expansion. A single large power wedded to the status quo will assist the balance of power and will offer resistance to any state which would disturb it. It could also hold out markets and funds to developing nations, enabling them to sell and borrow abroad. The functioning of an international trading system does depend upon a number of nations concluding that they can better advance their positions through economic development and trade than through recourse to war. A strong power standing for peace assists others to reach this conclusion.

But it is one thing to contend that hegemony of the redefined and lessened sort is helpful to economic and political stability; it is entirely another to claim that it is essential to it. When the United Kingdom first decided to devote herself to international trading as a national livelihood in the 1840s, there was no strong power overawing others, which bolstered such a choice. When Japan and the German Federal Republic moved in similar directions after 1945, it was not foredestined that the international economy would remain open or that depression would not once again produce the closure of the 1930s. There was a calculated risk involved: other countries would have to be persuaded to join the trading system and to support its requirements. Full convertibility with the United States dollar and an end to exchange control did not come until 1958. Thus while one could judge national monetary goals and values from the Bretton Woods discussions in 1944, it was not clear how far nations would go in actually implementing those goals. Countries that initially favored a nationally regulated system, or separate trading blocs, had to be convinced that a single, open, international economic system would work to the benefit of most countries.

If the establishment of openness required a leap of faith on the part of its partisans, so the prevention of closure also requires persuasion, concurrence, and agreement. If that agreement is forthcoming, and most major trading nations believe that the trend toward protection must be resisted, ultimately it will be resisted. Such opposition to national restrictions will be effective even in the absence of a single strong power which provides military and financial resources to the rest of the world. It is precisely this path of international agreement of the major economic participants— United States, Japan, Germany, France, Britain, and influential Arab nations—that has allowed the financial system to hold together in face of continual crisis since the early 1970s. No single state has been able to undertake the task alone. Hegemonic stability has not been needed.

Role of International Regimes

Some critics have argued that hegemonic stability is not necessary to the establishment and maintenance of an open international trading and financial system if an international regime exists to monitor and enforce compliant behavior among nations.[22] A regime exists in a given realm (trade, oceans, finance, oil, nuclear power, sea-bed mining, nuclear weapons transfer) when countries agree to give up independent decision making in that realm and to constrain their behavior according to certain established international norms. A domestic society is a clear example of a regime. The individuals in it give up certain forms of independent behavior—the right to kill, for example—and in return receive equal treatment and protection of domestic laws and police forces. Stable agriculture becomes possible under a regime of law. Property is protected as well as life. People are obliged to pay taxes to receive security and some minimum degree of welfare.

In international regimes, as well, there are obligations placed upon national behavior, and there are sanctions if countries violate their obligations, such as an inability to raise loans in international credit markets. If one country violates the rules of the International Civil Aviation Organization, it may not be allowed to fly airplanes into or over other jurisdictions. Regimes are required when independent and unconstrained decision making would lead to suboptimal outcomes for both parties. The establishment of a regime may be a means of overcoming the all too seductive incentives of Prisoner's Dilemma outcomes in trade, exchange rates, whaling, fisheries, and a variety of other activities.

It cannot be doubted that international regimes do constrain national behavior and tolerably manage to police compliance in a variety of international realms—usually those of an economic or technical character.[23] But international regimes do not cover all forms of international behavior. In security, for example, there is no regime which governs the military or armaments behavior of the United States or the Soviet Union. There is no body which polices intervention by one state in another's affairs and which could disallow the Soviet move in Afghanistan or the American incursion in Grenada. Wherever independent decisions are unconstrained—as they probably are in the issues of supreme national interest—regimes cannot be formed. Thus, only a very small portion of international behavior is subject to regimes at the moment. Nor is it clear that new regimes in important areas, such as security, conventional arms tranfers, arms races, aid to the Third World, are likely to be formed. Theories of international regimes, therefore, cannot be monistic. They always have to allow for the residual and most important part of national behavior—the unconstrained. We, therefore, are forced back to dualism as the minimum possible approach to an international theory which claims to deal with all aspects of national behavior.

Dualism: Political-Military and Trading Worlds

Each of the monistic approaches we have considered explains a facet of international politics, but each neglects evidence which points to disparate and unexplained behavior. The realist theory sees international relations in a manner akin to gas molecules colliding with one another in a heated chamber. Velocity, momentum, and collision are the abiding metaphors. Such an approach does not recognize that some molecules have already coagulated or combined, perhaps forming new compounds which are as stable and enduring as the simple molecules themselves. The two versions of Marxism-Leninism offer insights into individual and historical aspects of international relations. The Leninist theory of imperialism has broad application to the causation of World War I. The dependency theory has given an account of the failure of some Third World nations to develop independently since World War II. Each approach, however, fails to see that nations change policies: they do not incessantly repeat the old behavior and the old errors. Capitalist states were not bound to conflict with one another as Lenin said, but neither were they bound to collude as the apostles of *dependencia* claim. In fact, what is most striking is the detachment of international capitalism from the particular state: it serves no individual national interest but seeks instead, often in the guise of the multinational corporation, to redistribute production and funds in ways that serve its *own* interest.

The hegemonic stability theory offered reasons for both economic and international failure in the 1920s and 1930s. But it was not so easy to explain why the international financial system functioned long after Britain had lost her economic hegemony between 1890 and 1913 and why both the financial and trading systems continue to operate today in the absence of the premier dominance of the United States. The interdependent world economy may occasionally function well when a single nation can act as market and lender of last resort, but it appears that it can also operate when no single economy performs those two functions. If that were not the case, the world economic system would have broken down after 1870 and again exactly one hundred years later. Neither catastrophe occurred.

It is possible that only international regimes can save the world when the hegemonic leader loses his grip. In a variety of areas today, regimes supplement and perhaps even supplant the activity of the previous strongest nation. But international regimes form and reform; they are occasionally broken. Power changes and transformations alter their course. Thus, theories of regimes can never provide an adequate explanation of all of international relations. They are as much product as cause.

Dualism, thus, becomes a minimum causal explanation of the range of international behavior. There is, of course, more than one dualism. Robert Keohane and Joseph Nye seek to explain the variety of international politics with the dualistic categories: power and interdependence. In a power world states act as coherent units, force is a usable instrument of policy, and there is a hierarchy of international issues dominated by questions of military security. Interdependence refers to a world in which states can no longer fully regulate policy, there are multiple channels of access between societies, no hierarchy of issues, and force is generally unusable. The distinction between power and interdependent worlds, then, lies generally in the cohesion of units and the type of transactions between them. Power is the preeminent goal of a state-centric universe, but interdependence is a characteristic that only applies when states as entities have lost control and are unable to impose a hierarchy upon policy issues.[24]

In contrast, the dualism that is proffered here accepts the state as the final reference point of decision in the system: the difference between worlds concerns the means that are used to advance state interests. In an interdependent world states will be more likely to follow trading strategies, but they will not certainly do so as the history of the 1920s and 1930s demonstrates. Some states are primarily trading states and relegate efforts to improve security and the arms balance to the low end of the priority list; others are maximizers of power and territory and are in the arms race for all they can get. For them, trade is an ancillary and derivative occupation. Such "low politics" does not befit, so some say, a great power. The cost and benefit of trading as compared with the cost and benefit of making war greatly influences the choices that nations make in terms of respective emphases. They do not, however, entirely determine those decisions. Nations can learn and unlearn from history. They follow paradigms that hold or appear to hold received truth. But truth is influenced greatly by sudden and dramatic national experience—the Munich capitulation of 1938 spawned generations of power theorists and led to a universal denunciation of appeasement. Yet, as applied in the trading context, appeasement was the lubricant of adjustment to make sure that no partner to a bargain was greatly disadvantaged. Sudden and dramatic territorial losses will reenergize power and conflictual urges, and as a result nations will spend their substance preparing or perhaps even overpreparing for a war that none of them wants, paying huge opportunity costs in the trading sector. But the pendulum of choice can reverse once again.

PART II

PAST WORLDS

4

Historical Fluidity
and Change

One of the difficulties of most international theory is that it
has been analytical rather than historical in character: it has been
deterministic rather than contingent. Models have been offered
that described one historical age in theoretical terms but failed to
account for others. The dynamics of historical development has in
this way defeated any purely monistic approach. In fact, the
alternation between military-political and trading worlds cannot
be understood except in historical terms. Without gross oversim
plification, one can argue that the trend in the first part of modern
history (from 1500 to 1900) is for a greater concentration of power
in the hands of territorial states and their leaders. This period not
only sees an increase in the size of territorial states and a decline
in their number, it also witnesses greater control over the population
of these states. Thus the power of the national leadership grows
both extensively and intensively. Commensurately, the power of
supranational influences and forces, like the ecumenical Catholic
Church and the Holy Roman Empire, greatly declines. Medieval
universalism is replaced by the modern state, and loyalties become
national rather than international in character. It is not surprising
that this age is the epoch par excellence of the military-political
system. Nations compete with one another virtually without limit,

and continual warfare is the result. Until World War I, the system sustained in part by the balance of power is based on the rational waging of war. Governments deem it more efficient and acceptable to wage war than to accept the hegemony of one member of the system.

This does not mean that the trading system does not occasionally intrude or that no nations subscribe to it during this period. In the nineteenth century, mid-Victorian Great Britain became the first nation to place strategic reliance upon an external system of trade.[1] Her decision to undermine her own agriculture was not tactical in character but represented a long-term policy of importing cheap food from abroad, the better to enable her to concentrate upon her industrial forte. On the Continent, free and open international trading was a kind of icing on the domestic cake—it had a tactical, not a strategic character and could be quickly abandoned with the first whiff of domestic depression. Thus despite the rise of trading influences and potentials, not until the twentieth century could the system of international trade begin to gain widespread adherence. The military-political and territorial system preponderated down to World War I.

After the war, the territorial and military system received its first great challenge. The large British, French, and German empires ceased growing. No longer was there a trend toward a smaller number of states. In fact, out of the First World War comes a series of new states, salvaged from the breakup of the Austro-Hungarian Empire. The Russian Empire was temporarily challenged. The Turkish Empire had already become decrepit at the end of the nineteenth century, and a number of new nations had emerged in the Balkan region even before 1914. With the exception of the Austrian Empire and the German Empire, whose demise was confirmed at the Paris Peace Conference, the other European empires remained in place overseas and endured until after World War II.

But the trend toward an increase in the number of states and a decline in their size is not immediately matched by corresponding changes in domestic politics. In Italy, Germany, and Stalinist Russia a new domestic system of total control—totalitarianism—

is visited upon the population. This new system based upon propaganda, a black shroud obscuring outside enlightenment and information, with a monopolistic party using terror to stay in charge, allows the government to act in world affairs with a new and unlimited ruthlessness. Thus the horror of war which became well-nigh universal in the aftermath of World War I did not prevent certain states from continuing to behave in terms of the mandates of the military-political system. Totalitarian governments had no greater extensive power resources; they relied instead upon new intensive resources and gambled that the increment would enable them to win territorial victories. World War II proved them wrong, but even that horror did not disabuse all nations of the military-political system. Some remained its partisans, but increasing numbers of others, fed up with war, moved to embrace the new possibilities of the international trading system. As governments in many countries loosened control of their electorates, as imperialism broke down and more liberal political systems began to be installed in a host of countries in the aftermath of World War II, the domestic requirements for continued adherence to the military-political system began to be undermined. This modest liberalization, attenuating the connection between domestic electorates and their governments, also helped to lift the national gaze to the broader international horizons required by the new trading system. The openness of the international economy also facilitated the transition from political-military to trading states. The benefit of trading increased as its cost declined.

But the greater cost of war, as represented by World War II, did not immediately transform great power politics. The rise of the two superpowers—the United States and the Soviet Union—represented an evolution that conflicted with that in world politics generally. The size and power of the superpowers grew as the size and power of other states declined. While lesser European and Asian states joined the new international trading system, the United States and the Soviet Union, with large markets and apparent self-sufficiency in natural resources, did not feel any initial disposition to do so. They might stand on their own. With technological and military expertise at their disposal, they could think in terms of additional gains, sweeping opponents from the field. Nuclear weapons allowed superpowers to threaten others, and the initial primacy of the United States was so great that it seemed for a time that even the Soviet Union could not keep pace with her. It was therefore not surprising that military conflicts occurred in Korea and Vietnam, where the superpowers could test their strength and their endurance. Conceptualizing international shifts in territorial terms, United States legislators could bemoan the "loss of China" to the Soviet side or speculate that Soviet gains in Eastern Europe might ultimately tip the balance against America and the Western nations. At each opportunity, both sides would tend to think that an ideological shift in one small power or the other might allow the opposing superpower to organize the small state into its territorial orbit. Hence ideological issues in Asia, Africa, or Latin America were interpreted in territorial terms.

While the political-military struggle of the superpowers was being played out, however, many nations, although partly involved in such quarrels, began the quest for a new and peaceful means of national advancement. Instead of conquering new territory to be assimilated into national lands, such countries sought to improve their position by domestic production and international trade. As their industries became more competitive and could sell more effectively in world markets, they would gain a larger share of world trade and corresponding advantages in economic growth rates. They did not need physically to acquire new lands containing resources and markets as long as the international trading system provided access to what they needed on a free and open basis. With an open international financial system, one did not have to possess a territory to invest in it. This openness also fostered new instrumentalities, like the multinational corporation which owed final allegiance to no national jurisdiction while operating in many. Trading cities, though located within a territorial state, often displayed autonomous tendencies, seeking to benefit from the international division of labor.[2] Countries in East Asia like Japan, Korea, Taiwan, Singapore, and even Hong Kong rapidly moved into international production, benefiting from the investment of multinational corporations, some of national origin. They also increasingly engaged in international finance, as lenders as well as borrowers. Oil countries in the Middle East became sources not only of petroleum but also of investment funds.

The product life cycle describing the birth and development of new products, which was first detected at the Harvard Business School became a stimulus not only to international production and the multinational corporation, but also to the development of trading states. Originally, television was a product of American industry. The domestic market in hand, United States companies began to export to Europe and the developing world. Eventually, however, latecomers—European and Japanese companies—not only captured their own markets but began exporting to the United States. In this more competitive environment, American companies could survive only by producing TV sets in export platforms overseas (nations with expert work forces but low labor costs) and then exporting them to the United States. Textiles, television, and now automotive components are produced in this way, and at each stage the new developing trading country gets a larger range of comparative advantage. Eventually, automobiles may be entirely produced in the Eastern and Southern Hemispheres. Industries like steel, shipbuilding, and electric appliances are also moving toward these locales and away from their traditional centers in Europe and North America. As long as international trade remained open, and investment funds could be shifted easily from one jurisdiction to another, the incentive to trade for a national livelihood remained very strong, particularly for small countries that could not hope to sustain their industry or agriculture wholly on the basis of national raw materials and markets. They have to export to live. But larger and stronger countries like Japan and the Federal Republic of Germany have also elected a trading course in world politics. They no longer think of improving their national position through territorial gain but rather seek to use strategies of economic growth sustained by foreign trade to maintain and increase the standard of welfare enjoyed by the population. In this way Norway, Sweden, and Switzerland have surpassed the United States in per capita income, and the life span of the average Japanese has equaled that of the American.

The Trading System in International History

Given the great successes of the international trading system since 1945, one is tempted to wonder why these never occurred before. Why did trade not preponderate over territory in the early development and policy of the units of modern international politics? This seems a peculiarly appropriate question when we recall that trading city-states existed in the late medieval period of European history and that they flourished down to the end of the fifteenth century. Venice, Genoa, and the members of the Hanseatic League garnered great returns from commerce borne on the sea lanes of the world. The question seems intriguing from another standpoint. Some historians have speculated that a linear rather than areal organization of international politics might have emerged at the beginning of modern European history.[3] A confederal association of small states sustained by oceanic commerce might have obviated the rise of the territorial nation-state. Why did such a system not take form? One explanation is that the trading cities and city-states of the Renaissance engaged in conflicts akin to those of their territorial counterparts of a later period. Trade was not open and free; rather, individual city-states sought to monopolize it and to command key sources of supplies. In particular, any trading unit which could gain control of Eastern spices would win unexampled returns in Europe and the Mediterranean. Venice and Genoa vied for control in the fourteenth century, and Venice's victory in 1380 was not permanent. Portugal's Vasco da Gama rounded the Cape of Good Hope and found a sea route to India a century later thereby undercutting Venice's link to the East through Arab traders in the Levant. In much the same way, sixteenth-century Spain tried to establish a practical monopoly in gold and silver bullion, though she did it by territorial conquest of Peru and Mexico. But even where cities did not seek empires, there was no drive toward specialization or a stable division of labor between them. Instead, each sought to develop an exclusive market, or *entrepôt*, for the goods of others, to become the universal fair for the commerce of Europe. If all comers had to go to one place to exchange wares, the reigning *entrepôt* would gain a special bounty. So conflict was built into the trading arrangement. Only one city-state could control the sources of supply; only one could become the *entrepôt* for Europe. And so they warred to see who it would be.

Later in the seventeenth century when Amsterdam and Holland supplanted Portugal and Spain, the situation was the same. Holland seized the Indies, controlling and regulating the production of coffee, tobacco, cinnamon, cloves, and tea. She sought a monopoly in the sugar islands of the Caribbean but could not gain control of all sources of supply. At the same time, Amsterdam became the *entrepôt* for Europe—the universal warehouse for the world, where most of international exchange took place. Monopoly trading operations were an invitation to military conflict. Thus one reason why the linear trading system did not come to the fore at the beginning of the modern period was that trading city-states were in continual war and could not establish a stable and enduring pattern of cooperation among themselves. Moreover, the new monarchies that were gaining control of territorial states were more effective militarily than either antecedent feudalism or the trading states of the Renaissance.

The Rise of the Territorial State

The sixteenth and seventeenth centuries saw the development of new and stronger monarchies in Western Europe. City-states lost their political momentum and were absorbed into larger states. The successor states had far more power than their late medieval and early modern forebears. Although the seventeenth-century monarchy of Louis XIV was the first developed example of the military-political (territorial) state, it was only an early approximation of modern examples. The great French king inaugurated a period in which expansion in Europe and overseas became the *modus operandi* of monarchs strong enough to accomplish it. This expansion achieved its first crescendo in mid-eighteenth century, but it was not until 1914 that European empires divided the world among themselves.

In 1453 there were no strong territorial states in Europe, but fifty years later, Spain, France, and England had emerged in a reasonable resemblance to their modern selves. The territorial monarchs gained power because of new military, religious, and economic factors. Gunpowder had finally arrived from China and helped French and Hapsburg armies to begin the process of extinguishing the independence of the Italian city-states. Cheaper and more mobile cannon contributed to the revolution in warfare, and any ruler who "controlled a well-stocked artillery park could make his will prevail across comparatively enormous distances."[4] One result of this innovation might have been the unification of Europe under a single power. This did not happen because smaller states were often wealthy, and no power could monopolize the production of artillery. Holland, Sweden, and Denmark were able to master the fundamentals of the military revolution along with France and Spain. From 1500 on, however, geographic location, size, and wealth became determinants of ultimate viability. Despite new fortifications, cities which could be approached from land were likely to be vulnerable. Small duchies and principalities were likely to be wiped away.

The decay of medieval Catholicism also fostered the growing power of the new monarchies. When Martin Luther propounded his ninety-five theses at Wittenberg in 1517, a religious revolution began which culminated in the triumph of the Protestant Reformation. The German princes quickly saw that Lutheranism and Protestantism could be used to justify further independence, not only from the pope but also from the Holy Roman Emperor, who sought to enforce religious orthodoxy. The success of Protestantism as an international movement undermined the claims of the papacy and the empire, strengthened princes and kings commanding territorial states, and created a Europe of separate national sovereignties. This fragmentation meant that Europe would stay disunited and that any pretender who tried to unify it would face determined opposition.

Economic factors also favored the king and a strong territorial state. Spain showed how conquests overseas might extract wealth which could be used to enhance monarchical power and glory. Unlike Venice, Spain was not content with a monopoly of trade with new regions: she conquered and colonized captured areas. The output from the mines in the New World largely determined Spain's role as the great power in Europe. She demonstrated that an imperial and trading monopoly in luxury goods and specie could transform power relations on the European continent. Brother monarchs now aimed at empire, following the Spanish example. Economic factors thus operated in two different ways. They strengthened the great imperial powers which could provide new luxury goods or specie to European coffers. At the same time, certain trading cities and city-states temporarily gained as well. Little Holland transformed herself into the Dutch Empire and dominated European commerce until the mid-seventeenth century.

But the territorial monarchies, in the longer term, gained more. Militarily they were large enough to withstand assault, and they had large populations to support the military endeavors of their prince. Worn out from seemingly endless wars with Louis XIV after 1713, Holland could no longer compete with giant states like France and Russia or even with the larger British Isles. With new resources in tow, kings strengthened their grip and pressed for even greater administrative unity and centralization.

In the political field they met occasional resistance. There was a natural alliance between king and the small peasant communities spread throughout the realm. The king wanted taxes and grain supplies; the peasants wanted protection from the exactions of feudal lords and the establishment of a peaceful countryside, free from brigands. Grain supplies in local depots enabled royal horsemen to patrol the hinterland and provide security.[5] More ambivalent was the king's relation to the townsmen. The higher elements of the French middle class were offered employment and ennoblement in the King's service. This mode of reward was less costly to the monarchy than the historical distribution of land had been because it kept the territorial bases of his power intact. Monies raised by merchants could also be invested in royalty. In the sixteenth century kings became major consumers of funds accumulated by trade, and though they often defaulted on their loans, European royalty paid high interest to the moneylender. In this way, the rich townsmen had something to gain from an association with the monarch. But this link should not obscure the essential independence and distance from the monarchy that towns sought to create. They did not want royal control of their trade; they did not like tariffs and quality standards imposed on their goods and sought to avoid them whenever possible.

Attempts to control trade frequently led to elaborate efforts to circumvent the authority of the political and territorial prince. Spain and Portugal did not fully determine the policies of their urban allies, Genoa and Antwerp. The more kings sought to lay their hands on commerce, the more, like quicksilver, it slipped through their fingers.[6] Its ruling center migrated away from realms where kings had authority, first to Amsterdam and then to London. And the royal attempt to run the Spanish and later the French Empire on monopolist and mercantilist lines was not successful. The Spanish and French colonies traded illicitly with others. Even English settlements in North America evaded the restrictions of the British Navigation Acts. While Louis XIV was fighting the Dutch, his merchants at Bordeaux were trading extensively with them. Moreover, the monarchs' attempts to direct commercial capitalism were unproductive. The kings' resources were tied up in land, which was not a very remunerative use of funds in the second half of the seventeenth century.[7]

Another reason for the townsmen's distaste for monarchy had to do with a difference in attitude toward the national market. The king wanted a national market that could absorb the products of industry and agriculture and make for national self-sufficiency and independence. A large national market made cooperation with foreign nations less necessary. The great trading cities—even those inside territorial states—did not want to have to sell in the national market, if they could earn a greater return abroad. Their horizon was the world. In Venice, Holland, and England, the international market was far larger than the national political unit. In those countries trade would finally prove more important than military or territorial expansion, though this transition would take centuries. Total independence and self-sufficiency would not be sought when major markets and sources of raw material were largely overseas. In France or Russia, however, the state was much larger than the initial economic arena: the attainment of self-sufficiency meant an expansion, not a restriction, of the national market.[8] Thus the conquest of other people's territory did not interfere with essential internal trade. In France and Russia, areal concepts took precedence over linear ones, and few overseas trading ties were sacrificed in the process. The military-political and territorial model could find application under Peter the Great and Louis XIV, under Alexander I and Napoleon. Only countries which included great trading cities would harbor natural opponents to royal centralization.

Finally, the nobility remained opposed to royal authority, except in Russia. As French centralization proceeded, the nobles held on more tenaciously to their remaining privileges. The French Revolution ultimately took place because the king no longer possessed the capacity to reform France; centralization had reached the limit attainable under the social and legal systems of the old regime.

The transformation of the medieval into the modern can be depicted in at least two different ways. In one sense it represents the trend toward the consolidation and strengthening of the territorial state. National units coalesce and begin to compete for power, influence, and territory. In another sense it represents a reordering in the priority of international and domestic realms. In the medieval period, the world, or transnational, environment was primary, the domestic secondary. Within states or (prior to state consolidation) between lords of the manor there was chaos or anarchy. External to the state, however, the pope, emperor, ecumenical Catholic Church, and the hierarchical obligations of feudalism created a certain order.

There are only so many symbols or levels of authority to which people may be loyal. If they are primarily loyal to the pope, a supranational figure, they cannot be entirely loyal to the king, a national one. If they are loyal to the feudal lord, a subnational actor, they cannot be wholly loyal to the monarch. Thus to the degree that the medieval period created a successful federative unity at the international level, it must also have created anarchy within states. Only to this degree is international loyalty possible. But the transition to the modern is caused by a switch in the primary focus of loyalty. Modern international relations substitute loyalty to the political state or monarch for loyalty to either supranational or subnational units. Domestic cohesion, therefore, is partly obtained at the expense of international order. As a result, the primary concern of thinkers and statesmen since the Peace of Westphalia (1648) and even more since the French Revolution (1789) has been the problem of international conflict and disorder. Could international peace be obtained consistently with a measure of domestic support and tranquility? This question has not yet been fully answered. It is, however, interesting to observe that the growing international interdependence of the late twentieth century has helped to undermine domestic loyalties without as yet substituting a new focus of loyalty at the international level.

In the period between 1450 and the beginning of the nineteenth century, the transformation which led to domestic cohesion and international disorder took place in two stages. The first occurred with the undermining of universal forces and institutions: the Catholic Church, the pope, and the Holy Roman Emperor. New monarchies grew in scope and power during this period, but the nobility remained as a force for disunity and particularism within states. It was not until the French Revolution that centers competing for domestic loyalty were amalgamated and the nobility either revolutionized or forced to accept a dependent position in domestic politics. Strong kings and their chancellors emerged from this struggle on one side, and cabinets and parliamentary government on the other.

Internationally this period saw the establishment of the large territorial state as the integral unit of European diplomacy. It emerges as a successor to a mixed regime, in which territorial states compete for influence with trading cities and city-states. The latter give way politically and are gradually absorbed into more or less cohesive territorial states. But trading cities continued their economic relationships with one another, and during the nineteenth-century period of *laissez-faire* and free trade fashioned new and strong connections that formed the basis of the Victorian trading system of international relations.

Trading cities, however, could not have organized the world after the Renaissance because they did not control the hinterland, the agricultural areas on which their existence depended. Systematic and profitable agriculture needed a territorial organization of internal politics and the enforcement of peace by the king or his agents—this was the system that finally prevailed in the seventeenth century. In the period of more than three centuries after 1450 royal mercantilism increasingly curtailed the development of a separate trading system of international relations, eventually amalgamating it with a territorial system. By mid-eighteenth century, territory, empire, and mercantilism had combined to form one system presided over by the king. This system, modernized by the French Revolution, gave even greater power to domestic leaders and installed anarchy and conflict in international politics. Cohesive nation-states began to emerge from the fires of revolution and nationalism at the beginning of the nineteenth century, but there was little to make them cooperate; political modernity appeared to equal war. The Industrial Revolution then appeared to offer a new and intensive means of national development to states that had previously relied on extensive territorial conquest and empire building. These peaceful possibilities were not seized upon until much later, in the late twentieth century.

The Westphalian System of International Relations

Two factors increased the scope and power of the military-political and territorial system of international relations: the growing ease with which states seized territory and the greater support which kings and parliamentary leaders received from their people. The Peace of Westphalia, which ended the Thirty Years War in 1648, stimulated both tendencies. The lawyers of Westphalia reduced the pope and emperor to the status of territorial princes and recognized legal equality among states. Prior to Westphalia bishoprics, duchies, and principalities could claim only the status due their ruling house, while the Holy Roman Emperor presided over them all. Westphalia transferred the right of sovereignty from the emperor to the German princes. Conceding sovereignty, the jurists sought to prevent a repetition of the domestic devastation wreaked by the Thirty Years War. Sovereign rulers would prevent marauding bands or private armies from despoiling their countryside, towns, and cities, and they would not condone or launch such campaigns within the domains of a brother monarch. By limiting war in this way and making it more tolerable, they also made it more likely.

At the same time, the consolidation of central authority meant the end of divisive domestic and religious issues. The commercial classes triumphed in Holland after 1688, the Whigs in England, and royal power elsewhere. But in each case the end of religious civil war entailed the development of new rivalries in foreign relations. Now kings could turn to the quest for international power.

Three possible tactics might have been used to prevent war in the mid-seventeenth century. In the prior medieval period a hierarchy of state units ruled alternately by the pope and the emperor had overawed recalcitrant princes and frequently induced them to yield. Westphalia, however, had obviated that possibility. A new national leader of a territorial state might have been able to impose a hierarchy if he had been strong enough. But the separate sovereignties were too evenly matched. Finally, there might have been a growing specialization of commercial tasks, a new trading world that would have cemented cooperation among partners to the exchange. This awaited the provision of railroads in the nineteenth and twentieth centuries to match the prior benefits of oceanic shipping and allow all states to follow a trading vocation. In the seventeenth century none of these remedies was at hand. Military conquest remained the primary option for royalty and none pursued it with greater vigor than France's Louis XIV.

It was Louis XIV who set the standard for his royal peers in the second half of the seventeenth century: the pursuit of power and glory through military conquest. He evoked the balance of power in response to his campaigns. Smaller and less powerful states would band together to resist his incursions in Italy, on the Rhine, and overseas. The doctrine of the balance of power did not develop until later, but the act of opposing a monarch aiming at preponderance was consecrated even before the Peace of Utrecht

(1713) wrote "finis" to Louis's ambitions. France wanted to be the greatest seapower as well as the greatest landpower, but she succeeded in neither.

The Westphalian system of sovereign, independent states was a constant invitation to military expansion by the strongest powers and in this sense a constant incentive to follow the dictates of the military-political world. Since there were no hegemonic powers, no Leviathans, each ruler thought he might succeed in a program of conquest. But the incentive to wage war provided by the relative equality of states was counterbalanced by other powers' incentive to resist such expansion. In a system of four or five more or less equal powers, no state would be definitively deterred from waging war (it might after all succeed under given conditions of military technology), but no single state could hope to defeat all the rest. If they combined, the balance of power would erect a formidable barrier to continued conquest. What the Westphalian system did, in short, was to enshrine an arrangement in which war would be frequent, limited, but unsuccessful in toppling the balance. It would use up resources but not gain hegemony.

AN EIGHTEENTH-CENTURY VARIANT

The Westphalian system established the sovereign independence of states as the requisite feature of interstate relations. In the seventeenth century, monarchs sought to increase their independence through the conquest of new land. In the eighteenth century the objective altered slightly: kings and their counselors came to recognize that commercial profits could transform national power, and profits could be ensured through control of key commodity-producing areas. Hence empire became a goal equally with territory in Europe. A new strategy commended itself to the British; they would let their Continental allies do the fighting, supported by English funds, while British fleets carved out new commercial enclaves overseas. The subjugation of India would give Britain command of the subcontinent's tea and textiles. A monopoly of North American produce—tobacco, rice, timber, indigo, and grain— would enable Britain to extract a premium from their sale in Europe.[9] If London had been able to conquer the sugar islands of the Caribbean, she would have controlled production at the source and emerged with rents like those earned in later years by OPEC oil. In the Seven Years War, Britain ousted the French from North America and India and challenged their Caribbean plantations.

Britain used her maritime skills to fashion a dominance of overseas commerce that no one but the Dutch had approached. Near the end of the century, this dramatic increase in trade, operating upon a grain surplus and abundant British coal supplies provided the stimulus to manufacturing that set England on the road to the Industrial Revolution nearly a half century ahead of her Continental competitors.

But in military terms the British triumphs of 1763 were delusive. The American Revolutionary War, which culminated in the Battle of Yorktown and the surrender of Cornwallis in 1781, conveyed an entirely different lesson: that Britain could no longer dominate the world outside Europe and that the empire would be short lived. The defeat in America rested on two weaknesses: the inability of the British Navy to master a combination of other navies, and the weakness of the British Army in fighting in vast territories overseas. The navy had to be strong in too many places at once: in the Channel, the North Sea, the Mediterranean, the Indian Ocean, the North Atlantic, and the Caribbean. "Because she had insufficient strength to be superior everywhere and because she dared not withdraw from any of the four main theatres—the Channel, Gibraltar, the West Indies, the American seaboard—then she ended up by being too weak in every one of them."[10]

The Peace of Paris in 1783 was the first major reverse to British military fortunes in the eighteenth century. For a brief time British conclusions were similar to those of Holland after the Peace of Utrecht. Perhaps Britain should concentrate upon her commercial vocation and give up military and naval exploits. If Britain could not dominate the overseas world, there was no point in acquiring a vast external empire which would fall from the mother country's lap as ripe fruit from a tree. In the first three-quarters of the nineteenth century, the British Colonial Office dutifully ratified the sentiment: they readied their dependent territories for independence, believing that the American precedent would be followed in other cases.

But there was another lesson as well. The greatest setback of the Revolutionary War was not territorial. The years 1776–83 proved that commerce did not prosper in war: British trade suffered its greatest setback in the entire century during these years. William Pitt's doctrines were temporarily negated. War would destroy not enhance commerce. Had there not been a French Revolution, which spread political discontent throughout Europe, Britain would have reached pacific conclusions and reduced its military budget.

In certain respects the 1780s were not entirely unlike the 1980s. In both cases military expenditure relative to benefits had grown to levels that aristocratic, liberal democratic, and perhaps even communist regimes could hardly support. The choice in each case appeared to be greater accommodation in international relations or increasing domestic costs. In its next to last decade, it was still not clear what alternative the twentieth century would choose.

The Westphalian system, resting on the twin pillars of national sovereignty and independence was bound to foster war. Unless new territory was taken, kings and parliamentary leaders might become vulnerable to a major foe. Military expansion was an axiomatic response to this problem. At the same time domestic politics initially supported the choice. Wars were fought by hired mercenaries, leaving subjects to their own pursuits. Wars were bloody and expensive, but they did not devastate the countryside or plunder cities as seventeenth-century conflicts had done. Armies did not sortie far from their supply magazines, and they were hindered in their movements by long baggage trains which contained courtiers, courtesans, and troops of players. Parallel military columns meeting on a road could not always arrange battle with one another. They had to be wheeled ninety degrees to fight and by then the enemy might have moved elsewhere. Campaigns were more matters of maneuver and position than pitched battles, and the defeated army could usually withdraw in good order. The exactions of war upon the civilian population, at least, were limited.

It was thus possible for ordinary inhabitants to support their prince because little enough was asked of them. But nationalism and patriotism were rudimentary at best. Loyalties were personal, to the prince or princess, but not to France. Indeed, "nationality" as an honorific term had yet to be invented. Only in England was there a stirring of national consciousness based on the Glorious Revolution of 1688 and England's insular tradition. In this era of moderation, no monarchical project could be carried to extreme lengths for fear of arousing provincial opposition or for lack of funds. Little enough could be accomplished with a tax system that allowed privileged classes to escape payment and that was administered chaotically. Lacking money and hemmed in by aristocratic rivals at home and royal opponents abroad, the monarchs of Europe could maneuver only with difficulty. They had no means of mobilizing popular support over the heads of the particularistic nobility. The Continental wars of European sovereigns were thus limited and indecisive, and even the victors emerged in debt.

Thus in the third quarter of the eighteenth century one of the main supports of the Westphalian synthesis began to splinter. After 1648 the kings could devote new attention to international relations for the domestic religious and political problem had largely been solved. They could rely on the sufferance of their peoples for policies aiming at power and glory in the struggle with other monarchs. But military conflicts had become so expensive by the time of the Seven Years War (1756–63) that new sources of revenue were needed to pay for them. The British imposed new taxes on their American colonies and provoked the American Revolution. Louis XVI called the Estates General to vote for new taxes and brought on the French Revolution of 1789.

The emergence of the military-political and territorial system out of medieval universalism had involved two requisites: the establishment of cohesive state units and the relative ease of making war. Warfare was relatively easy and moderate in the old eighteenth-century regime. But its financial costs exceeded what unreformed domestic systems could pay. The political upheaval in France demonstrated that new support could be given to a revolutionary regime, thus freeing the military-political system from restraints and increasing domestic cohesion. This was the lesson to be absorbed by the nineteenth and twentieth centuries.

There was another possibility. If the wars of kings caused domestic discontent and brought on a financial crisis, one alternative was to cease making war: to turn to the creation and development of an international trading system in which peaceful economic development and commercial competition became the means of improving the national position. This logical outcome was neglected, however, until the British revived it at mid-nineteenth century.

Conclusion

Modern international relations emerged out of a fluid historical situation. In the mid-fifteenth century, the territorial state had not yet triumphed over universalist and local influences. Trading relations among city-states were as characteristic of international relations as the territorial state's drive for empire. Until the beginning of the sixteenth century it was not clear which tendency would predominate. By the end of that century, however, and even more so after religious struggles ceased a hundred years later, the king and the territorial state emerged victorious. This paved the way for an international contest for power and glory. Domestic centralization and support helped to institute anarchy as the ruling principle of international relations. This support was brought into question once again at the end of the eighteenth century, but reformist nationalism and militarism forged in the revolutionary and Napoleonic wars gave new scope for international conflict. The moderation of eighteenth-century conflicts yielded to Napoleonic battles which completely reshaped the political contours of Europe. Large new states like Prussia were fashioned, and small principalities absorbed into other countries. Not only the revolutionaries and Napoleon gained a new hold on popular esteem; the conservative autocrats, waving the banner of nationalism, also won a new lease on life. The domestic state was reformed to permit even greater conquests in foreign relations. The military-political and territorial system vanquished all alternative possibilities.

5

The Triumph of the Military-Political World

From the French Revolution until the 1930s the military-political and territorial system went from strength to strength. Revolutionary militarism could conquer more territory than the eighteenth-century monarchs had been able to take. The growing sense of nationality and nationalism—the consciousness of the difference between Frenchmen and Germans, Spaniards and Portuguese, Dutch and Belgians—strengthened the internal bases of power and gave new support to political leaders who represented the individual nationalities. The gradual concession of liberalism and popular influence upon government made, in a sense, the acts of the state indirectly the acts of the people. They were identified with its successes and failures as they had not been with those of eighteenth-century royalty. And even where liberal reforms were not accomplished, nationality served as a bulwark against foreign incursion, and patriotism often strengthened the hold on power of conservative leadership.

In one way, growing national sentiment should have impeded military conquest and put limits on foreign expansion. How could France attack Italy or Germany if German and Italian nationalism were well entrenched? But nationalism in the first part of the nineteenth century did not generally separate political entities into small obdurate nationalities. Rather, French military campaigns during the Revolution and afterward under the Napoleonic empire were largely directed (except perhaps in Spain) against territories where nationality extended beyond the confines of existing political boundaries. Germans would not particularly defend a single German principality since what they wanted was national unification and a larger Germany. Ultimately, French attacks against Prussia, Austria, and the smaller German states did evoke a nationalist and patriotic response, but it came so late in the Napoleonic Wars that political successors were not deterred from attacking other states because of fears of arousing a nationalist response. At the same time, Napoleon's military strategy heralded epic victories for those who would harness popular support to citizen armies and bolster them with new tactics of rapid mobility, sustained by forced marches and lighter and more mobile artillery. In the post-1815 period one country after another would learn the Napoleonic lessons and gird itself for effective military combat.

This did not occur immediately. In the aftermath of twenty years of war, Europe was ready for a respite and a period of reconciliation.[1] The European Concert of Powers leagued together to cooperate while warweariness and the common fear of revolution remained to worry conservative states. As long as war was believed to cause revolution, the unreformed empires would not initiate it. As long as revolution was also regarded as a reinforcing cause of war, the conservative statesmen of Europe would band together to put down domestic unrest.

Neither of these views lasted much beyond 1830. Revolution could not be prevented forever, as the upheavals of both 1830 and 1848 proved. But war was gradually seen to be dissociated from revolution and no longer as a cause of pervasive domestic discontent. From 1859 to 1871 four quick wars showed that decisive battles could be fought without inflicting social harm; two of the losers could even remain in power at home. Thus, the urge to avoid war slackened, and nations began to prepare to win it instead. After 1871 exclusive alliances were formed as a substitute for the previous all-embracing Concert. There were even some who courted war as a relatively anodyne means of reinsuring their hold on power. Unreformed conservative regimes saw nationalism and imperial adventure as a means of distracting attention from pressing social issues. In 1914, it was three largely aristocratic regimes, in Austria, Germany, and Russia, that felt they could not brook another challenge and went to war. Until the Great War, moreover, the appeal to nationalism and patriotism had been a relatively effective means of avoiding parliamentary and suffrage reform in Central and Eastern Europe. If liberalism could not be conceded, nationalism would be. Thus the political-military system of the nineteenth century managed to combine the ability to wage war with considerable social support. Even the Marxist German Social Democratic Party rallied to vote for the war provoked by the ruling classes in 1914.

Under these circumstances it was not surprising that imperial expansion in Africa, Southeast Asia, and the Pacific would be a popular phenomenon in most European countries. The extension of European "enlightenment" to "benighted peoples" in Africa and other continents suited the national image many countries held of their own as a superior civilization.[2] European imperialism had succeeded in dividing up the world by the first decade of the twentieth century and thereby of carrying one feature of the military-political world to its zenith. The average size of states had grown much larger (including their dependent territories) and the number of independent states had commensurately declined.[3] The program of territorial conquest inaugurated by kings in the sixteenth and seventeenth centuries had now reached its limit. And at the same time that states were getting larger, territorially, governments were also enjoying an unrivaled support for their foreign policies. It is in these two senses that the nineteenth century and early twentieth century represent the apex of the military political system.

The Triumph of the Military-Political World

Contrary Tendencies

The trend of the nineteenth century as a whole was to strengthen and deepen the hold on international relations of the military-political world. But the liberal political deductions from the French Revolution and from gradual English reform pointed in other directions. In one way, of course, they stimulated nationalism and strengthened the foreign policy of liberal-democratic states for they associated the electorate with policy decisions and outcomes. In another way, however, they began to sketch limits to foreign policy choice. If people had a role in government, they would support those policies with which they could identify. They would not support royal or cabinet policy willy-nilly. Support for imperial adventure or policies of national unification and aggrandizement was partly conditioned on the premise that they would be generally successful and not too costly. No one wanted a repetition of the Napoleonic struggles; no one wanted a foreign policy or a rearmament plan that bankrupted the nation. People were willing to support their leaders when it appeared that the cost of threatening war or of actual fighting was low and its benefit high. They began to raise questions when either of these two requisites was in doubt.

In the British case, the drawn-out struggle of the Boer War revealed the disadvantages of imperial responsibilities. But this was as nothing compared with the wholesale destruction caused by World War I. By 1916 and 1917 troops became hesitant to launch new offensives that past battles had proved were both unbelievably bloody and indecisive. It was not until after Russia collapsed in 1917 that Germany thought she could revert to an offensive strategy. Equally, it was not until the United States entry into the war in 1917 and the arrival of American troops in Europe in 1918 that France and Britain believed they could try to push the Germans out of France. In the 1930s this cautious sentiment was ratified by the Oxford vote in which students declared that they "would not fight for King and Country." After the Crimean War at mid-century, British "jingoism" or bellicosity was limited to the relatively costless enterprise of sending the fleet to Turkish ports, thereby demonstrating "resolve." People supported such maneuvers as they expressed revulsion at the "Bulgarian horrors," massacres inflicted by Turkish misrule of her Balkan population, because in fact there was little to be done. England was not going to fight Turkey, nor was she going to attack Russia, Turkey's enemy. The Crimean War in the 1850s had been a sufficient baptism into bloody and wearing struggles, even though it issued successfully from the British and French point of view. Thus already in the nineteenth century it had begun to be established that popular support of foreign wars could be guaranteed in liberal-democratic states only if those struggles were moral, short, and not too costly. The later pacifist implications of World War I rested on well-established nineteenth-century political premises.[4]

Notwithstanding such attitudes in liberalizing societies, the conservative unreformed governments of Europe were not directed by popular prejudices and did what they felt was necessary to stay in power. Full popular influence upon government and foreign policy awaited the domestic political reform that came after World War I.

But the most powerful tendency counter to the military-political and territorial system of the nineteenth century manifested itself in commercial and economic relations. On the whole the nineteenth century represented a further intensification of the military-political and territorial world system. Fighting became easier, and governments received considerable support if they followed nationalist dictates. The British, however, inaugurated an entirely new commercial system based upon free trade in the 1840s. This system was not ultimately to catch on in Europe nor did it determine the foreign policy of Continental states. But it represented the first country's conversion to a strategic policy of peaceful trade as a means of improving national fortunes. In the period 1830 to 1870 Britain was no longer an imperialist nation.[5] She did not seek extra colonies and was readying her previous dependencies (particularly her settler colonies) for self-government and ultimate independence. If free trade could be extended to her markets, sources of raw material, and food, Britain did not have to acquire new territory to gain the economic benefits. Free and open access would be a cost-efficient substitute. Much therefore depended on others' acceptance of an open trading system. Briefly the Continent came to agree with Britain and in the 1860s free trade began to catch on in France, Prussia-Germany, and elsewhere. In pursuit of this policy, as Toynbee points out, Britain was prepared to sacrifice her own agricultural producers. With the repeal of the tariff on grain (the Corn Laws) in 1846 Great Britain in effect decided that she would not herself feed four-fifths of her population who would become dependent upon imports of cheap food from other countries.[6] This was not an altruistic policy on her part. Under the law of comparative advantage, it allowed her to concentrate on an industrial and export strategy and to nourish her citizens with grain from America, Australia, and New Zealand. At the same time the policy depended on generally pacific international assumptions: that war would not disrupt trade routes and that it would not take place with Britain's traditional suppliers. Britain, in other words, reversed the mercantilist practices of the previous century. Cheap raw materials would now be the fuel for British industry, and inexpensive food would provide energy for the British worker. England's specialization in one realm would allow others to specialize in different ones, and free trade between them would benefit all.

This did not mean that war would never occur. Britain and France fought Russia in 1855, although the French provided the bulk of the land forces. England engaged in episodic war with China over the opium trade. But Britain never thought of waging a serious war on the Continent, and when one loomed in 1864, she backed away. Her trading strategy was in this way contrary to her presumed balance of power strategy, and it was not until her trading strategy had been considerably eroded at the end of the century as a means of foreign policy advancement that she began to take new Continental commitments and a preservation of the balance seriously.[7] Other countries had to make their hostility much clearer before Britain would modify the peaceful expectations that she believed would follow from general adherence to a world system of free trade.

The British trading system which flourished between 1850 and 1870 linked suppliers and markets in a network of cooperative interdependence. At the center of the network perhaps only Great Britain fully accepted and sought to work within the interdependent relation which her specialization entailed. This dependence was modified by the existence of the British fleet policing the sealanes, but the Royal Navy only guaranteed that goods could be delivered; it did not and could not force other countries to produce and sell particular commodities against their will. The American Revolution had occurred to rebut, once and for all, any attempt at such mercantilist control. Britain thus had to persuade her suppliers that they had an equivalent interest in meeting her needs, and she had to offer a trading incentive to them. This meant British industrial goods in the first instance, British loans or investments, and finally, acceptance that other countries would be allowed to develop a surplus in the British home market. Thus European nations, as well as America, Canada, Australia, New Zealand, and Argentina, could expect to benefit from trade with England. The balance of rewards was not only mutual but eventually came to favor the later industrializers.

How could the British agree to such radical transformation of the traditional mercantilist attitude? Because Britain could thereby concentrate on what she did best, producing textiles and machinery. The long production runs required to meet foreign demand for her goods generated additional economic growth and power. Wealth was developed intensively on an economic, industrial, and commercial basis without acquisition of additional territory.

Before the imperialist mystique caught on in the 1880s, Britain went to quite absurd lengths to avoid taking new colonies. She conceded responsible self-government to Australia, New Zealand, and Canada, hoping thereby to persuade them to share London's defense burden, and when they showed little disposition to do this she withdrew her garrisons. She did not accept the proffered cession of the Fiji Islands in 1861 and gave the Ionian Islands to Greece in 1864. In 1865 a Select British Committee recommended withdrawal from all West African possessions except Sierra Leone. By the 1860s a policy of "separation by consent" had become the policy of the British Government.[8]

Thus British policy at mid-nineteenth century overturned two hundred years of precedents. Spain, Holland, and France, to say nothing of Britain herself, had previously aimed at monopoly control. But England now substituted free access for control: if markets were open, they did not have to belong politically to a particular state. Imperialism was unnecessary and uneconomic. It provoked opposition and involved an avoidable expenditure of military force.

Those who have studied the history of the European state system have often been tempted to conclude that the strongest nation makes its bid for military hegemony at the peak of its relative power position. Such hypotheses would explain French late eighteenth-century and German late nineteenth-century bids for leadership. But Britain did not seek to dominate the Continent or her European colleagues at the period of her greatest relative strength. How could this be? The answer is that at mid-nineteenth century Britain was acting according to a nonterritorial model of international politics. The trading model which she espoused and sought to persuade others to adopt did not measure national success by the amount of land won by conquest. Trade, specialization, and access (rather than monopoly control) were sufficient to benefit productive national societies. In Britain's relations with her suppliers and markets is the first real example of the trading world of international politics.

The military-political and territorial world was predicated on the maximization of national independence. It rested on the drive for self-sufficiency by a homogeneous national unit, seeking a relative power advantage. The balance of power could never be secure in such a system because sooner or later states would awaken to find their power position had changed. War might then be necessary to bring political and prestige positions into correspondence with the underlying power distribution or to prevent loss of valued possessions. And even if power relations remained constant, nations seeking a better position would never be satisfied with the existing pattern, and war was the frequent means of redistribution. Since armed conflict was intrinsic to the military-political system, only the most powerful governor could suppress it. Under these circumstances it was not surprising that theorists of the military-political world commonly recommended world government or a total abolition of the interstate system itself as a solution.[9]

World government was not necessary in the trading world

because the conflict of interests among parties was limited. Trading nations seek an absolute improvement in their position and a better allocation of resources. They need not conflict if the sum of total benefits is increasing. Societies and populations wish the largest possible access to goods, and imports are essential to increase the total. Interdependence is preferable to independence and self-reliance at a lower standard of living. A trading world is easier to govern than one of military-political sovereign states. Trading states need to make economic adjustments and to finance temporary balance of payments deficits. The requirement for a trading world is a central bank or institutions which severally perform that function.[10] But world government—an international Leviathan—is not necessary. Economic rigidities are to be overcome, not territorial or military ones. This helps explain why Britain, the world's greatest industrial power, did not seek territorial hegemony and why its relations with suppliers and markets were generally peaceful ones at the peak of its relative power position.

Mid-nineteenth-century Britain and its associates offer the first full-blown example of the trading world of international politics. It could not have occurred earlier. Only after the American and French revolutions of the late eighteenth century were some nations increasingly organized to reflect the social and thus the consumer interest of their populations. Mercantilism had been a royal and aristocratic doctrine, assuming that societies were created from the top down, that subjects existed to serve the royal interest. Hence the state was organized for international purposes, to join in the game of nations, which was the real "sport of kings." Citizens or subjects should comport themselves so as to contribute to French or British advantage in the endless maneuvering for power among sovereigns. But the earliest free traders of the eighteenth century, David Hume and Adam Smith, looked at the matter from the bottom up. Wealth was not power but rather stocks of goods. The more goods, the better off the society. The liberal economic doctrine that they helped to develop directed the state to use its resources to benefit the society of consumers through unhampered international trade. The nation was to be run to help society, not the other way around. Thus the application of liberal doctrines partly awaited liberal societies who would put them into practice. They awaited liberal reform domestically, and it was the most liberal nation, England, that brought their doctrines to fruition internationally.

The trading world of international politics made its debut in the nineteenth century. But one should not conclude from this that it dominated international relationships or even all of British policy. The Continental states, despite their temporary conversion to freer trade continued to think in traditional military-political categories. England ruled the seas and did fight Russia in the Crimean War. This war was a great defeat for the apostles of free trade and international cooperation in what otherwise was a succession of victories at mid-century. They opposed and denounced it, but they could not prevent it.

It is perhaps surprising that the military-political and territorial system did not assert itself against contrary tendencies even earlier than 1914. Free trade did not endure beyond 1880, when the effects of the economic depression of 1873–96 led to tariff protection in a host of Continental countries. The British stayed on free trade, but Germany, Russia, Austria, France, and the United States increased their tariffs. Britain was led, somewhat against her will, to intervene in Egypt in 1882 to assure payment of her international debt. This occupation prompted France and Germany to begin the colonial partition of Africa in 1884–85. Britain then returned to an explicit policy of imperialism:

> as more countries turned away from laissez-faire and began to erect tariff barriers, the "open door" also began to disappear. Strategic and commercial reasons were brought into play. Precautionary claims had to be made to preserve each country's interests and to forestall rivals. It then became impossible not to join in the partition for fear of being left out altogether. The inevitable reaction was a tendency to divide up the remaining areas, unoccupied by Europeans in Africa and the Pacific.[11]

In the 1880s when colonial real estate was open and available, the European powers had few overseas conflicts. In the 1890s when it was beginning to be divided up, there were collisions in Africa and Southeast Asia. In the first decade of the twentieth century, the colonizing urge returned to Europe itself and expressed itself in a competition between Austria and Russia for influence among the territories gaining their freedom from Turkey in the Balkans. It was this struggle that eventually provoked World War I.

Even the British fell prey to annexationist sentiments, with adherents of Gladstone's Liberal Party beginning to endorse the cause. Lord Rosebery, British foreign minister, told the Colonial Institute in 1893:

> It is said that our Empire is already large enough, and does not need extension. That would be true enough if the world were elastic, but unfortunately it is not elastic, and we are engaged at the present moment, in the language of mining, "in pegging out claims for the future." We have to consider not what we want now, but what we shall want in the future. We have to consider what countries must be developed either by ourselves or some other nation, and we have to remember that it is part of our responsibility and heritage to take care that the world, so far as it can be moulded by us, shall receive an English-speaking complexion, and not that of other nations . . . we should, in my opinion grossly fail in the task that has been laid upon us did we shrink from responsibilities and fail to take our share in a partition of the world which we have not forced on, but which has been forced on us.[12]

As imperialism and nationalism were growing, military and technological factors allowed them even greater scope. Railways, the breech-loading rifle, and more effective artillery permitted armies to bring greater firepower to bear against an enemy and to do it more quickly. Prussian conscript soldiers proved more mobile than their professional Austrian and French adversaries. Decisive battles were fought within two to six weeks of the opening of both the Austro-Prussian (1866) and Franco-Prussian wars (1870–71). Neglecting the precedent of the United States Civil War, military staffs concluded that the next major war would be short and that success depended on military and railway timetables. The first power to complete mobilization would have a decisive advantage over a slower opponent. The lessons of 1866 and 1870 strengthened offensive preparations in every European capital. New territory could still be taken by military force and without social or economic disadvantage. Outside powers could not intervene quickly enough to affect the outcome. Such new military techniques also held the potential to upset the balance of power. Despite the countercoalitions which had challenged Napoleon I, Prussian-German Chancellor Otto von Bismarck encountered none; he moved too fast to be deterred by external powers. Bismarck also showed restraint: once Germany had completed her unification, he disclaimed territorial ambitions in Europe.

Thus it was surprising that a major European war, involving four or more great powers did not occur much earlier than 1914. For a brief period (at least until 1890) Germany and Britain helped to hold nationalist ambitions in check even while popular imperialism was beginning to work its influence upon the European body politic. In England's case concentration upon a trading vocation stimulated her to remain aloof from the Continent until the early years of the twentieth century and generally to try to settle the disputes of others. She did not want to interrupt her peaceful economic progress and trade by taking sides in war. Her reliance upon overseas suppliers and markets was ill-suited to national control of all materials that might be needed in war.

For different reasons Bismarck's Germany also sought compromise among European states. The "honest broker" could balance between rival camps only if trusted by both. Bismarck thus substituted a strong diplomacy for a hegemonic territorial or military position, a policy that was unfortunately abandoned by his successors. As Germany succumbed to the lure of territory after 1883 and even more after 1890, her central diplomatic position declined in proportion. The Great War was delayed in part because Bismarck's Germany devised a diplomatic system between 1871 and 1890 which held Europe together, effectively uniting the eastern and western halves of the Continent. Only France remained isolated, and even she accepted a temporary rapprochement with Berlin over colonial matters. Perhaps most importantly, Bismarck did not try to do everything. He did not seek dominance overseas but limited himself to Europe; nor did his power on land lead him to seek naval mastery. There was even a de facto division of responsibility with Great Britain. Britain could be supreme on the seas and maintain the largest overseas empire; Germany would be the strongest land power but would not seek additional European territory. Thus Britain could pursue her trading vocation a little longer for no one was trying to upset the balance of power in Europe. Britain's neglect of Continental matters in these years was largely attributable to German moderation and acceptance of the status quo. Without realizing it, Germany and Britain had developed a kind of reciprocal specialization that not only kept peace between them but also maintained the peace in Europe.

The Intensification of the Military-Political World

Thus the lineaments of an international trading system remained in place longer than they might otherwise have done. The cult of offensive war and the rise of nationalism and imperialism were foredestined to put an end to that system at some point. When tariffs were reimposed in the 1880s, nations, following the dictates of Alexander Hamilton and Friedrich List, agreed that nations ought to endeavor to possess within themselves all the elements of national supply. The national market was thus given priority over the international market, and Continental states proved, in particular, that their temporary conversion to free trade in the 1860s had only been a tactical concession, to be taken back when the depression of 1873–96 made it clear that all countries could not prosper. The growth of world trade slowed. From the 1820s to the 1870s the increase had been about 50 percent per decade; it fell to 37 percent from then until 1913.

High tariffs made return to a territorial policy axiomatic. Access to markets and raw materials would no longer be sufficient because that access was being progressively diminished. Only control of territory provided a guarantee that the market was captive. When France and Germany took colonies, England did not want to be left behind and moved to acquire a large share of Africa, partly to protect her position in Egypt. After 1815 there had been about sixty European states and about ninety or one hundred in the world as a whole. By 1914 the former number had been reduced to little more than a third. Successful imperialism outside Europe operated to control the rest of the world. Britain, France, Portugal, Belgium, and Germany ruled Africa. Britain possessed South Asia; France, Britain, and America governed Southeast Asia. Oceania was ruled by Britain, France, Germany, and the United States. Japan and Russia shared Northeast Asia, and China was open to penetration by many powers. Latin America was formally independent but informally under the powerful influence of the United States. A few great powers controlled the world.

Industrial developments and colonial acquisitions made for greater equality among powers. Britain was demoted from her premier position, but no single European state was strong enough to assume her role. In fact, although all powers were stronger, German and Russian growth outstripped the others. There had been no hegemonic system during the nineteenth century; instead there was a partial division of labor—an extension to the state system as a whole of elements of the trading system. Not until the 1880s was Berlin drawn into the colonial quest. But the problem was that as Germany grew stronger and surpassed Britain industrially, she trampled on the division of labor which had helped to mitigate previous rivalry. She moved from Continental policy to world policy and built a great navy to challenge Britain overseas. In response London expanded her army and began increasingly to dispute German leadership of the Continent. The growing homogenization of capabilities was made more dangerous by the homogenization of roles. More equal states, undeterred by one another, were seeking to compete in the same realms.

The late nineteenth century presented the dilemma of the military-political system of world politics as it had been forged since Westphalia. If states were bound to rival with one another, there would always be attempts at hegemony. Louis XIV and Napoleon had represented the fullness of this urge. The solution to the problem was to make states so equal that no move to hierarchy could possibly succeed. But how could one state prevent another from gaining more power? Only by defeating it and then reducing its size and strength. Hence the maintenance of equality and equilibrium frequently required war, and the ruling presumption of the Western military-political system was that war could rationally be waged. The objective of the state system could never be peace, certainly not peace as an overriding objective.

Until World War I this system caused war, but it functioned tolerably well in Western history. For until then wars had not been so costly that their occurrence represented a greater evil than the disequilibrium that they prevented. But the Great War of 1914–18 was such an evil: it killed so many that the basis of the Westphalian settlement was called into question. At the Battle of the Somme alone in 1916 the British lost more men killed than they did fighting Germany during all of World War II. And if the British suffered over nine hundred thousand battle-deaths in 1914–18, the French lost half again as many. After 1918 one began to question whether equilibrium was more important than peace. Thus the last years of the nineteenth century and the first decades of the twentieth showed that the operation of the military-political system could become intolerable. It was not surprising that in the 1930s the preservation of peace was uppermost in the minds of British and French statesmen.

But how should peace and stability be achieved? International theorists have been inconsistent in their vision of stable economic and political systems. Politically, and militarily, they have tended to believe that an evenly balanced system would be most stable, yielding only occasionally to war. Economically, they have maintained that a system of world economic interdependence needs a hegemonic power to distribute rewards to subordinate players and to keep the system open—to act as a market or lender of last resort. By this double line of reasoning the nineteenth century was stable because of a balance of power on the one hand and hegemony on the other. Both, however, could not be true. Britain could not be hegemonic while a balance of power governed Europe. In actuality, while Britain was never supreme over all others, she held an industrial advantage until the last part of the century. British leadership lasted until her advantage was cancelled, and then the prospects of military conflict increased. Equal states do not decisively deter one another. As Germany and Russia rose in rank relative to Britain, the amount of competition and conflict also grew.

100

The Triumph of the Military-Political World

But the leveling of world politics did not put an end to the system of economic interdependence or at least not immediately. That was because hegemony is required for stability only if there is no division of responsibility among participants. If there is a specialization of tasks among members of the system, even considerable equalization of their capabilities does not lead to conflict. Thus the international economic system could continue to function well enough until 1914. This was not a prolongation of the British trading system because the Continental adherence to it was tactical and not strategic. In the military and territorial sphere, the specialization which had marked British and German cooperation in the 1870s and 1880s no longer existed. Germany wanted a navy to gain a "place in the sun" and Britain an army to maintain the balance on the Continent. France, Russia, and Austria were also interested in improving their power positions. But because of the pattern of alliances—France, Russia, and England against Austria and Germany—they could not gain simultaneously. And while they were seeking greater international power their domestic supports were weakening. Both Austria and Russia felt compelled to expand into the newly independent Balkan area, Austria to prop up its multinational empire, Russia to act as protector of the Slavs. The emergence of an ultranationalist and slavic Serbia was bound to be a prime irritant for Vienna, but the Russians would support it nonetheless. When Serbian officials connived in the assassination of the Austrian archduke and heir to the throne, Austria determined to punish Belgrade once and for all. St. Petersburg, however, could not condone any more Austrian advances and prepared to mobilize. This prompted German mobilization under the terms of the alliance with Austria, and that in turn committed France, the ally of Russia. Britain also went to war when Belgian neutrality was violated by German armies on their way to France.

If any military conflict should have been "the war to end wars" then the war between 1914 and 1918 was it. Even the European victors did not gain: they used up their foreign investments, printed money, took out huge loans, and converted their industrial machines to war production, thereby leaving the international market to others, principally the United States. The losers suffered revolution and the Austro-Hungarian Empire broke into pieces. In the throes of revolution, Russia withdrew from the war and only the United States made a profit. In Europe after 1919 popular sentiment yearned for peace. The popular mood was so antiwar that the villains who had caused it were pilloried and punished. Germany was asked to accept responsibility for the war, and a crushing reparations bill was presented to her in the Versailles Treaty. The peace of 1919 was not a peace of reconciliation but rather one of vengeance. The weak liberal governments that governed Germany after the fall of the kaiser were as vulnerable to nationalist appeals as they were afraid of war. One could scarcely govern Germany without being against Versailles and the dictated peace. All governments tried to evade or to water down their obligations under the treaty. Hitler ultimately succeeded to power because the economic crisis of 1931–32 impoverished the very classes who would otherwise have supported a liberal Germany and because he stood for a repudiation of the Versailles settlement in all of its aspects.

Hitler's achievement of power in Germany in January 1933 has to be explained against another result of the Great War, the social discontent and chaos which emerged from it in Central and Eastern Europe. Two factors helped to explain this revolutionary ferment. The first was the postponement of domestic political reform. Nineteenth-century Germany never achieved responsible, parliamentary government. The French Revolution had not been extended to Central or Eastern Europe, and the conservative coterie who remained in power in Austria and Russia had been able to avoid political change.[13] It took World War I to unsettle these elites and remove them from power. Their failures in the war were sufficient reason for the riots or revolutions which broke out at its close. Austria-Hungary had not only refused parliamentary reform, she had also suppressed the subject nationalities: the Poles, Czechs, Ruthenians, Croats, and Slovaks. When the monarchy collapsed in 1918, the dependent nationalities revolted and Hungary staked out an independent course. Poland and Finland emerged from the Russian Empire's grasp. The smaller states which gained independence were scarcely viable economically and their leadership veered from the extreme Left to the extreme Right. The war and later economic crisis was the second factor responsible for this political disorder because the wartime inflation had impoverished the salaried middle class, the bulwark of moderate regimes, and rendered it susceptible to appeals from the political fringe. After the Russian Revolution of 1917 the specter of Bolshevism loomed in Germany, Hungary, and East European states. As Felix Gilbert writes:

> The situation in the Balkans and Eastern Europe held two particular dangers for the stability of Europe as a whole. Democracy there had succumbed because of the contrasts between nationalities, conflicts between a radical peasantry and a bourgeoisie anxious to foster industrialization, resistance of a landowning class to agrarian reform, fear of revolution and of Communism. The dictatorial or pseudodictatorial regimes which followed the democratic governments clamped the lid on these problems; they did not solve them. Thus, they were themselves unstable, and having come to power by force, they were threatened by force.[14]

The failure of reform in the nineteenth century had led to the danger of left-wing revolution in the twentieth century. Except in the Western democracies, limping victors in the war, the problem of political leadership everywhere was how to stay in power in the political and economic turmoil which ensued after 1918. Of the democratic regimes set up at the war's close in Central and Eastern Europe, only that in Czechoslovakia endured until 1939. In Germany the problem was acute because the Reichstag was polarized between the extreme radical parties on the Left and the ultranationalist parties of the Right. One group stood for revolution and the other for a repudiation of Germany's defeated status and a vindication of her international rights. The moderate parties in the center never had a majority after 1923.

It was not surprising that the territorial and military-political system emerged as an acceptable alternative to more than one state. If Germany, Italy, and Japan did not fulfill their territorial ambitions at the end of World War I, they might develop even more nationalistic and solidaristic regimes and try again. Since social change had apparently outpaced liberal or moderate reform as a panacea, revolution or nationalism remained as the realistic alternatives. Given this choice, nationalism appeared more attractive to middle and lower middle-class elements. The threat of social chaos tends ultimately to produce strong leaders. It did in Russia. In Italy and Germany it led to the Fascism of Mussolini and the National Socialism of Hitler. Discontent was ruthlessly suppressed and new reservoirs of domestic support were plumbed in Germany and Italy for a policy of political and territorial expansion.

It is difficult to imagine such a dramatic transformation of what should have been peaceful, even pacifist sentiment, into war-prone hysteria. But politics was polarized in the states which had not triumphed at the Paris Peace Conference. There was no solid middle ground to which the winners could appeal. The future appeared to belong to the "leader on horseback," the charismatic figure who could master the conflicting tendencies of modern politics and make the people bend to him.

It was strange that such conclusions should have been reached at a time when the conquest of new territories seemed as difficult as it ever had been. Neither Germany nor Japan appeared strong enough to challenge the great and even giant states that would oppose them. Neither could defeat the United States or Soviet Russia, and when Britain and France were added to their number, the prospect became still more bleak. Military and technological factors also offered little help to a new policy of territorial revision. Defense seemed to govern even the most well-designed offense, or so at least the military chiefs reasoned after World War I. Offensive war would use up men and material on an unprecedented scale without achieving its objective. The British invention of the armored tank gave the offense more mobility and firepower while protecting the soldiers who were spearheading it. But this recognition dawned only gradually and did not appear to allow one great power to humble another.

Some voices spoke out against these conclusions. Lord Hugh Trenchard, the British air marshal, believed that a strategic bombing offensive could be decisive. Captain B. H. Liddell Hart and Major General J. F. C. Fuller concluded that the tank could transform the art of war. Some strategists believed that the economic blockade, quite effective in World War I, could once again bring an enemy to his knees. But the strength of British and French seapower, to say nothing of American, was so great that it was Germany and Japan who had to worry about the effects of blockade. Thus the military balance and the apparent bias toward defense seemed to favor the very nations which desired to avoid war.

The military balance, however, was not the only consideration. Politically, the Paris Peace Conference created states which were neither fully legitimate nor strong enough to defend themselves. If the peacemakers had left the old empires in place (presuming this to have been possible) they would have had strong bastions in Central and East Europe but not ones which could command internal legitimacy. If they had followed the principle of national self-determination to its extreme they would have had even smaller but legitimate nations, with slavic nationalities each gaining their own state. But what about Germany? If national self-determination had been given full expression, Germany and Austria and the German parts of Poland and Czechoslovakia would have been united. This, however, would have produced a German superpower astride Central Europe, and France would not stand for this. Thus, some states were larger than a single nationality and some were smaller. Broadly speaking, the new states of Eastern Europe were too large to be ethnically legitimate but too small to be defended against determined attack by a great power.

The supposed supremacy of defense did not operate in the way that strategists thought it might. Perhaps France could defend itself against an attack by Berlin, but France could not prevent a successful German attack against a weak Czechoslovakia or Poland. To defend her eastern allies, France would have had to wage offensive war against Germany, compounding all evils and disasters of World War I. Even with a military balance tilting against them, Germany and Italy could expect to make gains by threatening or actually going to war with the small states on their frontiers.

Though this came later, the development of the blitzkrieg made territorial gains easier. Rapid enveloping movements led by new armored spearheads would punch through enemy lines and disrupt his ability to regroup. Troops on the frontier would be encircled, and logistic lines cut: the disorganization behind the lines would become a rout. If German forces could defeat one opponent at a time and do so quickly, aggressive war could become tolerable once again. After the Second World War began, Germany became convinced that she could win even against large opponents:

her speed and armored power could compensate for a smaller army. In 1940 Germany planned to (and actually did) defeat France in six weeks, and she expected to eliminate the Soviet Union by November 1941. That was nullified by the Russian winter and Stalin's counteroffensives. In 1939 Germany did not have a plan that promised victory against her main opponents, Britain and France, but she attacked anyway. One major factor tending to strengthen the military-political and territorial system was the installation of Fascism and National Socialism in Italy and Germany. War was not much easier to wage, but domestic support, procured by the apparatus of totalitarianism, was now much greater. Hitler had greater scope than any German leader before him, and he could use that support to make up for deficiencies in power.

Economics offered no alternative possibilities. In one way, World war I should have disabused European states of tariffs and controls and fostered a trading system of international relations. In turning their industries to munitions, Britain, France, and Germany had lost export markets to the United States, Japan, and the Scandinavian countries. British shipping, which had helped to balance prewar trade deficits, no longer carried the bulk of world tonnage. European investments abroad, many of which were sold to finance the war, no longer yielded the same returns. The inflation caused by the war had raised prices so that European goods were too expensive in export markets. There was no way to return to the halcyon days of 1913 when domestic economic expansion could be stimulated by foreign trade. After the boom of 1919–21 there was a collapse in demand. Less competitive industries could no longer be run at full capacity. In addition, European production had to be devoted to repaying debts, first to Britain and then in larger amounts to the United States. After the difficulties with inflation during and after the war, deflation seemed safer than letting prices and wages spiral upward. As a result European countries began to tolerate higher unemployment; until the Second World War Britain had never had less than one million unemployed, at least 10 percent of her labor force.

There were two ways in which the complicated structure of reparations and debts might have been sustained. One involved financial transfers: American loans to Germany, German payments of reparations to France and Britain, and British and French repayment of war debts to the United States. As long as such loans were popular on the New York financial market, this economic tripod might stand. But American stocks began to surge ahead in 1927, and American investors turned to them and away from German bonds. This meant that the structure could not be maintained by monetary means.

Another means was the transfer of goods. Britain and France could run an import surplus with Germany, taking German exports as reparations. The United States might in turn accept a British and French surplus in the American market so that they could repay their debts. Neither Britain nor France was pleased with the prospect of financing reparations by buying German goods, but the United States offered the final obstacle. America had become an exporting nation, and though she was a creditor on a grand scale, she did not wish to open her markets to the exports of others. Instead, she raised tariffs in 1922 and again in 1930 to the highest levels in United States history. This made it impossible for the allies to repay their debts.

In the end, late in 1932, nations accepted a mutual cancellation of reparations and war debts, but the damage to the German domestic order had already been done. Striving to pay reparations the German government of Chancellor Heinrich Brüning had embarked on a policy of domestic contraction, lowering prices and wages to gain competitiveness in world markets. This produced mounting unemployment, reaching a total of six million, more than 25 percent of the workforce and creating the discontent which led to Hitler's accession to power in January 1933.

In response to the economic crisis and the Great Depression, states resorted to economic nationalism. The depression of 1873–96 had brought new tariffs, and the Great Depression of 1929–37 had an even more malign effect. Nations responded with competitive devaluation, exchange control, and tariffs. They sought to export their unemployment to other countries. Between 1929 and January 1933 world trade was slashed by two-thirds, and it was not until the Second World War that unemployment was eliminated in Britain and the United States.

J. M. Keynes called the Great Depression "the greatest economic catastrophe of modern times," and its international effects were as disastrous as its domestic impact. Cut off from trade, some nations began to think how they might use military means to acquire economic resources. One aim of Hitler's policy "was to gain additional land in the East, whereby Germany would become self-sufficient in the production of food and also gain additional sources of raw material."[15] This policy marked a renewal of the military and territorial system. The two strong powers, Japan and Germany, were able to expand against weaker states unless and until the United States, Russia, and Great Britain combined against them. It was thus axiomatic that Japan would take much of Southeast Asia in addition to portions of China and that Germany would have a free hand in Eastern Europe until Russia turned against her.

Germany aimed at *Lebensraum* (living space) in Eastern Europe, seeking ultimately to make herself as independent of outside sources of supply as was the entire British Empire, taken as a group of nations. New German colonization overseas was impossible, given the British and American fleets; all Germany could do was to expand eastward to seize new grain, coal, and oil supplies. Japan's main trading partner had been the United States. America had provided her with steel and other metals in addition to oil and rubber. When in 1940–41 President Franklin Delano Roosevelt embargoed these items, hoping to halt Japan's military expansion in China, the Japanese moved to find an alternative supplier. Southeast Asia produced many of the needed materials, but the controlling colonial powers would not sell on Japanese terms. Since Japan had to obtain oil or give up her military position in China, she decided to strike against Southeast Asia. Such a conquest could be thwarted by the American fleet, so Japan first destroyed much of its Pacific Fleet at Pearl Harbor, hoping that the United States would eventually accept a compromise settlement. Once again military force was used to seize resources that were no longer available through international trade.

PART III

PRESENT
WORLDS

6

The Military-Political World

Tolerability of the Military-Political World

The Second World War was quite unlike World War I and had a different effect. The 1914–18 struggle had been a draining and indecisive defensive conflict primarily waged in Western Europe, and it was in the West where the tide finally turned. In contrast World War II was largely decided in the East, and the Western campaign was postponed by diversionary battles in the Mediterranean and North Africa. Trying to avoid the wearing and indecisive European struggles of World War I, the Western allies fought in Egypt, Tunis, Sicily, and Italy and let the Russians initially bear the brunt of German military power. Hence casualties in the West were far less than they had been after 1914. Western domination of the air also made a much greater difference than in 1914. Table 2 shows how the Western allies (with the exception of the United States) managed to reduce their battle losses in the Second World War.

In like manner the image of war after 1945 contrasted greatly with the anguished recollections of 1919. World War II had been moral; it had brought down aggressive and inhuman Fascist leaders. It was a necessary, a "just" war when compared to the stupidity and folly of 1914, where war took place even though

TABLE 2
Battle-inflicted Deaths

Country	World War I	World War II
England	908,000	270,000
France	1,350,000	210,000
Italy	650,000	17,500
United States	126,000	408,300
Austria-Hungary	1,200,000	—
Germany	1,800,000	3,500,000
Russia	1,700,000	7,500,000

NOTE: J. D. Singer and Melvin Small, *Wages of War* (New York: John Wiley & Sons, 1972), pp. 355–56.

many believed reasonable men might have found a solution. It was no longer necessary to amass one million men and one hundred thousand horses to fight a battle. The tank and greater mechanization and mobility meant that war could be faster and more decisive. It need not drag on for four long years. This, of course, suggested that the defending powers would lose ground at the beginning, but their losses could be made up by counterattack and invasion. And if America pledged to defend Europe in advance, an aggressor (German or Russian) could not hope to succeed. It was, after all, the United States effort that made the difference in both wars: they remained indecisive only so long as American power was not applied. Even after a formal United States declaration, there was in both cases a long period of American mobilization and rearmament before her forces were ready to fight. United States forces in Europe, however, would fight immediately and could be rapidly reinforced. Then a future aggressor would know that he could not prevail even in the initial stages.

This sentiment was consistent with the negative reaction to the Munich capitulation of 1938. When British Prime Minister Neville Chamberlain agreed to give the Czech Sudetenland to Nazi Germany, he proclaimed "peace for our time," but the reality was war and in deteriorating circumstances. Afterward many thought he should have stood firm. But Britain could not have prevented Germany from invading Czechoslovakia or Poland; she could only have attacked Germany in retaliation. It was much harder to take such an offensive move when the prevailing belief was that

Germany could defeat an assault from the West. After 1945 there was no such problem. With strong conventional forces and American troops in Central Europe, one could resist an attack from the East. It was thus much less necessary to appease aggressors—to postpone war until it could be fought on better terms.

In 1939 Hitler may have believed until the last minute that Britain and France did not mean what they said about Poland, despite the formal treaty of defense between London and Warsaw on August 25. Hitler had successfully called the Anglo-French bluff in the past. The Western powers had not reacted when challenged in the Rhineland in 1936, Austria in March of 1938, and Czechoslovakia in September of the same year. Was it certain that they would go to war over Poland? Even the British Cabinet and Parliament were unsure because it took them two days of debate after Hitler's invasion of Poland to decide to declare war.

After 1945, however, this would not be a problem. Deterrence involved having forces on the spot which would either have to fight or retreat. There was no way they could disengage. Again, United States and Western forces in Germany after World War II clarified the commitment. To take Germany, Russia would have to fight America, Britain, France, and a host of lesser countries. In the beginning, Western monopoly of the atomic bomb added reality to deterrence. The Soviet Union did not explode its atomic device until the late summer of 1949, and her nuclear capability remained inferior to America's until the late 1960s and early 1970s. With nuclear superiority, the United States could threaten or use nuclear weapons to bulwark its ground troops. Even if the Soviets had larger conventional forces, they would not dare to strike because of the nuclear risk.

Fighting wars, or at least threatening to fight them, thus held few dangers. And even after the Soviet Union became a major nuclear power, deterrence remained in place in part because of the presence of United States troops in many areas of the world. Would an aggressor wish to attack them even if he also possessed nuclear weapons? From the American standpoint, a nonnuclear war would be dangerous only in Western Europe, where as late as the 1970s the Soviet Union might have pushed Western forces into the Channel. Elsewhere, except perhaps in the Persian Gulf,

American conventional forces would have been sufficient to repel Communist attacks. Purely conventional wars, of the sort waged in Korea, did not disturb American military planners because command of the air, mobility, mechanization, and armor would tell the tale for the defenders. The Korean War was not a repetition of static campaigns like those of World War I. Battles raged up and down the peninsula, and the stand-off which ultimately emerged was a reflection of the limits placed on the forces, not intrinsic immobility or a defensive stalemate.

New defense doctrines led military and political leaders to contemplate strategic commitments on a much wider scale. Containment and deterrence even suggested that credibility was perhaps more important than capability. It was credibility that Britain and France lacked in 1938–39. Forces did not have to be fully capable of resisting attack; in the age of American nuclear superiority, they only had to certify that a conflict was in progress. Since no aggressor could be sure the United States would not use nuclear weapons or launch massive conventional attacks upon his homeland, he would hesitate. At a certain stage in the early 1960s American strategists almost seemed ready to believe that the rest of the world could be held safe from Communist military aggression by United States efforts alone. Under President John F. Kennedy's administration the United States prepared to wage two and one-half conventional wars at a time—in Europe, Asia, and the Caribbean. If America could fight both Russia and China, she could surely defeat anyone else.

One of the reasons for the reemergence of the military-political and territorial world after 1945 was the belief that war could be limited, that it would not be disastrous, and that deterrence might even avoid war. After the "loss of China" in 1949 these views became even more explicitly territorial in nature. The communization of China meant its territorial loss to the Western camp. Defense lines might now have to be moved to the offshore island chain, and it was not even clear that mainland Southeast Asia could be defended. American military and diplomatic leaders did not wish to lose any other important countries, in Europe, the Middle East, or as it turned out, Southeast Asia. American Secretary of State John Foster Dulles helped to complete a ring of defense pacts with forty-four other nations, on the assumption that United States treaties would help to deter aggression. Yet, if all that was necessary to establish credibility was to declare an American intention to defend another power then the commitments would not be very costly ones. The Soviet Union responded to the North Atlantic Treaty with the Warsaw Pact and also signed treaties with other Communist and some neutralist nations. For a time, it appeared as if alliance networks might almost deter on their own. Whatever may have been true in the Soviet Union, in the United States many believed that America could protect a worldwide glacis of territory without undue military or economic exertion.

Western deterrence policy was founded on the assumption that a few major defections might lead to a collapse of the alliance system as a whole. Hitler had tested France and Britain three times and at each point found them wanting. In the end, therefore, they had to fight to restore credibility, and World War II was the result. To avoid war after 1945 one had to respond each time and put forces on the spot to counteract the challenge. One could not let a few pawns be taken. But if one were going to defend the whole world, that defense had better be cheap and also successful. How could it be made so?

After the Soviet Union developed atomic and hydrogen weapons and a large force of intercontinental ballistic missiles, the United States could no longer claim escalation dominance—that is, that America would be more prepared to raise the nuclear ante than Moscow. For both, it would be a disaster. This focused attention on limited war, where instruments of mass destruction would not be used on either side. Limited war presumably meant conflicts in which one of the superpowers fought a smaller state or where two clients engaged in battle. If it were the first, then the superpower would presumably win because the outcome would depend only on what limits the superpower observed. If the second, the clients might reach a stand-off, depending on what was supplied by their superpower ally, or, as in the Middle East, one client might defeat but not destroy the other. In either case such proxy wars would not involve the two giants directly, and the dangers of escalation could be controlled. If clients did the fighting, the major power would not suffer the costs and killing, and his population would continue to support containment and military deterrence. Israel's wars against the Arabs neatly fitted this conspectus, and her victories were very popular in the United States, contrasting with the reception accorded the defeats of the Vietnam War.

As late as the 1960s one might still believe that the military-political and territorial model would win support in the United States because alliances and clients would reduce the burden on the American people. The Cuban missile crisis of 1962 probably strengthened this conviction. Though in retrospect the protagonists came near the brink of nuclear war, the policy community might conclude that "crises of resolve" were no bad thing. One does not have to fight, but the staging of crisis, if accompanied by crisis-management, serves the purpose of cost-effective deterrence. One did not have to fight the Soviet Union or invade Cuba; merely escalating the tension and readying nuclear and conventional forces put enough pressure on the Russians to make them back down. When the greatest power in the world commits itself, the other player folds.[1] Deliberate escalation and crisis management thus became the tools of an effective military strategy. In certain ways the Cuban crisis was even better than the Korean War. Only one American was killed, the U-2 pilot who traversed the missile fields in the later stages of the confrontation. Otherwise, it was a signal success for the United States. It served notice that America would not retreat in future crises and greatly strengthened America's credibility of response. Korea had done the same thing but at a much greater cost; it had also demonstrated that even a small, seemingly unimportant nation not within the United States defense perimeter might still be defended. After that it was no longer clear to Russia where the United States would *not* be involved. Cuba was, of course, in the area of primary American interest, but the United States response was so firm that its lessons might conceivably be applied in remoter areas, in Vietnam, for example. Another crisis of resolve there, so it was thought, would also be won by the United States. Again, there seemed little enough to do to maintain American defense lines and credibility around the world. Their cost was not supposed to be too great.

Meanwhile the Soviets were intervening in their own back yard in 1956 and 1968. The Hungarian and Czech invasions, however, did not necessarily mean that Moscow was unduly aggressive. Eastern Europe had been their sphere since World War II, and the trend of developments had actually served to undermine their paramount position. America should not be upset by an attempt to right the balance that was being tipped by domestic pressures in the satellite countries. The United States' planners recognized the problems that the Soviet Union faced, and some of them even declared an "organic" tie between the Soviet Union and the regimes of Eastern Europe. Again there was little to react against. There was also another method of competing with the USSR which did not require fighting. When trends seemed adverse, simply rearm. President Kennedy and his Secretary of Defense, Robert McNamara, had followed such a course in 1961–63. Internal technological and military development thus became a substitute for demonstrating resolve in combat. New military notions, like the doctrine of damage-limitation, served notice on the Russians that the United States would try to prevent them from gaining a nuclear capacity to devastate the United States. United States ability to limit damage meant that she might respond to an attack in Europe with strategic nuclear strikes on Soviet bombers and missiles, thereby limiting any response they might make on American cities. Rearmament and the new doctrines which went with it declared United States unwillingness to accept Russian nuclear equality. If the Soviets were going to keep up, they would have to rearm as well. Much has been written about the arms race: its tendency to increase inflation, to divert production from needed civilian projects, to distort the economy and employment in various ways. But if one had to choose between rearmament and war, those distortions were distinctly bearable.

Insofar as rearmament became a substitute for, rather than a prelude to, fighting, it had certain other advantages. It did not require an attack upon territory. One could gain power intensively, through the mechanism of industrial and technological development; one did not have to seize new lands with all the costs that their conquest would involve. It thus probably helped the military-political world last for another generation or two. Without the actual fighting that took place in Vietnam, it is doubtful whether rearmament alone would have sustained the peace movement in the United States or stimulated the antinuclear campaign in Europe. Popular revulsion is fostered by actual violence: the return to rearmament as a major focus of political-military policies probably improved their prospects at least in the short run.

But such evolutions in the attitude toward war and the ability of deterrence practitioners to reduce its costs did not tell the whole story. The actual changes in power among states as a result of the Second World War erected a new category of superpower: only the United States and the Soviet Union belonged to it. The trend of history since the sixteenth century or so had been to increase the number of great powers. Industrialization had allowed America, Japan, and Italy to join their ranks. Thus the results of 1945 were nearly unprecedented: for the first time since the bipolarity of Hapsburg and Valois kings of the Reformation, power was concentrated in the hands of two major states. The power rivalry would be replicated, and once again there would be few near-great powers which could influence the contest. Nor was the competition a wholly equal one. Russia had initially lost one-third of her territory and industrial power to Germany; her homeland and population had been decimated. Though she had very large military forces, her economy had been totally disorganized by the war and needed a long respite to regain strength. With the exception of the Pearl Harbor attack, none of the present or prospective fifty states of the United States of America had been bombed or invaded. Her industry was intact and booming. In 1950 her output equaled 40 percent of world gross national product. Though she demobilized after the war, her economic and technological strength was awesome and capable of rebuilding a formidable military machine in a short period, as she in fact did after the Korean War. In terms of their strength vis à vis others, both Russia and the United States were capable of thinking in terms of territorial expansion: the Russians because they had a land frontier with many weak buffer states; the Americans because they could intervene with sea and air power in far-flung trouble spots—from Korea to the Congo to Vietnam. Some believed the "loss of China" could be made up by gains in Africa and Southeast Asia.

The conferences during World War II showed how powerful the American-Soviet duopoly had become. At Yalta one could cavalierly realign the frontier of China, divide Germany into zones, and move Poland one hundred miles west. The two superpowers were so strong that, when in agreement, they could virtually partition the rest. Even when opposed, Moscow and Washington still had room for maneuver. The USSR expanded into Eastern Europe at the end of the war, with ideological but no military opposition from the United States. America fomented coups in Guatemala and Iran that restored American-leaning leaders to power, and in Africa she blocked Soviet penetration of the mineral-rich Congo (now Zaire). In the post-Nasser Middle East, Washington virtually excluded Moscow from any significant role. Yet America did nothing when the Soviet Union invaded Afghanistan. She did not react when China occupied Tibet in 1950. Events along superpower borders were very difficult for the opponent to control.

Through it all the Soviet and American conception of world affairs was preponderantly territorial in nature. Nations were "won" or "lost," and the abiding metaphor turned ideological conversion into military victory or defeat. After bipolarity had been established in Europe, many came to believe that the struggle between the two giants would be decided ultimately by the allegiance of the nationalist and nonaligned nations. If India, Indonesia, and major African states all lurched to one side, the balance in world politics would be tipped irretrievably. Thus the superpowers had incentives to contend the territorial contest, to search for victory over the opponent. They did not hesitate to intervene, to rearm, or to demonstrate resolve. Nuclear war would not take place, and the superpower taking the strongest line would win without war. The territorial design remained in place for a full two generations after World War II.

Fissures in the Military-Political World

The relative tolerability of World War II gave the political-military system a greater life span; it did not endow it with immortality. The special edge which the Soviet Union and the

TABLE 3
*Growth at Market Prices
in Selected Developing Countries
in US Dollars (billion)*

Country	1960	1980
	(GNP in billions)	
Spain	61	177
Brazil	62	308
Taiwan	8	45
Egypt	10	29
Mexico	64	233
South Korea	13	63
Nigeria	26	66
South Arabia	15	117
Venezuela	27	74

SOURCE: Directorate of Intelligence, *Handbook of Economic Statistics, 1983* (Washington, D.C., Sept. 1983), pp. 30–31.
In each case, in table 3, the country's output has more than doubled in a twenty-year period exceeding the rate of world growth. This growth holds up if it is expressed in real (that is constant dollar) terms.

United States possessed over the other major nations did not last. The trend which in the last three years of the war was fomenting a new superpower bipolarity changed direction and instead produced a greater equality among great powers. This was not because other states became giant military nations although some, like China and India, did develop a modern defense capability. It was because others improved their industrial performance relative to the Big

TABLE 4
Real Growth Rates Selected Countries

Country	1966–70	1971–75	1976–77	1978	1979	1980
European Community	4.4	2.7	3.8	3.3	3.4	1.3
USSR	5.2	4.3	4.0	3.4	0.4	1.7
East Europe	3.7	4.7	3.0	2.7	1.0	−0.1
China	8.3	5.6	2.7	12.4	7.0	5.2
Japan	11.3	4.6	5.3	5.1	5.2	4.8
Less Developed Countries	6.7	7.0	6.8	4.6	5.3	4.8

SOURCE: Directorate of Intelligence, *Handbook of Economic Statistics, 1983* (Washington, D.C., Sept. 1983), p. 35.

Two. Both the American and the Soviet share of world gross national product declined after the 1950s, though the decline was much greater in the American case. The United States went from 40 percent of world output in 1950 to about 25 percent in 1980. The Soviet Union declined from its 14 percent share of world GNP in 1960 to about 13.4 percent in 1980. In the same period two other major states, Japan and China, were together catching up. In 1960, the two had only about 39 percent of the Soviet share, but they increased this to 65 percent in 1970 and 76 percent in 1980. If she has not already done so, Japan alone will shortly surpass the Soviet Union as an industrial power in world politics. Russia is growing at 2 percent or less; Japan is growing at 4 percent or more in real terms.

But it is not only that other strong powers, like Japan, China, and France, have increased their share of world gross national product. A series of developing countries have also transformed their positions. In each case, as seen in table 3, the country's output has more than doubled in a twenty-year period, exceeding the rate of world growth. This growth holds up if it is expressed in real (that is constant dollar) terms. What is remarkable, as shown in table 4, is that developing country growth compares very favorably with that of China and Japan and is much superior to Soviet and East European growth rates. As table 5 demonstrates, this finding is sustained even if we separate the OPEC less developed countries [LDCs] from the non-OPEC developing countries:

TABLE 5
Developing Country Growth Rates in Real Terms

Countries	1961–70	1971–78	1979	1980
Non-OPEC LDCs	6.3	6.0	5.7	5.9
OPEC-LDCs	7.3	8.0	4.0	1.0

SOURCE: Directorate of Intelligence, *Handbook of Economic Statistics, 1983* (Washington, D.C., Sept. 1983), p. 7.

There has been a squashing together of the topmost nations in world politics. The Soviet Union is now stronger relative to the United States, making for a more equal bipolarity. But others have grown stronger still in respect of Moscow. The distance between the second and third nations in world politics is narrowing to a hair's breadth. And after the third country (Japan) come Germany, France, Britain, and China, with Brazil, India, and Canada not far behind. The leeway given to the two superpowers is declining. They might impose their fiat if they acted together, but increasing rivalry between them prevents that.

The use of force has in consequence become more and more difficult. Against each other, the superpowers face a reliable balance of nuclear deterrence that is not likely to be altered by any technological development currently on the horizon. Against other states, the spread of nuclear weapons imposes restraints on superpower nuclear threats, for example, against China or India. Of course, it may be argued that nuclear weapons will never be used because their employment plunges the world into a whole new amphitheater of risk. Most important among these is whether the "first use" will begin an automatic escalation to all-out war. But even if this were not the case, the first use can usually be countered by a "second use," leaving the initiator worse off. If each use of nuclear weapons can be offset by a retaliatory strike, some have become convinced that nuclear weapons will never be used, and that conventional arms will determine the outcome. If that were true a tremendous weight would fall on the structure of conventional deterrence, perhaps more than it can carry.[2]

But no matter what the doctrines of employment may be, no leader of a state possessing nuclear weapons can be certain that he will not use nuclear weapons *in extremis*, when the tide of battle has turned against him. And if the defender cannot predict his own actions, the aggressor can do so even less. He will have to admit the possibility beforehand that nuclear weapons, with all their escalatory potential, could enter the conflict. This, in itself is a powerful deterrent to the beginning of any kind of war among powers so armed.

Conventional war presents other problems and is not easily deterred or terminated, as a series of wars in the Middle East and the Persian Gulf demonstrate. The theory of the blitzkrieg, first applied by Hitler's generals in World War II, has also been used in wars between Israel and Egypt. Iraq saw no great disadvantage in attacking Iran in 1980. Several wars between India and

Pakistan have turned on the results of the armored battlefield. Some believe that the situation in Western and Central Europe is as unstable as that between other conventionally armed opponents. There is the difference, however, that in Europe both sides also possess nuclear weapons and the ability to use them. Still another difference is that armored maneuver in the urban areas of central Germany would be more difficult than in the Sinai Desert or in the Rann of Kutch. Parts of the North German Plain and the Fulda Gap have been filled with cities. In addition the modern electronic battlefield makes attacking tanks pay a heavy price to win territory. Precision-guided munitions allow antitank weapons to destroy their target with high accuracy and relatively low cost. In the future virtually any target which can be electronically accessed can also be destroyed.[3] In any event in major battles between the two blocs, uncertainties will dominate the outcome. No set of military advisers will be able to guarantee successful conquest before the battle turns nuclear.

For the great powers the political possibilities of war have been greatly reduced. As late as the first half of the twentieth century it had been possible to believe that a strong great power might be able to gain control of the resources it needed through military expansion. Successful imperialism seemed to demonstrate as much in the nineteenth century. In the 1930s both Germany and Japan resolved to find such resources: the Japanese in China and Southeast Asia; the Germans in Russia and Eastern Europe. Given the presumed weakness or disorganization of their opponents (the Russians having just gone through the purges of the mid-1930s), Japan's and Germany's initial decisions were not entirely surprising ones. Both countries, however, made the later mistake of attacking or declaring war on the United States.

In the world economy of the 1990s, however, it would be much more difficult to conquer territories containing sufficient oil, natural resources, and grain supplies to emancipate their holder from the restraints of the interdependent economic system. Only Russia possesses resources and oil in large enough amounts to think of attaining self-sufficiency through military expansion. For other states in North America, Western Europe, or East Asia, the required program of conquest is simply beyond their means. Such an aggressor would need the oil of the Middle East, the resources of Southern Africa, and the grain and iron of Australia, Canada, and the American Middle West. Too much dependence and too little strength exist to make that list achievable. This does not suggest that war could not occur for other reasons; but war to attain economic independence is beyond the capacities of all states except the Soviet Union.

If war between the existing blocs is unlikely in Europe, it makes little difference that the Soviet Union invades one of its satellites in Eastern Europe or acts to cow the Afghans. No new resources of significance will be won. And in Afghanistan, the net result will always be a deficit not a surplus for Soviet capabilities: Russia will spend more than she will gain in return. The only event which could decisively change the balance of world capabilities would be a Soviet conquest of most of the Eurasian continent.

The possibility of such a signal change in the balance has been appreciated since the British geographer Halford Mackinder tried to refute the navalist conceptions of Admiral Alfred Thayer Mahan in 1904. Mackinder sought to show that landpower would become superior to seapower as Continental states industrialized, built railways, and developed internal lines of communication. In particular he believed the territory from Eastern Europe to the Urals would become critical to the dominance of world politics. Mackinder wrote, "Who controls eastern Europe rules the Heartland; who rules the Heartland rules the World Island; and who rules the World Island rules the World."[4] The continent of Eurasia was divided in two parts: the central core, the heartland consisting of Russia and Eastern Europe; and the inner crescent containing coastal Europe, the Middle East, South Asia, mainland Southeast Asia, and China. Outside Eurasia lay the outer crescent, including the offshore islands of Britain and Japan and the continents of Africa, Australia, and North and South America.

Mackinder's contentions were not answered in any specific way until the American geographer Nicholas Spykman undertook to rebut them in 1944. Spykman did not believe that Russia held the key to primacy in world politics. The heartland was important, but more significant still was the inner crescent, which Spykman dubbed the rimland, including the rest of Europe, the Middle East,

South and East Asia, and China. Spykman was impressed by the industrial capacity of Europe, the oil of the Middle East, the resources of Southeast Asia, and the vast unharnessed power of China and India. In response to Mackinder, he contended that "who controls the rimland rules Eurasia; who rules Eurasia controls the destinies of the world." He observed, "Already the United States has gone to war twice within thirty years and the threat to our security each time has been the possibility that the rimland regions of the Eurasian land mass would be dominated by a single power."[5] The axis powers in the Second World War, Japan and Germany, had each sought to conquer an important portion of the rimland and if they had been successful, they would together have dominated the world island.

Spykman's notions probably overstate the importance of particular geographic areas in world politics. But it is interesting to inquire whether a heartland move to control the rimland would tip the balance of world power, as it is presently distributed. In 1977, the division of power as measured by gross national product of each region was distributed approximately as follows: heartland 25.2 percent; rimland 28.5 percent; outer crescent 46.2 percent.

Russia presently dominates the heartland, and if she could occupy the rimland as well, the world balance would shift dramatically in her favor. This would be not only because of the then existing division of power: 54 percent for the world island versus 46 percent for the outer crescent but also because there is no single leadership of the outer crescent. The United States and its maritime associates, Japan and Britain, maintain strong connections with the Oceanic countries, but they do not rule Africa, and United States leadership of Latin America is fragile. Under such circumstances, Spykman's fears would be corroborated. The question is whether the Soviet Union has the ability to make such startling gains. Two world wars left Russia in control of the heartland and a series of strong powers in the rimland. In neither war did the occupant of the heartland manage to conquer the rimland, and in World War I the pressure was in the opposite direction. But if preventing a single power from gaining possession of the rimland is central to maintaining a balance in international politics, one should observe that these lands have developed very rapidly for the most part and are now much stronger than they were. They have grown in strength relative to the Soviet Union. But they are also disunited among themselves, and there will not be a single rimland power capable of challenging the Soviet Union at least until China fully realizes its industrial potential. Their power depends increasingly on maritime strength. A victorious heartland would have to cut off the rimland from sources of supply and reinforcement overseas, a task which even a very strong state could not accomplish with landpower alone. Western and American participation in rimland defense complicates the task even further, making it nearly impossible to accomplish, and thus adding an element of stability to world military politics.

Another factor might have tempted wholesale aggression after 1945 in fact but in fact did not. As the two greatest powers became superpowers and gained more territory and a greater sphere of influence, the average state declined in size and its numbers increased. Until 1914, nations were being combined in ever-larger agglomerations of power, and European imperial nations and the United States had become the overlords of the rest of the world. The 1920s and 1930s did not alter this tendency very much, for the small weak states that emerged from the Paris Peace settlement in 1919 became tempting tidbits for aggression by larger states. After 1945, however, the Dutch, Portuguese, Belgian, French, and British empires broke up, leaving small successor states in their place. The decline in size of states and concomitant increase in their number was accentuated by political divisions between Western and Eastern camps. Germany was divided in three—a Polish part, an East German part, and a West German part. Superpower tensions produced divisions of Korea and, for a time, Vietnam. Tiny island nations emerged from their dependent status in the Indian Ocean, the Caribbean, and the South Pacific. African nations ended their colonial tutelage, but tribal divisions threatened the maintenance of their national integrity in some cases. Could such frail creations survive? On the whole they have done so. In part this is a tribute to the tension caused by the rivalry between the United States and the Soviet Union for the loyalty of uncommitted nations in Africa, Asia, and the Middle East. Nonaligned states have been able to extract favors from both sides without compromising their independence.

In Europe, where Switzerland, Sweden, and Austria were the only nonaligned nations, separate alliance systems offered support to countries not strong enough to stand on their own. The North Atlantic Treaty lent American assistance to Western Germany and the Low Countries, menaced by Soviet armies in Central and Eastern Europe. The Soviet Union assisted countries in the Warsaw Pact that, by its lights, were threatened either by Germany or the United States. Some Western nations were also grateful for American assistance in dividing and counterbalancing a Germany which would otherwise dominate Western Europe economically and militarily. American and Soviet troops armed with nuclear weapons ensured that no change in frontiers was possible without threatening a general conflagration. Small states, with small military budgets, were thus sheltered behind the armaments of giants.

But the division between blocs and the apportionment of smaller states between them was not the only reason that weaker countries did not fall prey to aggression by the strong. Deterrence was not the only cause of international stability; domestic political strength and cohesion also contributed to that result. In the nineteenth century territory after territory had fallen victim to European imperialism because European countries had arms, and European leaders could either co-opt or overawe leaders of traditional societies. After a show of force or a single pitched battle, tribal elites and sheiks usually agreed to accept British or French rule. Their ability to mold domestic sentiment produced political quiescence, at least for a time. Imperialist expansion was not an onerous process; new territories could be brought into the imperial fold almost effortlessly.

In the twentieth century, however, most of the populations of the Third World have been mobilized to political activity and also armed. Urbanization, industrialization, and the decline of the rural population brought new literacy and political participation to the mass of people. Traditional leaders were no longer in a position to deliver their subjects to a foreign overlord, and ethnic and linguistic factors became much more important. The result was a more formidable and obdurate polity, one which could be less easily manipulated by foreigners. Colonial wars, like those in Vietnam and Afghanistan, did not result in uniform victory for the intervening power. Further processes of political mobilization will make even hitherto docile Third World populations resistant to foreign influence and rule. Small new nationalist states have won a political legitimacy and support that their predecessors did not enjoy.

An aggressor thus faces two difficulties: can he conquer a country without destroying it? Can he rule it once it has been subdued? The victor's inheritance may sometimes be quite harsh. In the Third World it may involve draining and indecisive conflicts, particularly where the opposing superpower has given arms to the insurgent population. Once committed, the aggressive superpower feels obliged to continue to fight, even if there is little prospect that he can win the allegiance of the population and extract resources and support from them. In Europe, the threat or use of nuclear weapons complicates the aggressor's task. At the close of World War II, the Soviet Union could occupy warweary satellites of Nazi Germany and elicit some support from a reluctant, but passive population. Two generations in Eastern Europe have known nothing but Soviet rule. But if the USSR tried to move west, she would have to succeed with a *coup de main,* a sudden blow which paralyzed the opposition but did not destroy the country. A very long and drawn out conventional conflict might subdue the people, but few industrial resources would remain to be mobilized. A nuclear conflict would render up a wasteland. If, on the other hand, a sudden strike succeeded without damage to the victim's society, even highly structured industrial economies could be disorganized by popular resistance. In neither case, then, would the USSR be able to gain and employ coveted industrial resources. Administering a military blow to Europe in such circumstances does not serve Soviet purposes.

More sensible from the Russian standpoint is a strategy of overawing European populations with military power and commencing a new arms race. If Europeans think they are powerless and that the United States is not to be trusted, they are more willing to listen to Soviet projects and plans, particularly if these are attuned to European political sensibilities. Roughly speaking, this has been the Russian strategy since World War II. But since the Soviets have also intermittently refused negotiations to limit the arms race, their sincerity remains in doubt. Despite the

European peace and antinuclear movement, the Soviet Union has not been able to convince concerned Europeans of her pacific intentions and good faith.

On the other side, the United States, despite the rearmament programs of the Carter and Reagan Administrations, has found that new weapons have not improved the climate of opinion in either Russia or Europe. Some elements in the Pentagon have believed that an arms race would force the Soviet Union to yield because Moscow cannot afford to devote more resources to defense. Soviet growth rates have declined since the 1960s, and more military expenditure threatens Russian consumption or investment. If Moscow keeps consumption about level, then a heightened arms race undercuts the investment which will keep the Soviet economy productive and growing. It may ultimately bring the Russian economy to a grinding halt. At this point the United States could negotiate from a position of strength.

Neither the Soviet nor the American theory is likely to bring peace or capitulation, however, because adversaries toughen as they are pushed to the wall. Economic pressure on the Soviet Union has not made Moscow more pliable; in fact, Russian awareness of the Pentagon approach has stiffened her negotiating stance. In the past, countries have frequently gone to war, not because they saw a window to victory but because they felt time was turning against them, that they would be worse off in the future than at present. Germany, Austria, and Russia all felt this looming weakness in 1914; they accepted war not because any of them were sure to win but because they were afraid of what might happen if they did not strike. Even Neville Chamberlain drew a line against Hitler in March 1939 because he could not tolerate any further reverses. Thus a beleaguered Moscow might be much harder to deal with than one more sanguine of the future. Of course, one of the great advantages of dealing with Soviet Russia as opposed to Nazi Germany is that Bolshevik doctrine teaches Russians that they will win in the end anyway. The USSR does not have to take extremely provocative risks to retrieve a diplomatic or political position in the short run. Moscow knows how to yield and to reverse course without drawing any final conclusions about irreversible trends in world politics. Thus the military-political system is not made more palatable by rearmament as a means of demonstrating resolve. All arms races do not lead to war, but neither do they lead to productive negotiations or to a new course toward peace.

If rearmament is better than fighting, it has important opportunity costs, that is, costs that arise because alternative courses of action have to be given up. If one rearms, he cannot spend the money on economic growth, high technology in the civilian sector, or research and development. Military expenditures do not increase national productivity. A recent quantitative study of the relationship between economic performance and a series of explanatory factors concluded that military spending, as well as industrial maturity, were associated with low economic growth and productivity. General government expenditures, increases in employment, or high wages, however, did not correlate with declining performance. In seventeen industrial nations the study found "that those nations with a larger military burden tended to invest less."[6] "A negative correlation also exists between military expenditures and the growth in total manufacturing capital." "Nations carrying heavier military burdens also tended to have lower productivity growth."[7] In the United States the first half of the 1980s showed that high military spending contributed to high budget deficits and to high interest rates. If the domestic capital market was largely devoted to financing the government's deficit, there was little enough left for private entrepreneurs who wished to borrow money in order to invest. If capital was available, one had to pay a high price in terms of interest to obtain it. This meant that only the most productive projects, the ones yielding the highest possible returns, could be financed by borrowing.

At the same time, high interest rates bid up the value of the United States dollar because foreigners could get a high return from holding their money in the United States. This in turn made it very difficult for American exporters who found their goods too highly priced abroad. United States domestic growth was also cut back because exporters could not sell enough abroad. At the same time, again because of the overvalued United States dollar, imports were very cheap and American consumers bought the lower priced foreign product, depriving United States manufacturers of the home market. If one cannot sell abroad or at home, American economic growth could be brought to a premature close. It is perhaps not surprising that the industrial growth of the Soviet Union and the United States has been similar to that of the most stagnant major industrial countries since the mid-1970s. Thus, both countries have to consider not only their rivalry with each other but also the danger that other, much faster growing, and more productive societies, which spend much less on defense than do the superpowers, will ultimately surpass them and forge ahead in the industrial race in world politics. They have a common interest to scale down their competition and to devote more resources to economic growth over the long term.

Another factor which lessens the grip of the military-political and territorial world is the growing resistance of populations to their governments' foreign policy ventures. Through most of Western history since the eighteenth century, the ease of making war has been generally accompanied by growing nationalist and patriotic support for such wars. Even when war making became more difficult and costly, peoples in totalitarian states were still forced to lend it unstinting support. In more democratic states, however, the carnage of World War I led to popular revulsion. A half-century later few wars were more generally reviled than the war in Vietnam, 1945–75, and the governments that decided to intervene massively there ultimately lost their supporters and were discredited. Ever since the 1750s, this had been the implicit bargain: governments should win quickly and without too many exactions, or in time their populations would desert them. The British had managed to keep a foothold on the Continent and to engage in war over a long period only because they drastically limited their involvement on land and fought wars by supporting allies on the spot.[8] When, after the Crimean War, this policy seemed as it if might be breached, British governments returned to a policy of "splendid isolation" in regard to the continent of Europe and focused their efforts overseas. The Great War of 1914–18 violated past premises and led to popular disenchantment with war. Thereafter people had to be convinced that the country's existence was really at stake or they would not be tempted to take up arms. The early contests of the Cold War did not change foreign policies very much because they either did not involve much fighting or they did not last overlong. Only Vietnam was both intense and long lasting, and the challenge was posed once again.

Since then popular sentiments against war in democratic or quasi-liberal countries have offered a check to the onrush of the military-political system.[9] They have given ample testimony to their opposition to military policies in the United States, Western and Central Europe, and Japan. In time, such popular opposition may be extended to South Asia and Central America, where wars and insurgencies have disrupted domestic peace and produced international conflicts in the region. But an unanswered question is whether greater popular opposition to militarist foreign policies in democratic states will encourage the Soviet Union to reconsider military expansion, or if not that, to develop peace appeals so strongly persuasive that Western governments will find their populations turning pacifist and neutralist? If one side decisively rejects the military-political world, may not that make the other side adhere to it even more strongly? If the Russians could be sure of capitalizing on this rejection, it might well do so. But popular sentiments have not prevented rearmament in Europe, the United States, or Japan. Forces in existence and deployed in place will resist if they are attacked. There is little evidence that the Soviets could benefit from military expansion, and they might be defeated. Antiwar sentiment burgeons when one's own side is the aggressor. Soviet aggressive moves would only weaken the peace movement in the West. In Europe and elsewhere the Soviet Union cannot win quickly in a major war; thus it must either fight minor wars, as in Afghanistan, or act to reduce the risks of major war. In Eastern Europe, where Soviet reserve echelon forces would operate, there is little sympathy for Russian expansionism, and satellite troops would certainly not follow the orders of their Russian leaders. Again a peaceful stategy is preferable even from the Soviet point of view.

If the major powers face constraints in operating in a military and territorial world, the nationalist countries of the Third World may find fewer inhibitions. They may be willing to run more risks and suffer more setbacks in the first flush of nationalist inspiration. It is even possible that political and military modernization in a number of countries will increase the amount of military aggression. This was the outcome of European nationalism in the nineteenth century: in the process of rejecting Turkish rule, Balkan states came to fight one another. In certain respects this was because the leaders of the new national states did not always have a firm basis of support in the population. The military class cast up reformist leaders, but they did not always enjoy support from peasants and workers, let alone the middle class. Similarly, one might have expected post-1945 leaders in the Third World after achieving independence to seek other means of satisfying their populations. War might then appear as a natural expression of national frustration. In the 1960s and the early 1970s in South Asia and Southeast Asia, there were wars and confrontations. In the 1980s India and Pakistan remained poised against each other as Pakistan completed her atomic device. Vietnam has not hesitated to occupy Cambodia or to incur the wrath of China. In Africa, Somalia and Ethiopia have continuing disputes over the Ogaden region and Libya presses its military initiatives against the Sudan and Chad. In the Middle East different Islamic ideologies contend in the Gulf War and in Lebanon. What strikes an external observer is not that war occasionally occurs, but that it does so rarely. New, and to some degree, weak states depend upon external assistance for war as well as development. Where there are strong supporters of each side, as for example in the Arab-Israeli or initially in the Iran-Iraq conflict, war may continue for a considerable time. But when new states are entirely on their own, conflicts face a limit. Countries dependent on the world economy for markets, assistance, and critical raw materials are doubly hesitant to embark on military adventures unless, again, they have a strong backer. Foreign investment shies away from such turbulent contexts. Much more than the great powers, the small have had to decide whether they would primarily be military nations like Vietnam and to some degree Israel, or whether they would seek to improve their national positions through peaceful trade and economic development. Such decisions have been less military and aggressive than one might have expected on the basis of nineteenth-century European precedents.[10]

Conclusion

The rise of the military-political and territorial system after World War II rested on a series of new props. The Second World War was much more tolerable than the Great War of 1914–18; it was patriotic in a way that 1914 was not. The causes of war, insofar as they centered on the misguided "appeasement" of Germany, appeared as if they might be easily remedied in the post-World War II period. One should "deter" opponents by threatening "unacceptable damage." Deterrence in the first instance was a matter of resolve and credibility. If the opponent was certain one would intervene, he would hesitate to act. Communicating resolve, a relatively cheap endeavor, made the United States and the Soviet Union believe that they could deter counteraction in a wide range of contexts. They could sign treaties, put forces in new territories, and rest assured that they would not be challenged. In this way, bipolarity was itself a form of superpower imperialism in that it implied that the Big Two might divide the rest of the political world up between them. Between superpowers, bipolarity was also tolerable because events would never get out of hand. Crisis management, demonstrations of resolve, and negotiation would produce a stand-off or a settlement. It was thus acceptable to go on trying to fill up all the power vacuums in the world and to probe for a weak spot on the part of the adversary. Even if war occurred, it would be "proxy" war or war with a client of the other side; escalation would not take place and nuclear war would never occur. As the British Foreign Secretary George Canning said in the nineteenth century, the world could get back to a healthy state again: "every nation for itself and God for us all."

But the events after 1945 failed to confirm many of the suppositions of the political-military world. Bipolarity did not remain in place and the signal change since then has been the growth of other industrial nations to a position of near equality with the superstates. China's growth and nuclear capability inhibits the Soviet Union from exceedingly provocative and risky actions against either the United States or China. Russia must always be concerned that the use of nuclear weapons against one power might waste a proportion of its forces and so weaken deterrence against the other.

The military-political system assumed that war or aggressive territorial expansion would be acceptable. Between themselves, the superpowers could not tolerate war, but they might each, alternatively or jointly, expand their alliance systems to the rest of the world, instating a permanent world bipolarity. This did not occur for two reasons: other nations, politically, were able to reject superpower tutelage; other nations, economically, were strong enough to stand on their own. Foreign policy gains, thus, have been drastically pared for the two nuclear giants. There remains the possibility of a direct confrontation between them, but here, both nuclear and conventional deterrence has made such plans dangerous and unlikely to succeed. Further gains in the control of the world island have been made very difficult by trends toward growing industrialization and ideological and political independence. In the Third World, wars have occurred and boundaries have changed. East Pakistan has become Bangladesh; Cambodia's independent existence has been snuffed out. But in the world as a whole the small and weak states which have emerged since 1945 have tended to maintain their positions. The mobilization of popular sentiment has probably tended to restrict overly aggressive, expensive, and exhausting foreign policies. At the same time, it has provided a strong defensive sanction against occupation of another's territories. An aggressor now has to consider the difficulty he will face in ruling a supposedly conquered country. Rearmament may be a better alternative than fighting, but it involves paying high opportunity costs and neglecting other means of improving national well-being. It is a strange commentary on the successes of the military-political system that its two major territorial protagonists, the United States and the Soviet Union, despite spending enormous sums and participating in fighting in different parts of the globe, have done less well than some of their nonterritorially and nondefense oriented competitors in the past forty years.

7

The Trading World

The Second World War initially strengthened both the military-political world and the trading world, but the second impetus was more enduring. After most major conflicts in Western history, peacetime brought a respite, a period of consolidation and agreement. This period did not last long after World War I when the victors concentrated on keeping Germany down, economically and militarily. After World War II, a peace of reconciliation was effected with the defeated powers, Germany and Japan, in part because the Cold War with the Soviet Union broke out at its close. As a new enemy emerged, the Western victors effected a rapprochement with the reformed ex-enemy states. The new trading system might have been undermined at the outset as political hostility and the threat of war overshadowed all other events. It was not, because despite the antagonism between Soviet and Western camps neither side wanted another round of war. Both Western Europe and the Soviet Union needed time to rebuild their economies and restore their devastated homelands. On the Western side there was a much greater understanding of the means by which liberal economies with convertible currencies could contribute to the rebuilding process. Part of the pressure for open economies came from the United States, no doubt desirous of extending her export markets. Part was based on conclusions reached in the 1930s that when financial collapse cuts the commercial links between societies, all nations will suffer, and some will move to seize what they cannot acquire through trade. Economic crisis and depression had been the fare that nourished domestic desperation and brought radical and nationalist leaders to power in more than one state. Prosperity, on the other hand, contributed to stable governments and to a more relaxed foreign policy stance.

The 1930s had also witnessed a transformation in domestic politics in a series of states. The Great Depression of 1929–37 convinced both peoples and governments that employment and social welfare were major national responsibilities: they were too important to be left to the private market and the workings of free enterprise. Henceforth governments in democratic countries— indeed in many others—would act to ensure basic levels of social and economic living. They could do this not only through domestic pump-priming or Keynesian deficit financing: the economic outcomes in one country were likely to be affected by policies in other nations. Depression could easily be communicated from America to Europe as had in fact happened in 1929 31. Depression could partly be avoided by holding export markets open to countries in need. But it was even more important to provide the international funds that would temporarily solve their balance of payments deficits. They would then not have to place restrictions upon their own trade or capital movements, restrictions which would hurt other nations. "Exporting one's unemployment" was a recipe for disaster for the developed world, and it could be avoided by mutual agreement.

The creation of the International Monetary Fund at Bretton Woods in 1944 was a giant step toward a trading system of international relations. The new regime called for an open world economy with low tariffs and strictly limited depreciation of currencies. Tariff hikes and competitive devaluation of currencies were to be restricted by the General Agreement on Tariffs and Trade (GATT) and by the Fund. Unlike the situation after World War I, nations were to be persuaded not to institute controls by offering them liquid funds to float over any period of imbalance in international payments. They would then have a grace period to get their economies in order, after which they could repay the loans.

The plethora of small nations created after the war by the decolonization process in Africa, Asia, the Middle East, and Oceania were generally not large or strong enough to rely on domestic resources, industry, agriculture, and markets for all their needs. Unless they could trade, they could not live. This meant that the markets of the major Western and industrial economies had to take their exports and they in return would need manufacturing exports from the developed countries. The open international economy was critical to their growth and stability. This is not to say that there were no other factors which supported the independence of new nations in the post-World War II period. Military factors and superpower rivalries made the reconquest of colonial areas very costly; ethnic and cultural differences limited the success of attempts to subdue one country or another. But political and military viability were not enough. Small states could not continue to exist as independent entities unless they could earn an economic livelihood. To some degree economic assistance from developed nations or from multilateral agencies met this need. If tariffs and restrictions had inhibited the trade of new nations, however, they would not have been able to function as independent units.

But the open economy of the trading world did not benefit only small nations. The growth of world trade, which increased faster than gross national product until 1980, attracted larger states as well. As the cost of using force increased and its benefits declined, other means of gaining national welfare had to be found. The Federal Republic of Germany, following Hanseatic precedents, became more dependent on international trade than the old united Germany had been. The United Kingdom, France, Italy, Norway, Switzerland, Germany, Belgium, Holland, and Denmark had imports and exports which equalled 30 percent or more of their gross national product, nearly three times the proportion attained in the United States. Japan's huge economy was fueled by foreign trade, which amounted to 20 percent of her GNP total.

The role of Japan and Germany in the trading world is exceedingly interesting because it represents a reversal of past policies in both the nineteenth century and the 1930s. It is correct to say that the two countries experimented with foreign trade because they had been disabused of military expansion by World War II. For a time they were incapable of fighting war on a major scale; their endorsement of the trading system was merely an adoption of the remaining policy alternative. But that endorsement did not change even when the economic strength of the two nations might have sustained a much more nationalistic and militaristic policy. Given the choice between military expansion to achieve self-sufficiency (a choice made more difficult by modern conventional and nuclear weapons in the hands of other powers) and the procurement of necessary markets and raw materials through international commerce, Japan and Germany chose the latter.

It was not until the nineteenth century that this choice became available. During the mercantilist period (1500–1775) commerce was hobbled by restrictions, and any power that relied on it was at the mercy of the tariffs and imperial expansion of other nations. Until the late eighteenth century internal economic development was slow, and there seemed few means of adding to national wealth and power except by conquering territories which contained more peasants and grain. With the Industrial Revolution the link between territory and power was broken; it then became possible to gain economic strength without conquering new lands.[1] New sources of power could be developed within a society, simply by mobilizing them industrially. When combined with peaceful international trade, the Industrial Revolution allowed manufactured goods to find markets in faraway countries. The extra demand would lengthen production runs and increase both industrial efficiency (through economies of scale) and financial return. Such a strategy, if adhered to by all nations, could put an end to war. There was no sense in using military force to acquire power and wealth when they could be obtained more efficiently through peaceful economic development and trade.

The increasing prevalence of the trading option since 1945 raises peaceful possibilities that were neglected during the late nineteenth century and the 1930s. It seems safe to say that an international system composed of more than 160 states cannot continue to exist unless trade remains the primary vocation of most of its members. Were military and territorial orientations to dominate the scene, the trend to greater numbers of smaller states would be reversed, and larger states would conquer small and weak nations.

The possibility of such amalgamations cannot be entirely ruled out. Industrialization had two possible impacts: it allowed a nation to develop its wealth peacefully through internal economic growth, but it also knit new sinews of strength that could coerce other states. Industrialization made territorial expansion easier but also less necessary. In the mid-nineteenth century the Continental states pursued the expansion of their territories while Britain expanded her industry. The industrialization of Prussia and the development of her rail network enabled her armies to defeat Denmark, Austria, and France. Russia also used her new industrial technology to strengthen her military. In the last quarter of the century, even Britain returned to a primarily military and imperialist policy. In his book on imperialism Lenin declared that the drive for colonies was an imminent tendency of the capitalist system. Raw materials would run short and investment capital would pile up at home. The remedy was imperialism with colonies providing new sources for the former and outlets for the latter. But Lenin did not fully understand that an open international economy and intensive economic development at home obviated the need for colonies even under a capitalist, trading system.

The basic effect of World War II was to create much higher world interdependence as the average size of countries declined. The reversal of past trends toward a consolidation of states created instead a multitude of states that could not depend on themselves alone. They needed ties with other nations to prosper and remain viable as small entities. The trading system, as a result, was visible in defense relations as well as international commerce. Nations that could not stand on their own sought alliances or assistance from other powers, and they offered special defense contributions in fighting contingents, regional experience, or particular types of defense hardware. Dutch electronics, French aircraft, German guns and tanks, and British ships all made their independent contribution to an alliance in which no single power might be able to meet its defense needs on a self-sufficient basis. Israel developed a powerful and efficient small arms industry, as well as a great fund of experience combating terrorism. Israeli intelligence added considerably to the information available from Western sources, partly because of its understanding of Soviet weapons systems accumulated in several Arab-Israeli wars.

Defense interdependencies, however, are only one means of sharing the burdens placed upon the modern state. Perhaps more important is economic interdependence among countries. One should not place too much emphasis upon the existence of interdependence per se. European nations in 1913 relied upon the trade and investment that flowed between them; that did not prevent the political crisis which led to a breakdown of the international system and to World War I. Interdependence only constrains national policy if leaders accept and agree to work within its limits. In 1914 Lloyds of London had insured the German merchant marine but that did not stop Germany attacking Belgium, a neutral nation, or England from joining the war against Berlin.[2] The United States was Japan's best customer and source of raw materials in the 1930s, but that did not deter the Japanese attack on Pearl Harbor.

At least among the developed and liberal countries, interdependent ties since 1945 have come to be accepted as a fundamental and unchangeable feature of the situation. This recognition dawned gradually, and the United States may perhaps have been the last to acknowledge it, which was not surprising. The most powerful economy is ready to make fewer adjustments, and America tried initially to pursue its domestic economic policies without taking into account the effect on others, on itself, and on the international financial system as a whole. Presidents Kennedy and Lyndon B. Johnson tried to detach American domestic growth strategies from the deteriorating United States balance of payments, but they left a legacy of needed economic change to their successors. Finally, in the 1980s two American administrations accepted lower United States growth in order to control inflation and began to focus on the international impact of United States policies. The delay in fashioning a strategy of adjustment to international economic realities almost certainly made it more difficult. Smaller countries actively sought to find a niche in the structure of international comparative advantage and in the demand for their goods. Larger countries with large internal markets postponed that reckoning as long as they could. By the 1980s, however, such change could no longer be avoided, and United States leaders embarked upon new industrial and tax policies designed to increase economic growth and enable America to compete more effectively abroad.

The acceptance of new approaches was a reflection of the decline in economic sovereignty. As long as governments could control all the forces impinging upon their economies, welfare states would have no difficulty in implementing domestic planning for social ends. But as trade, investment, corporations, and to some degree labor moved from one national jurisdiction to another, no government could insulate and direct its economy without instituting the extreme protectionist and "beggar thy neighbor" policies of the 1930s. Rather than do this, the flow of goods and capital was allowed to proceed, and in recent years it has become a torrent. In some cases the flow of capital has increased to compensate for barriers or rigidities to the movement of goods.

In both cases the outcome is the result of modern developments in transportation and communications. Railway and high-speed highway networks now allow previously landlocked areas to participate in the international trading network that once depended on rivers and access to the sea. Modern communications and computers allow funds to be instantaneously transferred from one market to another, so that they may earn interest twenty-four hours a day. Transportation costs for a variety of goods have reached a new low, owing to container shipping and handling. For the major industrial countries, (member countries of the Organization for Economic Cooperation and Development, which include the European community, Austria, Finland, Iceland, Portugal, Norway, Spain, Sweden, Switzerland, Turkey, Australia, Canada, Japan, New Zealand, and the United States) exports have risen much faster than either industrial production or gross domestic product since 1965, with the growth of GDP (in constant prices) at 4 percent and that of exports at 7.7 percent.[3] Only Japan's domestic growth has been able to keep pace with the increase in exports (see table 6).

Foreign trade (the sum of exports and imports) percentages were roughly twice as large as these figures in each case. The explosion of foreign trade since 1945 has, if anything, been exceeded by the enormous movement of capital.

In 1950 the value of the stock of direct foreign investment held by U.S. companies was $11.8 billions, compared with $7.2 billions in

TABLE 6

Exports of Goods and Services
(as a Percentage of GDP)

Country	1965	1979
United States	5	9
Japan	11	12
Germany	18	26
United Kingdom	20	29
France	14	22

NOTE: Michael Stewart, *The Age of Inter-*
dependence (Cambridge, Mass.: MIT Press,
1981), p. 21 (derived from United Nations
Yearbook of National Accounts Statistics,
1980, vol. 2, table 2A).

1935, $7.6 billions in 1929 and $3.9 billions in 1914. In the following decade, these investments increased by $22.4 billions, and at the end of 1967 their total value stood at $59 billions.[4]

In 1983, it had reached $226 billions.[5] And direct investment (that portion of investment which buys a significant stake in a foreign firm) was only one part of total United States investment overseas. In 1983 United States private assets abroad totaled $774 billion, or about three times as much.

The amounts, although very large, were not significant in themselves. In 1913, England's foreign investments, equaled one and one-half times her GNP as compared to present American totals of one-quarter of United States GNP. England's foreign trade was more than 40 percent of her national income as compared with contemporary American totals of 15–17 percent. England's pre-World War I involvement in international economic activities was greater than America's today.

Part of what must be explained in the evolution of interdependence is not the high level reached post-1945, but how even higher levels in 1913 could have fallen in the interim. Here the role of industrialization is paramount. As Karl Deutsch, following the work of Werner Sombart, has shown, in the early stages of industrial growth nations must import much of their needed machinery: rail and transportation networks are constructed with equipment and materials from abroad. Once new industries have been created, in a variety of fields, ranging from textiles to heavy industry, the national economy can begin to provide the goods that previously were imported.[6] The United States, the Scandinavian countries, and Japan reached this stage only after the turn of the century, and it was then that the gasoline-powered automobile industry and the manufacturing of electric motors and appliances began to develop rapidly and flourish. The further refinement of agricultural technology also rested on these innovations. Thus, even without restrictions and disruptions of trade, the 1920s would not have seen a rehabilitation of the old interdependent world economy of the 1890s. The further barriers erected in the 1930s confirmed and extended this outcome. If new industrial countries had less need for manufacturing imports, the growth and maintenance of general trade would then come to depend upon an increase in some other category of commerce than the traditional exchange of raw materials for finished goods. In the 1920s, as Albert Hirschman shows, the reciprocal exchange of industrial goods increased briefly, but fell again in the 1930s.[7] That decrease was only made up after 1945 when there was a striking and continuing growth in the trade of manufactured goods among industrial countries.[8] Some will say that this trade is distinctly expendable because countries could produce the goods they import on their own. None of the trade that the United States has today with Western Europe or Japan could really be dubbed "critical" in that the United States could not get along without it. American alternatives exist to almost all industrial products from other developed economies. Thus if interdependence means a trading link which "is costly to break,"[9] there is a sense that the sheer physical dependence of one country upon another, or upon international trade as a whole, has declined since the nineteenth century.

But to measure interdependence in this way misses the essence of the concept. Individuals in a state of nature can be quite independent if they are willing to live at a low standard of living and gather herbs, nuts, and fruits. They are not forced to depend on others but decide to do so to increase their total amount of food and security. Countries in an international state of nature (anarchy) can equally decide to depend only on themselves. They can limit what they consume to what they can produce at home, but they will thereby live less well than they might with specialization and extensive trade and interchange with other nations.

There is no shortage of energy in the world, for example, and all energy needs that previously have been satisfied by imported petroleum might be met by a great increase in coal and natural gas production, fission, and hydropower. But coal-generated electric power produces acid rain, and coal liquification (to produce fuel for automobiles) is expensive. Nuclear power leaves radioactive wastes which have to be contained. Importing oil is a cheaper and cleaner alternative. Thus even though a particular country, like the United States, might become energy self-sufficient if it wanted to, there is reason for dependence on the energy supplies of other nations. Does this mean creating a "tie that is costly to break"? Yes, in the sense that we live less well if we break the tie; but that doesn't mean that the tie could not be broken. Any tie can be broken. In this respect, all ties create "vulnerability interdependence" if they are in the interest of those who form them. One could get along without Japanese cars or European fashions, but eliminating them from the market restricts consumer choice and in fact raises opportunity costs. In this manner, trade between industrial countries may be equally important as trade linking industrial and raw material producing countries.

There are other ways in which interdependence has increased since the nineteenth century. Precisely because industrial countries imported agricultural commodities and sold their manufactured goods to less developed states, their dependence upon each other was much less in the nineteenth century and the 1920s than it is today. Toward the end of the nineteenth century Britain increasingly came to depend upon her empire for markets, food, and raw materials or upon countries in the early stages of industrialization. As Continental tariffs increased, Britain turned to her colonies, the United States, and Latin America to find markets for her exports. These markets provided

> ready receptacles for British goods when other areas became too competitive or unattractive; for example, Australia, India, Brazil and Argentina took the cotton, railways, steel and machinery that could not be sold in European markets. In the same way, whilst British capital exports to the latter dropped from 52 percent in the 1860s to 25 percent in the few years before 1914, those to the

empire rose from 36 percent to 46 percent, and those to Latin America from 10.5 percent to 22 percent.[10]

The British foreign trade which totalled 43.5 percent of GNP in 1913 went increasingly to the empire; thus, if one takes Britain and the colonies as a single economic unit, that unit was much less dependent upon the outside world than, say, Britain is today with a smaller (30.4 percent) ratio of trade to GNP. And Britain alone had much less stake in Germany, France, and the Continental countries' economies than she does today as a member of the European Common Market.

In the nineteenth century trade was primarily vertical in character, taking place between countries at different stages of industrial development, and involving an exchange of manufactured goods on the one hand for food and raw materials on the other. But trade was not the only element in vertical interdependence.

British investment was also vertical in that it proceeded from the developed center, London, to less developed capitals in the Western Hemisphere, Oceania, and the Far East. Such ties might contribute to community feeling in the British Empire, later the Commonwealth of Nations, but it would not restrain conflicts among the countries of Western Europe. Three-quarters of foreign investment of all European countries in 1914 was lodged outside of Europe. In 1913, in the British case 66 percent of her foreign investment went to North and South America and Australia, 28 percent to the Middle and Far East, and only 6 percent to Europe.

In addition, about 90 percent of foreign investment in 1913 was portfolio investment, that is, it represented small holdings of foreign shares that could easily be disposed of on the stock exchange. Direct investment, or investment which represented more than a 10 percent share of the total ownership of a foreign firm was only one-tenth of the total. Today the corresponding figure for the United States is nearly 30 percent. The growth of direct foreign investment since 1945 is a reflection of the greater stake that countries have in each other's well-being in the contemporary period.

In this respect international interdependence has been fostered by a growing interpenetration of economies, in the sense that one economy owns part of another, sends part of its population to live and work in it, and becomes increasingly dependent upon the progress of the latter.[11] The multinational corporation which originates in one national jurisdiction, but operates in others as well, is the primary vehicle for such investment ownership. Stimulated by the demands and incentives of the product life cycle, the multinational corporation invests and produces abroad to make sure of retaining its market share. That market may be in the host country, or it may be in the home country, once the foreign production is imported back into the home economy. Foreign trade has grown enormously since 1945. But its necessary growth has been reduced by the operation of multinational companies in foreign jurisdictions: production abroad reduces the need for exports. In this way an interpenetrative stake has increased between developed economies even when tariffs and other restrictions might appear to have stunted the growth of exports. The application of a common external tariff to the European Economic Community in the 1960s greatly stimulated American foreign investment in Europe, which became such a massive tide that Europeans reacted against the "American challenge," worrying that their prized national economic assets might be preempted by the United States.

They need not have worried. The reverse flow of European and Japanese investment in the United States is reaching such enormous proportions that America has become a net debtor nation: a country that has fewer assets overseas than foreigners have in the United States. The threatened imposition of higher American tariffs and quotas on imports led foreign companies to invest in the United States in gigantic amounts, thereby obviating the need to send exports from their home nation. Such direct investment represents a much more permanent stake in the economic welfare of the host nation than exports to that market could ever be. Foreign production is a more permanent economic commitment than foreign sales, because large shares of a foreign company or subsidiary could not be sold on a stock exchange. The attempt to market such large holdings would only have the effect of depressing the value of the stock. Direct investment is thus illiquid, as opposed to the traditional portfolio investment of the nineteenth century.

After 1945 one country slowly developed a stake in another,

but the process was not initially reciprocal. Until the beginning of the 1970s, the trend was largely for Americans to invest abroad, in Europe, Latin America, and East Asia. As the American dollar cheapened after 1973, however, a reverse flow began, with Europeans and Japanese placing large blocs of capital in American firms and acquiring international companies. Third World multinationals, from Hong Kong, the OPEC countries, and East Asia also began to invest in the United States. By the end of the 1970s world investment was much more balanced, with the European stake in the American economy nearly offsetting the American investment in Europe. Japan also moved to diversify her export offensive in the American market by starting to produce in the United States. But Japan did not benefit from a reciprocal stake in her own economy. Since foreign investors have either been kept out of the Japanese market or have been forced to accept cumbersome joint ventures with Japanese firms, few multinationals have a major commitment to the Japanese market. Japan imports the smallest percentage of manufactured goods of any leading industrial nation. Thus when economic policy makers in America and Europe formulate growth strategies, they are not forced to consider the Japanese economy on a par with their own because Americans and Europeans have little to lose if Japan does not prosper. In her own self-interest Japan will almost certainly have to open her capital market and economy to foreign penetration if she wishes to enjoy corresponding access to economies of other nations. Greater Japanese foreign direct investment will only partly mitigate the pressures on Tokyo in this respect.

It is nonetheless true that interpenetration of investment in industrial economies provides a mutual stake in each other's success that did not exist in the nineteenth century or before World War I. Then Germany cared little if France progressed and the only important loan or investment stake between major powers was that between France and Russia, a factor that could hardly restrain conflict in 1914. It is very important at the moment that the Arab oil countries have substantial investments in Europe and North America because their profitability will be influenced by changes in the oil price. Too high oil prices, throwing the industrial West into depression, would have the effect of cutting returns on Arab

TABLE 7

Dependence on Foreign Minerals (50 Percent or More)

Country/ Region	Bauxite	Copper	Nickel	Zinc	Tin	Cobalt	Iron Ore	Man- ganese	Chro- mium
United States	X	—	X	X	X	X	—	X	X
Japan	X	X	X	X	X	X	X	X	X
European Economic Community	X	X	X	X	X	X	X	X	X

SOURCE: Directorate of Intelligence, *Handbook of Economic Statistics, 1983* (Washington, D.C., Sept. 1983), p. 13.

overseas investments. It would therefore restrain OPEC from precipitate price increases. American business interests with a large stake in Europe would hardly encourage their government to take steps to export American unemployment to other industrial economies for this would only depress their own holdings abroad. A recognition of the degree to which all industrial economies are in the same boat has led to a series of economic summit meetings of seven developed nations in hopes that policies of multilateral growth could be agreed upon to benefit all. These have not solved economic problems, but they have contributed to much greater understanding of the difficulties and policies of other states and perhaps to a greater tolerance for them.

Between the developed countries and the Third World, energy and mineral interdependence fostered a more equal relationship. Australia was the leading producer of bauxite and a huge provider of iron ore in 1982. South Africa was an important source of manganese. Otherwise many of the world's minerals were found in developing nations like Zimbabwe (chromium), Zaire (cobalt), Malaysia (tin), Guinea and Jamaica (bauxite), Zambia (cobalt), Brazil and India (iron ore), and Gabon (manganese). Indian production of iron ore exceeds that of the United States, and Brazilian output is nearly three times as much as America's. In 1982 the twenty-four OECD countries imported eighteen million barrels of oil per day from the OPEC countries and Mexico. Only the United Kingdom and Norway, among Western industrial countries, were virtually self-sufficient in oil supplies. In this way the Third World obtained a considerable leverage in Western industrial economies,

149

and they were bound to obtain more as industrial dependence on imported minerals and oil increased with time.

Yet the great dependence of industrial economies upon each other for markets and the need for Third World minerals and oil would not produce political interdependence between countries in all circumstances. If governments were committed to reducing or eliminating their interdependence with others, the network of economic ties could actually be a factor for conflict. One of the fundamental differences between the Western and democratic industrial countries in 1914 and today—was the lack of commitment to maintain the structure of international economic relations prior to World War I. War between such economies was accepted as a natural outcome of the balance of power system. No pre-1914 statesman or financier was fully aware of the damage that war would do to the European body economic because of the belief that it would be over very quickly. Few bankers or finance ministers interceded with their foreign office brethren to seek to reduce the probability of war.

But the economic interdependence of 1913 had little restraining effect in another respect. Depression and economic disturbances were believed to be natural events like earthquakes and floods; they were not expected to be mediated by governmental intercession or economic policy. It was not until the 1930s that one of the chief functions of the modern democratic state became the achievement of domestic welfare with full employment and an avoidance of inflation. Because it was not the business of government in 1914 to prevent economic disruption and dislocation, little effort was made to minimize the efffect of a prolonged war upon society, and no effort to prevent war altogether. Between Western industrial countries and Japan today, war is virtually unthinkable. Even if economic interdependence was lower after 1945 than it had been in 1913 (and this is not the case), the political significance of interdependence is still much greater today. Governments in the present era cannot achieve the objectives of high employment without inflation except by working together.

There is another change of great importance. In the second half of the nineteenth century sixty million citizens left their countries in Europe to migrate overseas. Labor mobility in this way provided a reservoir of trained and untrained manpower for the regions of recent settlement: North America, Australia, and Latin America. International labor mobility was considerably less than this after 1945 (certainly as a proportion of population), but what flow there was reversed direction. Instead of the industrial countries seeking to send their surplus population overseas, the greatest population growth was in the Third World and the pressure was to move people to countries in the industrial North. Hispanics migrated to the United States in great numbers. West Indians, Africans, and South Asians to the United Kingdom. South Asians to the Middle East, and Vietnamese refugees to many countries. This flow provided a pool of low-wage and generally non-union labor for the work places of the industrial and large scale agricultural world. Wage rates were probably depressed as a result and domestic labor may have suffered, but remittances to the home countries made a huge difference to the balance of payments of countries like Egypt, Mexico, Turkey, Greece, and Pakistan. Caribbean nations improved their positions as a result. Nor did Northern or Middle Eastern employers wish to cut off the flow.

The consequences of the new trend were mixed. On one side, unskilled labor migration to Northern economies has probably increased unemployment there and held wages down. On the other, it has allowed Western industrial economies to maintain some of their original advantages in low cost agriculture, steel, and automobiles that might have been relinquished through high labor costs. Developing nations have reduced the pressure of population growth in this way, but the technological skills that the migrants gain are often lost to the mother country. Only some of the population returns, and the technology is not always shared.

In the nineteenth century the vast emigration from Europe to the Americas and Australia brought relatively skilled labor to underpopulated spaces. It encouraged the use of machines and labor-saving devices because labor was scarce. Labor-scarce economies fostered capital investment and economic growth, and the Third World of the nineteenth century developed very rapidly. In today's Third World, population pressures are much greater, and in some cases the population which leaves will be greatly missed.

Development will be much slower. The balance wheel to equilibrate the mechanism, however, could be provided by foreign capital and the multinational corporation. If major smoke-stack industries do move to the Southern and Eastern Hemisphere, the Third World will benefit as the North is forced to find an alternative occupation. New agro-industries will develop in Spain, Israel, and Central America. In time, not only light industry but also computers, trucks, and civilian aircraft may find a comparative advantage in South America. It is too early to assert that the balance will be an equitable one. The North may benefit more than the South, as has been the traditional outcome. But access to the Northern labor market may be critical for surplus populations in many Third World countries. Even more important will be the Third World's ability to sell in such markets.

Equally, if Northern industry is to be revivified, it will depend on finding new and growing markets outside North America, Europe, and Japan. Ultimately, the South, India, and China provide its opportunity for salvation. Thus, whatever the inequity of current arrangements, it is not easy to see the South trying to manage on its own, to de-couple or de-link its fortunes from Northern markets and capital services. It is also hard to imagine a situation in which Northern industrial stagnation does not prompt a new attempt to sell industrial goods in the still growing market of the less developed countries.[12] The capital and debt crisis of the Third World does not indicate lack of economic dynamism in Sao Paolo, Mexico City, or Caracas but rather an unfortunate concatenation of economic circumstances. The South needed to borrow when interest rates were low and to pay back when the dollar was high and the American economy was sucking in imports. The constant rise in interest rates has unfortunately deprived Southern industry and specialty agriculture of advantages that it should rightly have enjoyed. When the combination of rescheduling, refinancing, and debt repayment is eventually complete, there will still be a great economic impetus to investment in growing Third World economies.

This will leave Northern industrial economies without their traditional metier. Can they develop new ones? It now appears that trade in services, not goods, is the fastest growing part of the world export market. Services such as transportation, financial management, data processing, insurance, income on foreign investment, and other "invisible" items are also the most rapidly growing part of the GNP of many industrial countries. As technological development becomes critical to a nation's place in the structure of international comparative advantage, the transfer of technology and technological advice will become very important. Intraindustry specialization will shift quickly from one time period to the next and the rewards to those who advise on industrial strategy will be considerable. It will become necessary to know precisely what other countries are doing, and what they plan for the future. In civil aviation, for example, there is probably an international market for one or at most two new aircraft with the same range, carrying capacity, and fuel efficiency. If many firms enter the competition, most will be bankrupted by the struggle for sales and leases. To know what to do depends on excellent advice and an understanding not only of the market but of the intentions of other companies. In time there will be exchanges of resident aliens, specialists in given product lines who will spend long periods in other countries, reporting to their home country or firm. Their activities will affect the balance sheets of foreign trade. As information becomes a critical invisible export, leadership in foreign commerce will become even more keenly contested than it is now. The physical movement of goods will have a smaller role in determining a country's position in the export hierarchy.

It is even possible that new labor-intensive industries will begin to develop as sophisticated consumer tastes require individuated products that cannot be produced on an assembly line or Japanese "quality circle." Small shops or component plants will take on a greater part of the manufacturing process.[13] Countries like Sweden, Switzerland, and Italy, boasting highly trained labor forces and craftsmen, may gain new advantages in international specialty trades. Careful workmanship may add greatly to the value of the product without requiring vast expenditures of energy. Like the service sector, the specialty sector will offer new opportunities for countries to find competitive places in the structure of international trade.

Taken all in all, the world economy since 1945 has produced

the greatest increase in wealth since the Victorian economy of the mid-nineteenth century. Rates of industrial growth have exceeded those of prior decades and a host of new states have increased their per capita incomes, status, and welfare. The forty-year boom since 1945 has brought extremely poor countries like India and China into the industrial age. It has repaired the devastation of war in East Asia and Western Europe and given countries like Japan, Korea, Germany, and France an entirely new mode of existence. The new vocation of trading nations has beckoned to many societies and those that have responded have won incredible new rewards, frequently larger and more long lasting than those of their military and territorially oriented brethren.

8

Force or Trade:
The Costs and Benefits

The growing preference of states for a trading strategy in international relations stems not only from the benefits of commerce; it reflects the difficulties represented by the continuing stalemate in the military-political world. Since 1945 a few nations have borne the crushing weight of military expenditure, while others have gained a relative advantage by becoming military free-riders who primarily rely on the security provided by others. While the United States spent nearly 50 percent of its research and development budget on arms, Japan devoted 99 percent to civilian production. Meanwhile the Soviet Union's growth rate slowed from 6 to 4 to 2 percent per year and her industrial investment languished, as a result of the 12 to 14 percent of GNP per year which she spends on the military. Japan, with less than 1 percent of its GNP devoted to armaments, further enhanced its trillion dollar economy through trade and productivity gains. In the West, and particularly in the United States, large government deficits, caused in the most part by immense military spending of nearly $300 billion a year, generated high interest rates which slowed investment, hiked currency values, and limited American export competitiveness. All these expenditures raised the opportunity costs of a military-political and territorial system.

In the American case particularly, a reduction in the budget deficit was required in order to lower interest rates, which restrained both investment and exports. There are two ways of combining low inflation with economic growth: through monetary tightening and a stimulative fiscal policy (that is high government deficits); and through a more relaxed monetary policy which would bring interest rates down while reducing the fiscal stimulus that otherwise could cause inflation. In the mid-1980s it seemed impossible to continue the first course without very high interest rates that would choke off investment and put an end to the recovery from the recession of 1981–82. But the second course—reducing deficits and allowing interest rates to fall—could not take place without limits on government spending, and these in turn were dependent upon restricting the defense budget. Higher taxes would help to limit deficits, but only by also constricting consumption and investment. They could not stimulate growth and control inflation at the same time. Ultimately, as Congress was aware, the defense budget needed to be cut.

The disadvantages of high military spending in sacrificing other economic opportunities, however, are not its only costs; direct costs are also involved. The industrialization of warfare, with concomitant acceleration in the expense of weapons, has imposed its own burdens. Until the mid-nineteenth century, the cost of uniforms and food for troops and horses was the main expense of war, and, as Russia showed, a populous power could be strong without a well-developed industry. But by World War I industrial strength had become a decisive factor in war, and it was production during the war that determined its outcome. It appeared that the machine age could produce weapons almost indefinitely, and the problem became finding soldiers who would fight. After the early battles of World War I, conscription brought in new recruits when needed, but these became less willing to sacrifice themselves as casualties mounted and the battle lines remained more or less fixed. New means of offensive war had to be found, or there would be a political resistance of great magnitude. The armored tank was then developed to protect men in the forward battle area. Increased protection, firepower, and maneuvering speed were heralded as substitutes for massed infantry attacks. But the new tanks, artillery, and airplanes that performed these functions became very expensive. In constant dollar terms, tanks went from less than $50,000 per unit in 1918 to more than $2,000,000 in 1980.[1] Fighter planes that cost less than $100,000 in 1944 rose to at least $10,000,000 per copy forty years later. Paradoxically, as manpower became more expensive politically, the weapons that were to replace it became even more costly. This would not have been a major factor if weapons had lasted longer, but tanks and aircraft were subject to enormous rates of attrition on the battlefield. Ships became obsolescent and were rendered vulnerable to attack by surface missiles. In the end, all but the very strongest powers needed economic help to purchase armaments for long wars. Israel could not have continued to fight after two weeks in 1973 without shipments of arms from the United States. British rearmament would have ceased without Lend-Lease financial assistance from the United States in World War II, and the Soviet Union still has to acknowledge the enormous help it received from military equipment provided by Western powers. In wars after 1945, Vietnam, Israel, Egypt, Jordan, and Syria could not have fought without huge amounts of outside help.

Rapid innovation in weapons technology, producing AWACS (Airborne Warning and Control Systems), precision-guided munitions, and new forms of defense has made the battlefield a more hostile place for attacking tanks and planes. To survive, tanks must carry more armor and move faster, but this takes more fuel which is expensive to transport. Enormous utilization rates in wartime require that large numbers of weapons and supplies be stockpiled before hand. But powers hesitate to buy too many copies of any one weapon for fear that it will become outmoded. In modern war, there is no relatively fixed design, like the battleship *Dreadnought*, which could be bought, with minor improvements, by a decade of European naval ministers.

The conventional battlefield has become even more uncertain than its early twentieth-century predecessor. Technology that might appear to give the advantage to a sudden offensive thrust— such as the tank and jet aircraft—could well be nullified by antitank and antiaircraft defenses.[2] Defensive abilities to counter a tank attack by destroying second echelon forces, logistics, and supply bases behind the lines could transfer the initiative to a defender who might then be able to unleash a counteroffensive into enemy territory. Unlike the German Schlieffen Plan in 1914, which assumed that the surprise turning of the French left flank with a huge force would bring victory in six weeks, no contemporary commander can predict the outcome against a comparably equipped enemy force. Instead, uncertainties dominate the outcome.

The one outcome that is not uncertain is that the peacetime stockpiling of military hardware will become more expensive, rising at least 3–5 percent above inflation per year.[3] This will progressively reduce the number of weapons that can be deployed and provide extra incentives for arms control. The economic costs of a military-political world are not its only defects; political costs are also rising. In Western states there has been a growing revulsion against fighting in overseas wars that are not quick and decisive. Ever since World War I and particularly since World War II, the political costs of military service have been increasing. Patriotism has been a fluctuating asset and one which declines with the length and indecisiveness of war.[4] Political and international limits on conventional conflicts, dictating that they not violate nearby frontiers have limited the scope, but probably increased the length of engagements. The results have typically been inconclusive, reflecting the political stamina of respective opponents. Often the same conflicts break out again and again. Futile wars have not inspired the loyalty of those who are forced to fight in them; only short, dynamic, and successful conflicts command approval and support.[5]

The decline of military loyalty is also a product of political ineffectiveness and uncertainty. In an environment of growing interdependence, modern governments have been unable to fulfill the demands of their populations for economic welfare, security, and peace; domestic alienation has grown. Tax revolts have fed on governmental inefficiency and bureaucracy. If the government cannot provide for their needs with tax revenues, the people prefer to keep the money. In many countries, informed citizens resent military appropriations of billions per year, believing that such expenditures only feed the arms race as the opponent is forced to respond in kind. The security dilemma—where a defensive protection for one state means greater offensive power against another—

suggests that more expenditure may actually mean less security.[6] Western political support for arms reduction has grown greatly.

The pervasiveness of interdependence has another effect. As late as the 1930s, it was still possible for nations to calculate that they had a reasonable chance of seizing and holding by force territories containing needed raw materials and markets. In Japan's intervention in China in the 1930s she sought to conquer a vast market for her goods. This invasion was doomed to failure because she could never absorb China ethnically, politically, or militarily. But her move into Southeast Asia held some hope of success so long as the United States stayed out of the war. Hitler's drive into East Europe might have succeeded if he had not invaded the Soviet Union as well. In Rumania and Poland he sought the oil and coal that would enable Germany to ride out a long war with the Western powers. Except for the Soviet Union such ambitions are now beyond the reach of any major industrial nation. At present it is much easier to obtain needed access to raw materials and markets through trade than to try to control them territorially by force.

The defects of the military-political world do not stem only from its inherent weaknesses but also from the counterattractions of the trading world. However, despite its benefits, the trading strategy may not be elected by major and minor powers. Russia and to some degree the United States remain wedded to the older orientation. Borrowing precedents in the seventeenth and eighteenth centuries, Russia has westernized but has cut herself off from any significant dependence upon trade with European countries and the United States. In a pinch the Soviet Union could do without American or Argentinian grain, Western and Japanese technology and credit. She does not need to have Western consumer goods, and her need for imported oil, at least in the short run, has been exaggerated. The Soviet Union can maintain basic consumer production and an increasing arms budget with some sacrifice of her investment sector. Soviet leaders have been prepared to make this sacrifice in the past, and they may be willing to undergo more belt tightening in the future, as deficient Eastern European economies facing a shortage of cash demand more aid from Moscow. Ultimately, of course, the Soviet Union's ability to give such hard currency aid is a function of her ability to export. If this comes into question, Soviet leaders will once again face the temptation to use force to acquire what they cannot buy.

A major crossroads is now approaching in international relations. The current system is inconsistent, with trends pulling in opposite directions, some favoring trade, others oriented toward territorial control. Since 1945 an environment of economic openness and growing interdependence has sustained many small states that would otherwise have disappeared beneath the waves of international turbulence. If the military-political world had been fully in charge, these small states would have given way and been absorbed by larger states. The weak states of the nineteenth century fell prey to European imperialism; their counterparts might have been eliminated in a new burst of imperialism after 1945, if the military-political world had triumphed.

In the past the military-political world was efficient. It was cheaper to seize another state's territory by force than to develop the sophisticated economic and trading apparatus needed to derive benefit from commercial exchange with it. Nomads and barbarians proved that lesser-developed nations could, by honing their military skills, defeat better-developed states and economies. Force made up the disadvantage and allowed peripheral nations to seize the benefits of Western economic systems. Rome gave way to the barbarian tribes on its borders. The trading world of the Mediterranean was interrupted once by Islam and again by the rise of the Ottoman Turks. Portugal's new naval skills allowed her to intercept Eastern Mediterranean trade at its source, and undercut the link between Venice and India. In their incursions into North Italy, France and the Hapsburgs hoped to seize the most developed and civilized region of Europe. Throughout history the deceptive brightness of a civilization nearing sunset has tempted aggressors to seize what they could not emulate. In a similar way Western civilization has afforded a constant temptation to the Russians.

In one of those reversals to which history is prone, however, the pathway of aggression is no longer smooth. Western or Eastern riches do not lie at the feet of any organized power with fleets or horsemen. At least since the seventeenth century, economic development and cultural advancement have been associated with military power, and, as the record of imperialism shows, the better-developed initially subdued the lesser-developed regions of world politics. In the later twentieth century, the balance has become more even: Western weapons and technology have confronted Eastern numbers and ideological zeal. Where both sides have access to modern weapons, staying power decides the outcome. The very arms race has itself complicated the seizure of new territory, for arms are now readily available in world markets, and defenders have as much access to them as aggressors. Both sides may spend more, but the result is still indecisive. The costs of the military-political world are not likely to decrease, and they may increase further. The trade-off between military-political and trading worlds will be more significant because the particular nations that might choose one can always choose the other. The great economic nations will have military choices. The great military nations will have trading choices.

Such decisions are also influenced by changes in domestic politics. As wars have become more difficult and costly to win, domestic support for such wars has declined. The size of the state may have peaked in 1914, but domestic cohesion and support for state policy continued to grow spasmodically until the 1930s, when it reached its coercive apogee with the National Socialist regime of Adolf Hitler. For a time it appeared that World War II might have provided a different lesson in the exemplary fighting of the "good war." But the campaigns afterward were neither so morally unambiguous nor decisive. The result was that citizens in democratic countries came to resent and oppose them. Wars had to be short and decisive like the Falklands or Grenada to gain approval. The weakening of support for military activities in the West might appear to redound to the interest of the Soviet Union. It has scarcely no public opinion to take into account when it plots its foreign interventions. But the USSR has political opinion of another sort to consider, that in the satellite countries of Eastern Europe. There economic resentments, as well as political restiveness, have provided about as much challenge as the local regimes with Russian support can handle. Any adventurous gesture or misstep in foreign policy could set a new fuse burning, and the Soviet Union may yet have to give greater financial assistance and subsidized energy to assuage political and economic discontents there. Her allies in Eastern Europe now add to Soviet economic and political liabilities, and it is not clear how risky ventures in other areas would reduce their costs. Even the Soviet Union and the internal system of Communist repression have not solved the problem of popular laxity, indifference, and lack of support. Such trends do not increase the benefits or reduce the costs of the military-political system.

Since 1945 the world has been paralyzed between trading and territorial imperatives. One group of states has largely focused on trade, keeping their military expenditures limited; another group, particularly the superpowers and certain Middle Eastern states, has engaged in arms races, military interventions, and occasional war. If the balance starts to tip, the world could slide all the way to the military-political and territorial pole. Weak states in Africa, Southeast Asia, or the Middle East could then fall prey to successful military powers allied to one of the superpowers or to one of the two giants themselves. Successful aggression by one group of nations would call for counteraction by the other, and the globe could then be plunged into another period of massive conflict. The onset of a sudden world depression causing nations to clamp on trade restrictions could lead some to think in terms of military remedies to their economic problems. An intensification of the world debt and financial crisis could precipitate such an economic collapse and trigger, as it did in the 1930s, a resurgence of military expansion. But such an outcome is not foredestined. The very success of economic and trading nations might serve as a beacon to those who had traditionally pursued their great power callings through military rivalries, arms races, and nuclear crisis. In time it might even be possible to bring the superpowers to mitigate their rivalry in military-political terms and to express it through peaceful economic competition. The trading world would then have transformed international politics. Which strategy will be dominant cannot presently be predicted, but if history is any guide, indecision and ambivalence is unlikely to endure. After the 1870s the territorial system reasserted itself against the British trading system, as it did later in the 1930s. Unless critical great powers agree to contend their struggles in different terms, such a transformation is possible once again.

PART IV

FUTURE WORLDS

9

Prospects for Atavism

The current equipoise in international relations can scarcely be maintained: the balance will shift in one direction or the other, toward trading or territorial worlds. Many apostles of the Westphalian system have contended that the territorial and military drives of nations will reassert themselves, perhaps in the context of a new collapse of the world economy; that if war does not take place between East and West, it will ultimately break out between North and South. These pessimists hold that conflict will only be avoided if the West concedes, which, some believe, it has already indicated it may be willing to do. Finally, the most apocalyptic prediction is that nuclear war will eventually occur, for technological or political reasons.

None of these forecasts of a final relapse into international violence or appeasement should be taken as received truth. The prophets of doom have predicted the end of the world many times before. There is nothing automatic in the resort to war; it depends upon national decisions that do not need to be taken. If the probability of war cannot be reduced to zero (and it never can be in a system of particular states), the probability of peace is much greater simply because a structure of general peace is the sine qua non for the success of *any* international policy. War only succeeds if peace quickly follows and damage is held in check, and in the nuclear age such a sanguine outcome cannot be guaranteed. Aggressors are deterred by the overarching uncertainties.

In order to put such pessimistic arguments into perspective

one must first recapitulate the historical trends which have brought us to our current ambivalent and divided condition. In Western history the territorial state gradually consolidated itself from the Renaissance to the modern period. Medieval universalism and feudalism broke down, leaving integrated and more or less homogeneous political units in their place. The preexistent ecumenical ties of economics and religion were attenuated or completely severed. The rise of vernacular languages sustained by the printing press generally supported the new political units which emerged from the medieval period. Military technology ratified the change and the Thirty Years War allowed Protestant states to cast off Catholic tutelage and to lay the foundation in the twin treaties of Westphalia for a new international system based on sovereignty and independence.

Consolidation in turn prepared the groundwork for expansion at home and overseas. Mobile cannon and the siege gun reduced one fortress after another. Centralizing monarchies expanded outward, conquering new land and peasants while developing and perfecting administrative systems to extract tribute from the population. Intensive rule accompanied extensive acquisition. A greater popular role in government after the French and American revolutions gave people a stake in the changes wrought and lent greater support to state policy. In the late eighteenth and early nineteenth centuries revolutionary military force acquired a special legitimacy: it brought new political institutions to the neglected and downtrodden who were in turn promised a role in the new political collectivity. Insofar as coercive power operated within the ambit of a cultural or linguistic group, the result could be solemnized by nationality. As long as such groups remained vague or variant in composition, there were few ethnic barriers to expansion. Conquest frequently succeeded in coopting upper or middle classes to imperial or foreign rule: without a meshing of such classes with the lower stratum, that rule could be successful in Europe as well as overseas. The large, latent, and unmobilized fraction of domestic politics passively endured the result achieved. The experience of common participation in war sometimes solidified tenuous national bonds. During this period of political consolidation, the number of sovereign units in European politics declined and their size greatly increased.

Prospects for Atavism

At some point after 1914 the process began to reverse direction. Consolidation was followed by partial disintegration. Territorial units became smaller, particularly as their latent groups were mobilized to full political activity. The size of states declined after 1919, and particularly after 1945, and continues to decline today as more small units break off and join the welter of already independent states in world politics. Disintegration has occurred in still another sense: the cohesion of the modern state has lessened, and the services that it performs for the electorate have lost both their monopolistic character and their effectiveness. This change has been more relative than absolute: states have continued trying to strengthen themselves internally (and some, like Nazi Germany and Stalinist Russia, attained new apogees of totalitarian repression), but the challenges they have had to surmount have exceeded the capacity of all but the most powerful regimes. People support their governments less loyally in part because of the disastrous and bloody wars to which they have been subjected. They are less ready to answer calls to serve the national interest and have been less willing to regard the government as a sufficient protector of their security. Modern nuclear, ballistic, and terrain-guided weapons have made "security" a chimera, and safety has come to depend on the beneficent policy of other states, as well as on the protections offered by one's own.

In addition, the rise in economic interdependence has meant that individual states do not have the jurisdiction to control economic forces which might determine their level of socioeconomic living. Geographic jurisdiction was not sufficient for this purpose in the nineteenth century when it had reached its maximum extent; it is much more deficient today when the size of states has declined. Broadly speaking, in the industrial and technological period of modern history, there has been a rise in connectedness among societies: what any one does axiomatically impinges upon others. Economic and technological developments have become worldwide in scope. But political units and jurisdictions have been reduced in size. Thus interdependence has vastly increased. Governments cannot cope with this situation, and their populations have become partly disaffected as a result.

The proponents of the military-political and territorial world react to this devaluation of the governing power in apocalyptic terms: by insisting that jurisdiction be increased correspondingly to tasks. In an era of worldwide economic forces this means that each military-political power must presumptively conquer the world. If that cannot be accomplished then one strives to reduce the scope of problems and tasks by limiting the degree of interdependence. This is what the Soviet Union has been seeking to do over the past forty years. But to work against the forces of interdependence instead of with them produces autonomy only at a level of meager competence and well-being. One is condemned to mediocrity by virtue of insisting on omnipotence within a small sphere.

Nationalism, of course, supports such benighted endeavors. Nationalism creates and supports smaller and smaller political units at precisely the time when such units must be larger to be self-supporting. Nationalism creates and reinforces political stability in the Third World where the scope of economic jurisdiction is far too small. It becomes a problem only where it leaves the misleading impression that successful political aggression and war would somehow create a state large enough (an all-embracing Islamic Republic?) to achieve total independence. As this dream fades, interdependence becomes more acceptable.

What is the solution to the problem of world politics at the end of the twentieth century? World government would be a panacea because the scope of jurisdiction would then equal that of needed domain. But world government is unlikely because it violates one of the most potent trends of modern politics: the trend toward smaller political units. To respond to popular needs, governments must bring their services to the people, something they cannot do if they are too large and impersonal. All nationalist movements today (with the exception of Pan-Islamic Fundamentalism) look toward the creation of smaller units than those which already exist. Political legitimacy requires small units; political efficacy a world state. Peace therefore will elude us so long as the military-political system continues as usual.

A Resurgence of the Westphalian Synthesis?

Will territorial drives reassert themselves? Some argue that they are unavoidable so long as international politics divides humanity on the basis of separate, legally sovereign states. States and a state focus are necessary, so it is said, because they organize personal identities and provide a home for individuals in an otherwise anomic world. They provide protection through the perpetual mechanism of the balance of power, in which war and conflict occur but are in some measure controlled. Even if war and territorial change take place, so long as peace is reestablished, the results are not disadvantageous. Economic growth and development, so it is said, may be stimulated by periodic wars, occupations, and changes in frontier. Finally, there has been a periodicity to conflict in the modern world: periods of peace and warweariness ultimately give way to a new round of war. Many believe that this cycle has not been broken.

Such views provide a challenge to the future ascendancy of a peaceful international trading system. They depend upon an irrevocable tendency to return to "violence as usual" among states. Such a mechanistic reassertion of past trends, however, is not only unlikely, it is pernicious and need not occur. The vistas of peaceful growth and development are attractive enough to provide an alternative vision and course of action.

It is still necessary, nonetheless, to consider such possibilities and the arguments for them. According to such interpretations, the myth of the territorial state has been one of the most pervasive fictions of modern politics. In certain ways it may even have been a necessary one: if a person could not be defined successfully by religion, function, or caste, he had to be defined by place. Thus the geographic state-locale (as opposed to the feudal relation or status as a religious communicant) ultimately conferred identity. To be sure, cities and city-states offered such identifying designations to their members—in the Southern United States, one may still meet a "Tennessean" or a "South Carolinian." As civil wars gave way to international wars, the larger jurisdiction became the more acceptable one. One could not be a Philip Nolan (a man without a country) and still have political and therefore personal roots. Thus the parceling out of the world in terms of territorial states performed an emotive function long after it had failed to fulfill political, economic, and security purposes. Late twentieth-century cosmopolite jet-setters may spend their lives hopping from one jurisdiction to the next, but they still mostly identify with their country of origin. Citizens may bemoan the failure of their national state to solve important social and international problems, but that will not lead them to change nationalities. Information about the outside world may be greater than it once was, but the media of communication are still national and filter information through parochial lenses.

According to this view, the territorial and military world helps to organize one's perceptions. In the past the excesses of the military-political world as expressed in war usually led to a remission—a period of peace in which warweariness and economic needs combined to bring a degree of international relaxation and consensus. After the Napoleonic Wars, the Concert of Europe briefly functioned to settle disputes and hold Europe together. By 1854, however, even the British, the most commercial of European peoples, were ready for a good, short war, and found one in the Crimea. After 1919 the respite was shorter still, too short to rehabilitate the world economy or build lasting connections among nations. If the dial of the international barometer periodically shifts from "fair" to "foul" weather, so it must veer from this point of view toward war and conflict once again. The two generations that have passed since the end of World War II already seem a longer than average "era of good feeling" between wars. As national frustrations mount, spurred by interdependence, as well as the negative policies of other states, some countries will be ready for a new bout of war, a new clash over territory, and their citizens will support them.

Even if war does not mechanistically occur, some contend it will be produced by the balance of power as states go up and down the international scale and the newly powerful are tempted to assert themselves. A test of wills, conventional war, or nuclear crisis will occur sooner or later. Even trading states switch national vocations when their territory or prestige is challenged. The basic characteristic of a territorial division of the world is fluidity and flux. States do not remain in the same relation to each other, and even if they did, they would still be dissatisfied. The best and most representative government, Rousseau argued, will still forward the interest of its citizens as against those of neighboring peoples.[1]

The apostles of conflict maintain that the narrowness of national purview of particular states leads even the most enlightened governments to make war, and governments are not always enlightened. According to one interpretation of Western history in a "command economy," the government in the guise of all-knowing protector usurps the surplus that society produces and directs it to military manufacture and war.[2] In World Wars I and II, for example, the state took over economic functions, but after 1945 it did not fully restore them to the private sector. Instead, the arms race continued to extract the surplus and to prevent citizens of many countries from enjoying better lives. In the Orwellian version of this theme, Russian and American elites conspired to spend the surplus and reinsure their own hold on power. Unlimited war between giants was ruled out, but continual battles were fought on the periphery of world politics. In the Orwellian scheme, war and hate were necessary to ensure domestic obedience; a state without enemies could not live.

If this catalogue of arguments is not sufficient to bring a return to Westphalian clashes over territory, it is supplemented by still another perspective. Some writers contend that the stimulus of war, a change in territorial frontiers, and foreign occupation may be necessary to break up special-interest coalitions which have divided up the social product and stunted economic development.[3] According to this somewhat Treitschkian view, the countries which did not lose wars, experience territorial change, or undergo social-revolutionary transformation (those, in short, which did not receive a great political shock or stimulus) failed to maintain high rates of economic growth. In the past century Britain, the United States, Australia, and New Zealand were specially disadvantaged in this respect: seldom if ever losing wars, never suffering military occupation or change in frontiers, they were unable to break the power of their special interest coalitions, which became stronger over time. In contrast, the countries which lost wars, suffered foreign occupation, or change in frontiers, like Japan, West Germany, Italy, and France, did much better economically. If this view is correct, economic factors alone might appear to commend international violence to shock the system into renewed economic growth.

Finally, the proponents of continuing territorial violence contend that the ability to move beyond Westphalian notions and toward new trading strategies in world politics and economics depends upon the continuing undesirability of force. Physical attack must remain costly and largely unsuccessful. In the years since 1945 the nuclear balance has ensured that outcome for extremely threatening actions: the invasion of Western Europe or attacks on the homeland of one of the superpowers. Even this deterrent stability depends upon the certainty of retaliation. If nuclear weapons are too horrible ever to be used (even in defense) then they no longer deter. "No first use" strategies leave the outcome to be determined by the conventional balance. Thus a determined aggressor will ultimately come forward and a new territorial clash occur between great powers.

What can one say in rejoinder to this militarist catechism? A resurgence of Westphalian territorial conceptions along such lines cannot be entirely ruled out. But it does not appear likely. Most fundamentally, such a mechanical reassertion of past tendencies and trends neglects the role of social learning: the ability of one generation to innovate to remedy the failures of its predecessors. If nuclear war is too horrible to be contemplated, nations will consider other means of improving their positions. If the balance of power is typically maintained by seizures of territory (and these produce all-out war), then other means of equilibration will be found. If economic growth has previously been stimulated by losses in war, other stimuli need to be unearthed. Nor is it true that an individual's identification with his nation requires him to support all its excesses. An identification with place does not entail unlimited loyalty. What is perhaps striking about the lineaments of the trading world, at least as they have been extended since 1945, is the degree to which they are consistent with fundamental national identities. Germans do not have to be French to engage in trade with Bordeaux or Marseilles, or English to trade with London. No one denies the ethnic chauvinism of the Japanese, but that does not make them unreliable trading partners or suggest that they will ultimately return to the sword. The Venetians were zealots in trade, but that did not render them incapable of compromise.

The warweariness theme ultimately predicts a new generation of nationalist and inexperienced leaders who will return to warlike ways. Perhaps. In the Third World where nationalism is the strongest, military aggression has sometimes occurred. In relations with great powers, however, Third World leaders have been careful to avoid ultimate provocations, and their defense and economic well-being have usually depended upon support from one or more of the major developed states. Among the great powers themselves one sees little readiness to issue frontal challenges and few hints that the period of warweariness is over. Even the balance of power does not function as it once did. Territorial compensation was once the means of maintaining the balance.[4] But that means depended upon the population of the transferred province loyally cleaving to its new overlord. Ideological or military conversion today does not always last. Mozambique, a declared Marxist state, is seeking new relations with the West. Egypt threw over her suffocating ties with Russia in 1972. Iraq has come to reconsider her radical Islamic credentials now that she has been challenged by Iranian Shi'ites. The fact that ideologies must be tempered by ethnic and economic perspectives means that Marxist victories often do not endure. Russia propelled Somalia out of her orbit as she sought to embrace the new Marxist regime in Ethiopia. In Europe, Communist parties have a national as well as a pro-Russian orientation, and it is not clear where these would come down in a crunch. Balance of power mechanisms no longer operate through exchanges of territories with docile populations. Rather, arms increases, economic growth, and technological progress are the normal means of equilibration, and these do not require an assault on the territorial status quo.

The command economy does not hold the world in thrall. In fact even the internal economy is no longer "commanded" by national governments. Perhaps the best measure of the militarization of society is the proportion of the Gross National Product expended on arms. In World War II the United States spent more than 40 percent of its GNP on the military, and during the Korean War the fraction, after declining in 1946–49, rose briefly to 13 percent. Since then, however, the military budget of the world's most powerful nation has been limited to 10 percent or less, and in recent years American decision makers have found it difficult to expend as much as 7–8 percent of the GNP on defense. In the Soviet Union where a smaller economy sustains an equally large military budget, the fraction in the 1970s reached 12–14 percent of the GNP. With the exception of Israel and Vietnam (two nations which subsisted on aid from allies) the proportion for most other states did not exceed 5 percent, and in Japan it did not reach 2 percent of GNP. In the last decade some Third World nations have increased their arms expenditures, but the total for the developing world as a whole did not increase more rapidly than the associated rise in GNP.

One does not wish to play down the excessive military expenditures in which the world has indulged over the past eighty years; indeed, one of the prime reasons for the growing acceptability of trade and exchange as a national strategy in many countries has been the increasing cost and decreasing benefit of purely military approaches to national advancement. Here it is not merely the enormous amount devoted to armaments which counsels caution but the failure to derive commensurate rewards from a military approach. The war in Vietnam did not help the American position, nor has the war in Afghanistan aided the Soviets. The Persian Gulf encounter between Iraq and Iran has caused a large number of casualties, but it has not been decisive. Individual campaigns in the Arab-Israeli wars favored one side or the other but did not provide a final victory for either. The large territories occupied by Israel did not produce stability in Israeli politics or further the ideal of a Jewish state.

At the same time, despite the command economy interpretation, world trade increased rapidly at two different time periods: during the nineteenth century up to about 1875, and after World War II. In the latter period, world commerce grew more rapidly than the gross national product, leading to an increase in exports as a fraction of the GNP for many countries, including the United States. In addition the entire literature on interdependence among nations conflicts with the command economy thesis. The latter points to state regimentation of economic trends. In fact the major tendency of the past half-century has been in a reverse direction: the increasing ability of economic forces to elude state control. In an interdependent world the state is no longer in command and its ability to control economic events is declining.

Nor is war or territorial change required to induce new economic growth by shaking up special interest coalitions. Germany, Japan, and Italy had large and well-organized industrial enterprises that were not broken up after 1945, yet their economic growth was a signal factor of the period since the war. Perhaps this is because interest coalitions were broad or encompassing enough to take an enlightened view and thus act to restrain prices. Such an explanation would also help one to understand why Sweden, a country which suffered no wars or revolutions in the last one hundred years did better than Britain or the United States in sustaining economic growth. But this modification is not sufficient to save the hypothesis: some countries with narrow coalitions of business or labor have restrained greedy appropriations of the social product by special interests. In Denmark, Sweden, Germany, and Japan, trade unions and farmers' organizations sought to "boost quality in the interest of export promotion" while restraining wage increases.[5]

One of the differences between successful and unsuccessful growth seems to lie in countries' assumptions about the feasibility of economic self-sufficiency. Cartels flourish where autarchy appears attainable. In such conditions coalitions do not have to worry about being challenged by a wide international market or foreign competitors. If countries must export to live because they are too small to be self-sufficient, narrow special interest groups are an expensive luxury. As one observer remarks:

> Postwar Germany, Italy and Japan succeed economically not because of totalitarian episodes or foreign occupation, or integration into a larger unit but because *losses* of territory or empire, or the hope of

empire left them with factor endowments that indisputably forced them to trade.[6]

From this standpoint Britain and the United States had the cushioning disadvantage of relying either on their large national market (the United States case) or the countries of the Commonwealth and Empire (the British case) and as a result were not, after World War II, initially stimulated to develop a powerful export trade with a wider world. In diametric contrast, "were such small states as Belgium and The Netherlands, whose situation had long condemned them to trade and whose coalitions were therefore old hands at the enhancement of productivity."[7]

In this particular respect the prospects of a trading world are greatly enhanced. Because the size of the state is on the average declining and because a huge number of small states won their independence after 1945, the pressure to trade to sustain an independent national existence has been overwhelming. War and revolution were not necessary to force them into rapid economic growth: there was sufficient stimulus from the change in frontiers and the fact that new nations were now on their own.

Since 1648 war has been a major modus operandi of nation-states. If creeping nuclear paralysis now lent initiative to the most determined conventional aggressor, war would once again take place among great powers. Such an eventuality, however, is wholly unlikely. Even states which had formally renounced first use of nuclear weapons might be impelled to employ them in response to conventional aggression. Knowing this, an aggressor will hesitate to attack.

A reversion to territorial expansion, war, and conflict among great powers would represent a return to the world of Westphalia and the campaigns of Louis XIV. But that world is not inexorably upon us. There are other and less dangerous means of balancing power, developing the economy, or protecting the mobilization base. The seizure of territory may not succeed, or the guerrilla conflicts which ensue may raise the cost unacceptably. The fluidity of the power balance may be offset by the fickle obedience of the people to imperial governors.

Prospects for Atavism

A Collapse of the World Economy?

If conflict does not occur through a reassertion of traditional military and territorial imperatives, some believe that it will come as a result of a world economic crisis, a collapse of world prosperity and trade. According to this view, economic crisis is much more regular and predictable than war. Europe saw general peace between 1815 and 1914, but there were ups and downs of the economic cycle every twenty years or so. In the twentieth century recession has followed boom with depressing automaticity. The world financial system was overstretched in 1929–31. Many believe that the mounting burden of Third World debt today could cause a default not unlike Austria's in 1931, except that a substantial number of the world's largest banks would also fail. The portended Crash of '79 may be replayed in 1989 or 1999. Then each country would call in its debts, credit would be drastically curtailed, and business activity would come to a sudden halt. As a result, some predict that tariffs would rise to mountainous heights, and each nation would ration its supply of foreign exchange. International trade would be cut as each state acted to seize its own market from foreigners. Then trading strategies would be jettisoned in favor of military-political ones. The temptation to use force would rise proportionately. Small states could survive only under the protection of the great powers, and there would be de facto amalgamation of one country with another. The final outcome, according to this view, would be the formation of gigantic supracontinental trading blocs, blocs with markets large enough to herald self-sufficiency. One currency would be used in one bloc, a second in another, and there would be little or no trade between them.[8] The constant danger of worldwide economic crisis would under these circumstances plunge nations back into mercantilism and militarism.

But even if economic cycles did not bring collapse, there are those who would predict it on other grounds. A system of long-lasting trading interdependence is based, according to this view, upon nations accepting the full force of international competition and resisting the temptation to put on tariffs. It also rests, some argue, upon the presence of a hegemonic leader of the system who offers a market of last resort and serves as a lender of last resort to countries experiencing balance of payments difficulties.[9] Since some countries will be tempted to defect from such a system and to become protectionist "free-riders" and since hegemonic leaders frequently have to act against their own interest to keep the system open, many believe it will fall prey to its own internal contradictions.

From this point of view an international trading system is a fragile instrument, and it is not likely to withstand the buffeting winds of inflation, depression, or individual failure to realize the benefits of comparative advantage.[10] Disadvantaged countries will ultimately desert the trading arrangement and seek to improve their position through tariffs, quotas, and exchange controls. When these devices are adopted by others as well, they will bring the demise of the open trading system.

Finally, some claim that domestic pressures will bring collapse. Even if national governments were not tempted to become protectionist by the incentives of the international economic game with other states, their populations and interest groups will force them to put on tariffs and quotas. Since the 1930s many observers have concluded that business and labor will always demand higher tariffs to reduce unemployment. Traditional industries rail against imports from the new steel, textile, and automotive industries of the Third World, and in periods of recession would have considerable help from labor unions. Voluntary restraint agreements in the 1970s and 1980s proved the reality of such notions.

Altogether, therefore, the economic pessimists conclude that both the cyclical and structural character of international economic relations prevents any sustained period of prosperity and open trade among nations. An economic collapse is around the corner, bringing with it a reversion to militarism in world politics.

There is, however, little reason to reach such premature conclusions. If depression occurs with the monotonous regularity suggested above, the world economic system should already have collapsed. In 1974 and again in 1980–82 it withstood substantial downturns without a reversion to tariffs which would permanently restrict the general growth of trade. If the pessimistic view is correct, the plight of indebted Third World nations should perhaps already have produced one or two critical defaults, but in the Mexican, Argentinian, and Brazilian cases multilateral rescheduling and refinancing averted a crisis. In another period of great political and economic stress, the 1970s, the trading system continued to operate even though the United States could no longer carry the burdens associated with keeping it open. In certain respects it is astounding to recall that a whole range of retaliatory tariff increases did not follow in the wake of the United States devaluation and import surcharge of August 15, 1971. Equally, after the oil crisis of 1973 one might have expected new tariffs designed to win a favorable balance of trade for countries dependent upon importing oil in large amounts from the Middle East. In the 1980s the maintenance of an open trading and capital system is even more remarkable because the United States is less able to assist debtors and countries in balance of payments difficulty than she was in the 1970s. In fact debtors, including the United States, have received new money from multilateral sources, public and private, suggesting that a single hegemonic power is not necessary to prop up the system and make it work.

This outcome also casts doubt upon the incentive to free ride in an open trading system. Free-riding works so long as one can assume that the collective benefit will not be withdrawn, so long as others are willing to pay the costs of keeping the system open.[11] Whatever may be true of the Third World (which has been conceded a certain leeway in this regard), major industrial nations do not have the luxury of eating their cake and having it, too. If one trading power returned to a permanent policy of protection, the others might follow and the collective good of free trade would then be lost. Major participants in the system, thus, are hesitant to make a strong unilateral move against it. Social learning facilitates such a choice. Having lived through the 1930s with its "beggar thy neighbor" policies, nations today are reluctant to repeat such follies. They would rather bear the costs in the short run, hoping that by keeping the system open they will benefit in the long run. Multilateral tariff cutting has continued, the system has remained open, and capital flows have been more unconstrained than ever. Despite unemployment and recession, therefore, the trading system has remained in place since 1945, avoiding a general collapse. It has proved more resilient than its detractors imagined.

Conflict and War Between the First and Third World?

Even if economic collapse and a return to Westphalian brutality and national expansion can be avoided, there are some who see conflict issuing from other causes. According to protagonists of the *dependencia* school, war may become the ultimate means of forcing the North to take account of the plight of the South.[12] From this perspective, as indeed from many others, the beneficial results of world trade and growth have not been equally shared. Many countries in the Southern Hemisphere remain desperately poor. Some scholars point to the easier route traveled by nineteenth-century developing countries: the United States, Australia, South Africa, Canada, New Zealand, and small Central and East European states. The terms of trade for agricultural goods were favorable in the nineteenth century,[13] and American growth was financed by exports of cotton and grain. In the twentieth century and partic-ularly after World War II, the terms of trade may have turned against agricultural products and in favor of industrial ones, with the already industrialized nations in the North winning new (and undeserved) returns, while the South failed to profit from sales of its low-priced commodities. Today many parts of South Asia and much of Africa languish in poverty; many in the Third World see no solution to their suffering in the mechanisms of world trade. The pessimists believe that any attempt to increase food production would only diminish its price in world markets and leave underlying poverty unchanged. If no economic remedies can be found, the Third World is likely to turn to military alternatives, to the further spread of nuclear weapons, and to terrorism. This could bring new military conflicts between the North and the South.

Despite the opinions of experts and nay-sayers, however, the South may lie on the threshold of powerful new agricultural development. Small landholders from China to Bangladesh to the Punjab have recently increased their yields. If repressive government policies in Africa which discourage peasant production and provide few cash incentives to produce more grain were changed, the drift of labor to unproductive cities might be reversed and the import of food halted. Kenya and Zimbabwe have recently improved production while their neighbors struggle with antiquated policies. Mexico, Brazil, Korea, and India have built industry on the profits of small- as well as large-scale agriculture.

Ultimately, high labor costs in the North will direct heavy industry to the Southern and Eastern hemispheres. Even if this does not take place immediately, the Third World will be assisted to develop more rapidly in order to repay the debts it owes to Western banks, governments, and international institutions. It is in the narrow financial interest of creditor states that developing countries export enough to service their debts. This, however, puts the potential economic solidarity between North and South in too restricted terms. The North cannot resume its own economic progress unless the Southern market for its goods develops rapidly.[14] This cannot occur unless the South grows faster than it has done since the early 1970s. Hence some have seen justification for a new Marshall Plan linking Northern capital and technology to the industrialization of the poorer regions of the world. Even if such public-aid projects do not materialize, there will still be wide opportunities for private and multilateral investment in developing countries that will in turn yield dividends in greater international trade.[15]

Increasing military conflict between North and South cannot help the Third World's position. If developing nations use up machinery and arms (largely imported from the North) but have no export income with which to replace them, the military effort cannot be sustained and economic development is sacrificed in the process. Some extremely nationalist or xenophobic regimes may be willing to pay this price for a time, but it would be suicidal over the long term. Third World development ultimately depends upon selling to expanding markets in the Northern Hemisphere, on winning new comparative advantages in smokestack or other industries. A strategy of military hostility or radical "de-coupling" between South and North would only set back the timetable of economic development.

The Paralysis and Failure of Democracies: Pitiful Plutocrats?

When the Third and First World have so many common interests, one must believe that they will reach a lasting accommodation despite the arguments of the pessimists and the apostles of dependency. In East-West relations, however, there is another theme of despair: Western democracies will connive in their own capitulation to determined communist antagonists. Some believe the West is so weak and divided that it cannot respond to Soviet pressures. Jean-François Revel, in *How Democracies Perish,* writes:

> Democracy probably could have endured had it been the only type of political organization in the world. But it is not basically structured to defend itself against outside enemies seeking its annihilation, especially since the latest and most dangerous of these external enemies, communism—the current and complete model of totalitarianism—parades as democracy perfected when it is in fact the absolute negation of democracy.
>
> Democracy is by its very nature turned inward. Its vocation is the patient and realistic improvement of life in a community. Communism, on the other hand, necessarily looks outward because it is a failed society and is incapable of engendering a viable one. The Nomenklatura, the body of bureaucrat-dictators who govern the system, has no choice, therefore, but to direct its abilities toward expansion abroad. Communism is more skillful, more persevering than democracy in defending itself. Democracy tends to ignore, even deny, threats to its existence because it loathes doing what is needed to counter them. It awakens only when the danger becomes deadly, imminent, evident. By then, either there is too little time left for it to save itself, or the price of survival has become crushingly high.[16]

According to this assessment, Western states have been on the defensive at least since their failure to knock down the Berlin Wall in 1961. They did not respond effectively to the Hungarian Revolution in 1956, the Russian invasion of Czechoslovakia in 1968, or the Russian suppression of the Afghan government and people in 1979. This view asserts that they do not spend enough on arms, despite a massive military buildup by their adversaries. They are too ready and willing to trade and to lend (on concessionary terms) to their enemy, just for pecuniary advancement. A sizable segment of Dutch public opinion, questioned about Soviet policy in Afghanistan and Poland in 1981, decided that Holland lacked a moral right to criticize the USSR "as long as housing conditions in Amsterdam fail to meet the highest standards of modern comfort, as long as women remain exploited and legal rights of heterosexual married couples are denied to homosexual married couples."[17]

From this dismal point of view it is precisely the economic weakness and underlying political instability of the Soviet empire that make it dangerous. It has to make up for these frailties by success in foreign relations, or it cannot survive. But the apostles of gloom assert that there is no resolution in NATO, either political or economic. The Western allies compete to offer favorable economic terms to the Russians while hesitating to deploy the very military systems that would partially offset the Soviet conventional and strategic predominance. Afraid that the Soviet Union will stir up European public opinion against them, Western governments do not even carry out what they have agreed to do among themselves. This view is Spenglerian in its sweeping dismissal of Western weakness, irresolution, and plutocracy. According to it, nations without fiber will be discarded by history. From this standpoint, the danger is not reversion to militarism and territorial conflict; it is the obverse. Nations obese with economic plenty will not fulfill the necessary dictates of the balance of power. The ultimate conclusion, so pessimists declare, is either political collapse and acceptance of Soviet hegemony or a test of strength brought on when its outcome is an already foregone conclusion. In either case, the exponents of Western decline believe that there will be a return to military or political conquest.

But is the position of the West as unsatisfactory as all that?

The "Decline of the West" argument has been held by many distinguished historians, by Arnold Toynbee as well as Oswald Spengler.[18] Henry Kissinger may have conceived his task in similarly Metternichean terms: to slow down the revolutionary impulse and prolong the life of essentially conservative regimes. The uniqueness of the view of Jean-François Revel is that it combines a full recognition of Soviet economic and political weakness with admiration for its international strength. This doleful view, however, greatly exaggerates the number of high cards in the Russian hand and minimizes the underlying cohesion and vitality of the West. There is no doubt that changes in the German attitude in recent years have betokened an unseemly desire to get along with Moscow regardless of Russian policies. The Low Countries find it difficult to carry out their part of cruise-missile deployment in response to the deployment of a large number of Soviet SS–20s even though arms control talks were initially broken off by the USSR. In the wake of martial law in Poland, West European firms honored their Soviet pipeline contracts despite Reagan Administration attempts to bar European subsidiaries of American firms from doing so. It is not yet clear that Western high technology items will be effectively prevented from reaching Moscow. The Western reaction to the Soviet intervention in Hungary in 1956 was more severe and lasted longer than the pallid response to the Russian seizure of Czechoslovakia in 1968. The Russian invasion of Afghanistan in 1979, however, certainly spurred Western defense spending, in Europe as well as in the United States.

Ultimately what do these gestures toward Moscow amount to? They reflect the long-standing desire of most Europeans to avoid exacerbating political hostilities with the East. Such abstentions do not detract from Western security nor change the military balance. Forces remain in place; governments and parliaments vote and augment defense budgets. New technologies are deployed and force readiness is increased. Congressional sentiment in the United States favoring large cuts in American troops in Europe in 1975 has been muted in the last few years. Western rearmament has been surprisingly large and continuous in face of domestic cuts in spending. The balance between the two armed camps in Europe was more equal in the mid-1980s than at any time in the past generation. The Euro-strategic balance (which has never been even) moved glacially toward that distant goal in 1985.

What do societies have to do to defend themselves? Issuing belligerent pronunciamentos does not provide defense, though at one point Leon Trotsky thought it might. A society protects itself and retains vitality by providing (together with allies) the forces needed to offer a credible defense or a nuclear response in a crisis. It also does so by following dynamic strategies of economic and technological growth which will serve as a beacon to bureaucratic or inert economies, societies mired in worker lethargy and deficient capital investment.

Spenglerian defeatism also masks real uncertainties and vacillation in the Kremlin. Despite what right-wing critics have often claimed, the Russians do not always know just how to handle a crisis. In June 1941 Stalin wavered helplessly, unsure of what to do as Hitler's armies invaded Russia. The Soviets did not react to the Berlin Airlift in 1948 because they were afraid of precipitating a military incident which could lead to war. They moved missiles into Cuba but also withdrew them, tails between their legs, in 1962. They staked much on their alliance with China only to have it explode in their faces. Their move into the Middle East in association with Colonel Gamal Abdel Nasser of Egypt did not pay off, and now the most revolutionary force there is led by the vehemently antimodernist and anti-Russian Ayatollah Khomeini. In 1967, 1970, and 1973 the Russians were careful to avoid provoking the West and the United States, and Israeli or Jordanian victories emerged in those instances. The Russians did not react or cancel their invitation to Richard Nixon to visit Moscow after the mining of Haiphong harbor in spring 1972. The shooting down of the Korean airliner in September 1983 and the manifest inability of Soviet policymakers to explain or justify it produced worldwide condemnation and led the Russians to retract into a shell, for a time paranoiacally denouncing erstwhile friends as well as adversaries. After canceling both sets of arms talks in a huff, they agreed in 1985 to resume them without any Western concessions.

Some criticize democratic societies for allowing antidemocratic and subversive elements the political freedom to contend against Western policies, but in that open debate, as John Stuart Mill foresaw, the absolutists have never won out. A healthy skepticism in Western electorates has not played into communist hands, nor has it shifted governmental policy by much. The very economic and political openness of democratic countries provides the attraction to depressed Soviet peoples that has made them dissatisfied with their regimented life. It should not be otherwise. Far from declining, the West has provided the example and the stimulus to economic change in China and also Eastern Europe. Ultimately the Soviet Union may have to regear its economy to remain in effective competition with the West and Japan.

Nuclear War?

Violent nationalism, economic crisis, military conflict between North and South, and craven obeisance before the USSR may all be avoided in future international politics. Yet, many point out that war, even nuclear war, could occur for other reasons. According to some, accident, miscalculation, or mechanical malfunction will doom humanity. At a certain point computers, subordinate commanders, or crazed men locked in a missile silo will take over and begin a war with no political cause. Some note that the very procedures adopted to make sure that the chain of command continues to function in a nuclear crisis could so decentralize decision as to free it from political direction and control. There are only a few command and political centers, tempting an opponent to consider what one observer has called a "nuclear decapitation" strike,[19] hoping that his opponent's system would then shut down. Unfortunately, the remedy for such a threat is a degree of predelegation of nuclear authority to others, a power that has already, so it is said, been given to nuclear missile submarine commanders.

This leads to another danger. Some students of the subject have pointed out that the less robust the system of command and control, the greater the temptation to adopt "launch on warning" or "launch under attack" procedures. This would shorten decision time to 5 to 15 minutes with the fate of the world held in the hands of a single decision maker. Some have concluded that, under these circumstances, sooner or later there will be a nuclear war. Such hair-trigger readiness will ultimately lead to a cataclysmic blunder. This conclusion takes on some additional weight when experts recall that radar detection systems have on several occasions given false warning of an impending attack. One component of the strategic defense system would involve automatic launch of interception vehicles by computer.[20]

But historians point out that this is not the only danger. If either party were to conclude that the political and strategic balance in world politics was turning against him and that a conflict was ultimately inevitable, he might adopt a reckless stand in a crisis and an escalation process would then begin. None of the Great Powers was actively seeking a war in 1914, but some believed that it would come sooner or later. The assassination of Archduke Franz Ferdinand outraged Austria and led her to plot a small war against Serbia. After that, events began to unroll, and none of the major powers was able to stand aside.

Still other experts are worried by attempts to gain a one-sided nuclear superiority. In the 1960s United States advocates of superiority tried to find means by which America could "limit damage" to her own and allied populations through counterforce strikes on Russian missiles, airfields, and submarine bases. But the American threat to escalate a conflict without hitting cities has lent Russia incentives to build a larger force both to attack United States strategic bases and to devastate the American population after absorbing a strategic attack. This in turn prompted further United States expenditure to maintain the capacity to "countervail" Soviet capacities at each rung of the escalation ladder. The mutual striving for superiority has led only to parity. Therefore, some conclude that political and technological factors might interact to produce the worst of all worlds: the provocation of crisis in the first instance, and the technological inability to handle it in the second. They believe that nuclear war may well occur.

But fears of inevitable war are overblown. There is no reason to believe that failure to achieve superiority will produce war.

Contrary to many exponents of nuclear strategy, Thomas Schelling contends that in bargaining the weaker party is often stronger.[21] Because he has fewer resources, he can concede less than an opponent well endowed with capabilities and alternatives. Schelling takes the case of Joseph Conrad's *Secret Agent* who, though he manufactured nitroglycerin for terrorists, was immune from capture by the police. They knew he always carried a small quantity of the explosive on his person, and if police seized him he would detonate it, killing his captors as well as himself.[22] In a similar way, Israel with a few nuclear bombs may actually be able to deter the Soviet Union since *in extremis* she might deliver them on a number of Russian cities using one-way missions by F–15 or F–4 aircraft.

This does not mean that in general weakness is better than strength, but it does suggest that exponents of strategic superiority have entertained a one-sided view of their subject. Weakness is worse than strength in all situations but one: where mutual agreement is absolutely imperative. If one state can simply destroy another and emerge unscathed, no bargaining is necessary and victory goes to the stronger. If, however, owing to the possession of a substantial retaliatory capability, a less-powerful country in danger of being defeated can threaten to bring his adversary down with him, the balance begins to shift. The country with the smaller arsenal is forced to threaten full-scale retaliation first and thus obtains greater leverage in the negotiations. This suggests two conclusions: superiority is not necessary, and in the actual practice of the arms race since 1970, it has been unattainable.

Is such nuclear equality dangerous? Not if both sides continue to recognize that the greatest danger to both would be an all-out conflict that neither could win. If, therefore, a conflict escalation process began in Europe or elsewhere, there would be an overwhelming incentive on *both* sides to halt it short of unlimited exchanges on populations. It is true that both sides retain the capacity to hit the other's command, control, and intelligence centers early in a nuclear encounter.[23] But they do not have to use it, and the vulnerability of nuclear forces is not such that they will be forced to, willy-nilly. Attacks on command centers would lead the headless horseman of unlimited war to ride out on the plains of Armageddon; missile attacks much worse than those depicted in "The Day After" would destroy the Northern Hemisphere and perhaps precipitate "nuclear winter."

Because of the mutual interest both sides have in bringing a conflict to a close before such an exchange takes place, such mindless escalation need not take place. As the Cuban missile crisis and also the Yom Kippur alert illustrate, the superpowers are excruciatingly careful when they negotiate under the pressure of nuclear crisis, and they are attentive to the other's interest, as well as their own.

This is not to say that a nuclear exchange could never occur or that irrational factors or accident might not bring some sort of clash. But there would be no automatic and reflex response to a nuclear detonation. Leaders would be more interested in finding out what had happened and why it had happened than in levying immediate punishment.[24] Both sides would retain an overwhelming desire to bring the conflict to a halt.

The Soviet Union is often portrayed as a country eager to win a nuclear war, one which maintains and strengthens "war-fighting" capabilities. At the level of doctrine this is undoubtedly true, but at the level of actual forces, no set of American strategic leaders would change their capacities for those of the USSR. The Soviet Union does not possess either tactical or strategic superiority over the United States. In part, the emphasis upon "winning" or "prevailing" in a nuclear war is designed to bolster Russian confidence: if Moscow had no doctrine of how to fight once war began (and could only initiate a fruitless and suicidal exchange on populations) she might not feel capable of deterring the United States. In response the United States has also developed such doctrines and sought to retain limited counterforce options in the event of war.[25]

The result has been a mutual arms race in recent years with escalating strategic and conventional expenditure but without practical results in terms of a change in the balance. Economics, in rejoinder, would suggest further consideration of parity or even slight weakness in a strategic bargaining context. In any event, the prophets of doom have been gainsaid by the relative moderation of both superpowers in a crisis, moderation in finding a settlement well short of a central clash. If anything, in such crises the Soviet Union has been more moderate and tractable than the United States.[26] This mutual restraint, caution, and above all firm conviction on both sides that nuclear war is *not* inevitable has completely changed the strategic equation since 1945.

In 1914, several Great Powers believed that a general war would come sooner or later, and some were willing to accept it under what they thought were favorable conditions. This was not a complete misjudgment: war in the Western military tradition had been inevitable, owing to the consequences of the military-political system. Shifts of territory had been crucial to the equilibration of that system, and those shifts could only take place through war. In the 1990s, however, territory will not be the only means of rebalancing power; it will be the crudest and ultimately the least effective means. Nuclear war, therefore, is not inevitable.

Conclusion

One of the surprising things about the evolution of international history in the past two hundred years has been the persistent and anachronistic hold of the Westphalian territorial system. It has continued to capture the imagination of statesmen and peoples long after the territorial state retained sovereignty in any effective sense. That conception, of each state-unit acting like a little atom, self-sufficient and autonomous, is belied by recent history, and it cannot last much longer.

10

Recalcitrant Nations: Russia, the United States, and the Third World

Knowing that some of the worst evils that might befall the world can be avoided, we still cannot guarantee a shift toward the trading world and away from the territorial one. Regardless of what small trading powers in Europe and East Asia do, many important nations will not be tempted to change their orientations in world politics. The great territorial and military powers may well continue their competition for the allegiance of allies and geographical regions of the world, hoping that they will finally tilt the balance against their foe. Russia has had a centuries-old aversion to unprotected territorial frontiers. She apprehensively extended her sway into Siberia as early as the sixteenth and seventeenth centuries conquering fur-producing realms that were sparsely populated but might be occupied by an outsider. In the West she was on continual guard against invasion from the better-developed lands along the Baltic. The Russian steppe and plains provided an open highway in either direction, and the Ural

Mountains offered no barrier to enemy invasion. She organized a powerful and repressive state to control such vast territories.

The American preoccupation with territory was initially confined to the North American Continent, where the local French or Spanish bastions could threaten her so long as they remained on the mainland. In the nineteenth century the major concern was expanding westward to the Pacific. The move west, like the Civil War, was military in its implications because Mexico and the Indians (to say nothing of Canada) were put on notice that they might have to fight against the encroachments of the United States. Russia retracted from her exposed position along the North American coastline and sold Alaska to the government of President Andrew Johnson. With the end of the frontier in 1890 and the admission of the final Western state (Arizona) in 1912, the territorial vacuum was filled politically. Then, in the 1920s and 1930s the American market was sealed off to others and a policy of continental development based on practical economic self-sufficiency was put in place. Such a major territorial land mass might find the resources, markets, and industries that it needed at home.

Since 1945 the Third World also had reasons for isolation or alienation from the rest of the world. New nations had different attitudes and ideologies from those of the founding European members of the international system. In many cases they rejected the postnationalist quietism of European politics and sought aggressively to protect their territories and ethnic unity against outside influences. Governments were new and untrained; their political support was questionable. Political institutions could sometimes be tempered in battle, as were those of the French revolutionaries after 1790. India, Pakistan, Indonesia, Egypt, Libya, Iran, Iraq, Syria, Ethiopia, Somalia, Nigeria, Vietnam, and North Korea have demonstrated their hostile attitudes toward other political units in one or more military conflicts. Some countries and groups have committed acts of terror against other nations. The Pan-Islamic revival, sponsored by the Shi'ites in Iran, would sweep away all the particular Arab "state-lets" and create in their place an all-embracing Islamic Republic. In furtherance of the Islamic cause both Iraq and Pakistan have worked to develop atomic bombs, and Libya has tried to acquire such weapons from other powers. Where political frontiers are fluid or contested, new nations might fight over them, continuing the pattern of Third World instability that began in the Balkans before World War I.

In each of these three cases, Russia, the United States, and the Third World, the obsession with territory and the territorial balance has raised profound questions concerning a country's willingness to adopt an entirely different philosophy of national security and advancement.

Russia

Of present-day great powers, the Soviet Union is the most resistant to participation in a trading world on a continuing basis. She works to reduce her dependence on the outside world and to develop her own resources and technology on an autarchic foundation. Russia does not want to become dependent on foreign grain, oil, or technology and has sought to increase her national energy production and to duplicate the technology of Western industrial nations. In Afghanistan and Poland she has given evidence of a desire to extend a protective buffer of pliant regimes around her exposed frontiers. Her only significant industrial export has been arms for the Third World. Nowhere has she indicated that long-term trade, exchange, and specialization with Western and industrial nations would be in her interest. As a result, the territorial and military orientation of her policy has given rise to fears that she will once again seek to take over, for example, in the Persian Gulf, the oil or raw materials that Russia will increasingly depend on for her livelihood in the 1990s. New military aggression from Soviet borders could change the entire shape of world politics in the late twentieth century.

Such attitudes are not new. They are based on historical and cultural dispositions of long standing and they will not be easily modified. They could be accentuated as the Soviet Union is increasingly pressed by Western, particularly American, rearmament expenditures and finds that she can no longer, or for only a short period of time, sustain both military and economic phases of the competition. If the prospects for Russian long-range security decline in proportion to short-term ones, we might have a situation akin to that before World War I, where major powers concluded that time was no longer on their side. Historically, Russia was always suspicious though she was also envious of the West. Cut off from the sea, she pursued military and land-locked vocations and tried not to depend on trade.

> In relation to maritime access, Russia is the most disadvantageously situated of all large powers. The grand duchy of Muscovy, which was to give rise eventually to modern Russia, had no access whatever to the sea. In the nineteenth century, Russia, after having expanded for six hundred years, had a seacoast extending thousands of miles in the Arctic which was almost useless for transport purposes. She also secured ports on the Baltic and Black seas which were suitable for peaceful trade but which lacked free exit. The straits connecting the Baltic with the open sea were dominated by Denmark, those of the Black Sea by Turkey; and Europe saw to it that neither of these two countries would fall under Russian rule. Thus, strategically, the ports formed a liability rather than an asset.[1]

Nineteenth-century railroads added greatly to internal transport and communication; they also provided means of carrying Russian soldiers to the front, in East or West. They did not have the same impact as in France, where railways provided means of turning peasant small-scale production into grain and dairy exports. France, initially a large military-political and territorial state, under the impetus of better communcations and transport, has moved aggressively into the world economy as an exporting nation. She made this transition in two stages. First the railways brought foreign goods to the local market town and thereby undercut higher cost and smaller scale French production. It took more than fifty years for the second stage: for France to modernize her agriculture and industry to export both heavy industrial equipment and specialty agricultural products. The Soviet Union has certainly not gone through this second stage and remains vulnerable to improved national and international means of communications. Free trade in industrial products would almost certainly undermine many of their Soviet counterparts.

Russian and later Soviet imperialism was thus in part a reaction to Western industrial and economic superiority. If one could not compete on an equal basis with Western industrial economies, free access to the markets of other nations was not enough: one had to possess those markets physically. Hence, Russia's rivalry with Japan for influence in Korea and China in the late nineteenth century could never accept the principle of the "open door"; she had to have political and military enclaves to be sure of holding her own. Russian policy in Persia (Iran) in the nineteenth century and after World War II was additional evidence of such convictions. She would undoubtedly have liked to stay in Manchuria after the Japanese surrender in World War II, but her relationship with the new Communist China did not permit it. In Eastern Europe, the Soviet Union initially extracted raw materials, physical plants, and industrial goods from more developed economies, providing inferior Soviet products in return. Her net return was positive. Only in the mid-1970s did the pendulum swing the other way, with East European economies needing infusions of capital from Moscow, as well as oil, on concessionary terms. The Soviet Union has thus become an economic guarantor, and that role has forced her back into the international market to earn the necessary foreign exchange. Perhaps ironically, the USSR has had to try to replace the Western capital that no longer flows easily to East European countries.

The Soviet internal system of repression is also a tribute to Russia's inability to compete effectively in the marketplace of political ideas. There would be no reason for the Iron Curtain if the Soviet political system and ideology could sustain themselves on the basis of free and open competition with other nations. A single party, a monopoly of the media of communication, and strict regulation of entry and exit from the political system are the means of enforcing orthodoxy in the Soviet Union. If Russian citizens were able to compare Communist achievements with their counterparts in Western Europe and to decide freely which system they preferred, the Russian bureaucracy would collapse of its own weight. Thus the internal apparatus of coercion, like the external one, seeks to make up for Soviet deficiencies: to make an unacceptable system tolerable to the mass of the Russian population.

Historically Russian suspicion, verging on hysteria, has been stimulated by fear of invasion from the West. Charles XII of Sweden plunged far into Russian territory before finally being defeated at Poltava in 1709. Napoleon followed the same course in 1812, only to withdraw when he could not sustain his position after taking Moscow. After World War I, a series of Western powers intervened in Russia, and Poland saw its chance to win greater territories. For a time the Polish offensive carried as far as Kiev, and Poland ended the war in 1921 with millions of Russians inside its borders. The Nazi German invasion of 1941 was the most dangerous and the most nearly successful of Western thrusts into Russia, but it was still only one of a series. Traditionally the Russians took the defensive in such battles. They did not wish to meet major Western armies and reserved their offensive operations for weaker powers like Turkey, Hungary, Persia, or China, and even these were sometimes unsuccessful.

There are many who believe that the Soviet Union could never seriously modify its stance toward the outside world without risking the position of the Communist party in its governing apparatus. Any change in policy, particularly if it involved seeking a longer-term economic relationship with the West and the industrial world, would alter Soviet economic priorities and make them vulnerable to the vagaries of the world market. If Russia had to improve both the quality and the quantity of Soviet-produced goods to meet Western tastes, new investment would have to go into the consumer and capital sectors, undermining the past concentration upon military production. However, such choices have occasionally been made. Count Sergei Witte, Russian finance minister, lowered military spending and sought external financing for a massive railway building program in the 1890s. The ruble was made convertible into gold.

> His plan was not to expand manufacture of dubious efficiency and moderate technology but to raise the level of free-enterprise capitalism to the best international standards—and then by taxation to draw back a share of the resulting wealth into the public coffers.[2]

The entire program depended upon an infusion of foreign capital, making up for the deficiency of domestic savings. Under the stimulus Russian industrial production increased by 7.5 percent per year between 1888 and 1897, achieving the highest rate among major powers in Europe.

In the late 1950s and early 1960s under Chairman Nikita Khrushchev, there was another attempt to revivify Russian industry and agriculture through a policy of economic decentralization, cuts in the military budget, and new investments in the chemical industry. Khrushchev emphasized economic competition with the Western world and stressed that the Soviet Union would win because it would outproduce the capitalist nations. Khrushchev's foreign policy ventures were remarkably unsuccessful and his agricultural policy a failure. His dismissal in 1964 was laid to his "harebrained schemes" as well as his tinkering with the bureaucratic apparatus. But his opponents agreed that it was not so much his objectives as his means of attaining them which caused opposition. Under circumstances in which nuclear war would be a catastrophe for both sides, the idea that the Soviet Union might prevail economically had much to commend it from a communist point of view.

Could a communist country permit international supply and demand to influence or even determine its economic choices? To do so might in the longer term undercut its control of basic industries. China, however, has found means of adjusting its even more collectivist economy to the requirements of the external market. Maintaining control of the "commanding heights" of the economy, China has begun to allow supply and demand to determine the production of consumer goods. She has targeted certain industries, like textiles and raw materials, for export production and has become more cognizant of Western tastes and quality standards. The basic unit in agriculture has shifted from the state-controlled "commune," or collective farm, to the individual family producing unit. Under the new changes:

> the number of industrial product categories subject to planning are to be cut from 120 to 60 and farm product groups from 29 to 10. Key items such as coal, oil, steel, cement and fertilizer are expected to remain under strict controls. Consumer goods are more likely to be allowed to float with supply and demand. But once a producer has sold the assigned quota at fixed prices, he is to be free to sell

the surplus at flexible prices. . . . Another rumored change would give Government-run corporations, such as those engaged in foreign trade, greater autonomy from their ministries so that they could concentrate on business and assume direct responsibility for making a profit.[3]

Such trends have clearly had an impact in Soviet Russia. In the late 1970s and early 1980s a debate began between traditionalists and modernizers concerning the effects of the new and generally acknowledged "scientific and technological revolution" on both the world and the Russian economy. Modernizers have stressed that the old approach of independent Russian production of every commodity is no longer adequate. As one Soviet trade official wrote in 1979:

> The trend toward the international division of labor, and the application of international value criteria in assessing the expediency of a given large-scale program, permit individual countries gradually to rationalise the structure of their economy and to maximize investment effectiveness. Today, no industrial country needs to develop an entire production process from scratch, if, in exchange for its own goods, it can acquire an appropriate product or license for its manufacture from countries already producing it. [A nation] can then more rationally concentrate its investments and resources in other areas, so as to gain a leading position in specialized world markets.[4]

Another official went further to argue that in the coming decades Russia will find it increasingly "inadvisable or even impossible to produce the whole spectrum of goods necessary to satisfy the country's growing production requirements and individual demands."[5] But dependence on the West or Japan for many of these items would in turn require a Soviet export strategy and that would mean partly gearing the economy to Western demand.

Some observers believe that the USSR faces intrinsic dilemmas in moving in this direction. Rulership depends upon a mixture of coercion and information.[6] The more an élite relies on coercion, the more it dries up the supply of information about what is really going on in the country because people tell it what they believe it wants to hear. The more an economy depends upon information for rational decision making, however, the more the leadership must avoid coercion and provide inducements in its place. Over time, such a strategy would change the nature of the internal regime and the governing role of the Communist party within it. At first glance, there seems no way in which Soviet rulers can gradually accommodate the information demands of the market in their economic decisions.

Such conclusions, however, are premature. On similar grounds Soviet specialists have argued that the growing role of Soviet technocrats and rational decision-making procedures would undermine the rule by the Party.[7] Apparently it has not done so, any more than defense adjustments to the outside world have obviated Party controls. The Communist party has fashioned a strategy of dealing with the West which includes both economic and military elements. A decision to increase the importance of economic instruments and downplay military ones could also be taken and implemented by high Party functionaries.

Soviet decision makers, like their American counterparts, are concerned to find a mix which offers the most effective strategy. If Japan and China continue to persevere with fundamentally economic tools of statecraft, this will have an impact upon Soviet policy. China's economy has recently grown much more rapidly than that of the Soviet Union. She has concluded an agreement with Great Britain over the future of Hong Kong that would preserve the latter's capitalist institutions for at least a fifty-year period after reversion to the mainland. It is possible this pact could set the framework for an eventual rapprochement between Beijing and Taiwan in which China would gain the benefits of Taiwan's incredible export success and Taipei a degree of internal economic autonomy. Communist China would then preside over a mixed, partly free-enterprise and partly Communist-controlled system. Her decision to give greater latitude to exporting cities like Shanghai also shows that she is ready to combine market with dirigist influences. Can the Soviet Union do much less and still maintain her position as a great economic as well as military power? The answer remains unclear, but the stimulus to change is there. As Seweryn Bialer, a leading Soviet specialist, argues:

> adjustments have to be made if the system is to remain effective.
> . . . Should actual Soviet growth and energy shortages in the 1980s

fall within the range of the most pessimistic projections, the Soviet Union, without the reform and a successful one at that, is condemned not simply to a process of "muddling through" but a process of "muddling down."[8]

United States

As a continental nation located thousands of miles away from her ideological and commercial partners, the United States might have developed her seapower and merchant marine to become a trading nation in the tradition of Holland and Great Britain. She did not initially do so and, like Germany in the late nineteenth century, relied upon high tariffs to protect her growing industries. Foreign trade represented a very low percentage of gross national product because the expanding home market at first seemed sufficient for United States manufacturers. This was not the case for American agriculture, however, and beginning in the nineteenth century cotton and grain were prime export crops. Yet even here as the American textile industry grew, it could take more and more cotton from the South and would in time supplant the sales that British garments were making in the United States clothing market. As American industry diversified to machines, automobiles, and electrical equipment, the home market absorbed these products as well. As late as the 1920s and 1930s, many American businessmen were content to depend on customers at home; they felt no need to export. Before 1945 United States foreign trade remained less than 10 percent of its GNP. The completion of American industrialization removed the market that foreign manufactured goods had traditionally enjoyed in the United States.

This evolution was foreshadowed by the Civil War in which the protectionist North defeated the cotton exporters and apostles of low tariffs in the South. The Southerners had wanted to import British and other foreign manufactured goods and took Northern equivalents only under protest. After 1865 cotton and grain exports continued, but they had little political effect in fashioning a long-term foreign trade strategy for the United States. It was not until after the Second World War that American capitalists began to develop an export offensive, first in Europe and then in the rest of the world. At this point although the United States market was growing, there was a vast demand for American products overseas, a result of the disorganization of local production caused by the war. Even this considerable effort, however, did not shake United States manufacturers out of their comfortable and steady dependence on the American market. It was not until American consumers started a love affair with foreign-made automobiles, electrical appliances, calculators, and office equipment, that United States industry began to realize how extensively it had to retool to beat competitors at home and abroad. If it could not be sure of capturing the home market, it had to look overseas for new customers.

Politically and geographically the United States also had few early justifications for a military-political policy. Even more isolated from the European Continent than Great Britain, the United States for a century had assumed that affairs in Europe would not greatly influence North America. Four thousand miles away, the United States could not be attacked by another great power and could content herself with isolationist or Fortress America attitudes. When World War I and II impinged upon United States security, American intervention was rapid and decisive but also relatively brief in character. Thus, some United States planners were emboldened to think that a major, even a hegemonic role in world politics could be sustained by occasional bursts of American intervention. One did not have to fight long and draining wars to maintain this ascendancy; United States rearmament would be well within the great capacities of American industry. In short, no major social objective at home would be sacrificed by such a role, and the maintenance of full employment might even be served by it. Economic growth and the welfare state could go on as before.

It was not until the burdens of superpower policy began to mount in the 1970s that any other response was considered. Then, the political as well as the economic costs of major and continuing intervention abroad had to be taken into account. The result was a partial return to brief and hopefully decisive interventions, with no new long-term commitments. The "rescue" of the *Mayaguez* by President Gerald Ford in 1975 jeopardized more lives than it saved. President Jimmy Carter's abortive attempt to free the United States hostages in Iran in 1980 was another attempt to engage in forceful, but limited operations against opponents. President Ronald Reagan's Grenada operation succeeded in protecting American citizens and also overturning the left-wing government there. Israel had followed a similar strategy in its brief but violent wars, none of which lasted more than three weeks. Only in the Lebanese invasion of 1982 did Tel Aviv get bogged down in a holding operation, while Israeli casualties mounted. The result in the American case was to substitute rearmament and military doctrine for long-term intervention. Developing new weapons and new strategies of employment, United States planners tried to obtain "escalation dominance" over Moscow, remaining superior at each level of the ladder, conventional or nuclear. But the costs of such a strategy were very great and led to Soviet responses to regain parity. Both sides ended up spending much more than necessary, given threats from the rest of the world. Since each superpower was the other's major foe, they could have saved a great deal by scaling down the arms race, while maintaining the same balance at a much lower level.

But as the United States Government has moved toward minimal engagements, the populace has come to question the need for an international role. In the aftermath of the energy crisis and political disaffection with Vietnam, many young Americans preferred to set up small self-sufficient communities where consumption of food and electricity would be limited to what they could produce themselves. Then America would not have to be involved in a struggle for power in world politics and the wellsprings of American values could rejuvenate an adult generation that had lost its way.

For most, however, this response was neither desirable nor necessary, though it did provide one answer to the problem of finding a more efficient strategy of involvement in world politics. Another and more promising approach would have the United

States revert to an economic and trading strategy in world politics while still maintaining basic deterrents against war. In that case, both the Soviet Union and the United States would benefit, and it would leave America with funds to revive sagging industries or to find a substitute for them in the service or high technological trades. High technology provides a considerable stimulus to the economy but not to new employment. The effects of new investments in Silicon Valley in California or Route 128 near Boston would not be the retraining of vast numbers of unemployed workers, but it would stimulate the economy and provide new incomes that would be spent in travel, recreation, and a variety of other consumer services and businesses. Indirectly, service employment appears to hold one answer to the problem of finding new jobs in the 1990s. As opposed to defense work, which is inherently cyclical and temporary in character, jobs created by new private investment would also be in fields where they might earn foreign exchange and contribute to a new export offensive.

Thus a new trading strategy was not beyond America's reach, nor was it inconsistent with trends in domestic politics. Some sectors of business and organized labor opposed the entry of foreign lower-priced goods. They favored high tariffs or voluntary restraint agreements in the automobile, steel, and perhaps in other industries, like machine tools, suffering strong foreign competition. Labor turned against international "sourcing" of components and wanted all mechanical parts to be built at home. But tariffs and quotas would undoubtedly lead to retaliation, and United States industry would simply lose out abroad. Lacking the stimulus of worldwide competition she would fall further behind. Instead, an export drive in services, high technology products, including semiconductors and advanced information systems, would better serve American needs at the end of the twentieth century. At the same time specialized agricultural exports from the South, Midwest, and Far West could win markets in many areas of the world, in Japan and Russia, as well as Europe and the Far East. With more investment capital, a somewhat lower dollar, and lower United States interest rates, many entrepreneurs would begin a new competitive surge.

The Third World

In certain respects the Third World may be the more resistant to trading strategies over the long run than the Soviet Union. The USSR is a developed and partly modernized state. With new and unformed political institutions, ethnic divisions, and impoverished electorates, Third World states face basic problems of national unity. Except for the struggle for national independence, which was foreshortened by imperial concessions in some cases, new states have not undergone any really formative national experiences. War and conflict with outsiders provide the crucible that many new states still need to unify their diverse populations. It is even possible, as some have suggested, that the world is doomed to repeat the battles of the seventeenth century, in which new European states were forged out of medieval universalism. In this view emergent states always have to fight to establish coherent governments, and peace only returns when the nation-building phase is complete.[9]

A particular and virulent version of this thesis can be observed in the contemporary Middle East where, some observers tell us, "extremism" in Lebanon, Iran, and within Arab politics generally is prevailing against moderation. The Shi'ites, the Syrians, the extremist wing of the PLO, and Iran are winning, so it is said, against the moderates, represented by Jordan, Egypt, Saudi Arabia, and to some degree Iraq. These extremists have so polarized Middle Eastern politics that they have brought forth an equally intransigent and apocalyptic Israeli response on the West Bank and to some degree in Lebanon. The Pan-Islamic movement would return the Arabs to the stringent religious teachings of the seventh century, including the doctrine of the Holy War against infidels. This movement rejects Western influences of all kinds, even Western economic and technological progress if it is to be purchased at the expense of Moslem fidelity. It was perhaps not accidental that the reactionary revolution expressed itself first in Iran under the shah where Western ideas, consultants, and technicians had preponderated over nativist elements and the clergy in running the country.

But the drive to purge Islamic society of Western influences can be seen under the surface in many countries, including Egypt, Jordan, and the states of the Persian Gulf. If such heady elements boil up, moderate regimes will be dissolved in a new social cauldron. Islamic states may be amalgamated, and both Israel and Western access to Arab oil might be sacrificed in the process. Islamic fundamentalism may herald a kind of new Protestant Reformation, and religious wars may similarly follow in its wake.

But even if such religious messianism and militarism do not engulf them, Third World states will still find great difficulty adopting a capitalist international trading system or confining themselves to a trading strategy in world politics. The very commercial system that benefited Northern and Western economies appears to condemn Third World counterparts to permanent poverty and dependency. Agricultural and commodity prices remain low in the structure of world comparative advantage. Industrial development often takes the form of "branch plant industrialization" where Western multinational corporations provide capital and technology and then return the profits to the home country.[10] Even where industrial development is largely self-sustaining, it frequently accentuates class divisions and leaves the middle and lower sections of the society worse off. Such "dependent development" might impose its own limits to growth, for the working and middle classes might not have enough income to purchase the products of their own country's industry and agriculture.[11] From this perspective, some have argued that "de-coupling" the Third World from the Northern economic system might better serve the interest of developing countries.

Such challenges make it much more difficult to accept a trading strategy among Third World nations. Some countries have greatly profited from just such an approach, particularly East Asian countries and ASEAN (The Association of Southeast Asian Nations). Others, such as Brazil, Mexico, Turkey, Egypt, and India, lie on the threshold of startling new growth. The countries of the Persian Gulf have won very high per capita incomes and their support of Iraq in the Gulf War almost certainly guarantees that Iran will not prevail. Such an outcome would on the whole represent a triumph for moderate Arabs and perhaps cement a new relationship between Iraq (historically one of the more radical regimes) and Egypt. It would leave Syria and Libya isolated. Nor is it clear that Islamic radicalism in Lebanon can possibly produce a political victory there. Christians and Sunnis are too well entrenched to succumb to an Iranian-inspired Shi'ite conspiracy. In fact, some degree of moderation on the part of all parties will be required if an internal political settlement is to be found.

It is true that the international development process frequently accentuates divisions within Third World society, but it is equally true that autarchic development is probably impossible. An agricultural surplus must first be produced for investment to take place. This surplus means that not all agricultural producers are needed to feed the population and some are available for work in the towns. The surplus can be used to build an infrastructure—roads, railways, ports, and communication facilities—which will allow products to be shipped overseas.[12] The proceeds from these sales can be used to finance import-substituting industrialization. In the early stages of their development, all countries but Britain and Hong Kong protected their infant industries. But manufacture for the home market alone is generally inefficient unless the market is very large or the industrial process very labor intensive.[13] If large-scale production sustained by large amounts of capital is required, exports become the means of sustaining domestic development. In some cases, countries, like Ghana and Argentina, which neglected their agricultural exports in favor of a high-cost and inefficient import-substitution strategy, actually lost markets to other producers and to the United States, Canada, and Australia. At minimum, markets have to be available for agricultural exports and capital, as well as for industrial ones. These require a major link to the outside world.

Countries which stayed in the import-substitution stage and did not move rapidly to exports suffered correspondingly. India, Chile, and Uruguay continued to protect their hothouse industries as recently as the 1973 oil crisis and were late in moving to an export strategy. Others such as Singapore, Taiwan, and Korea removed many of their import restrictions in the 1960s. Exports bulked very large in their manufacturing sectors, and despite their meager resource endowments they also profited from exporting primary or agricultural goods. None was afraid to start an export industry with labor-intensive techniques.

In the future the non-oil developing countries, hungry for capital and machinery, may well serve as an increasing market for the engineering goods of the industrial countries. Equally in semimanufactured consumer sectors and in smokestack industries, like steel, shipbuilding, and increasingly automobiles, they may find a comparative advantage in exports to the developed North and West. International economist, Bela Belassa forecasts their rate of growth at 5.5 percent versus the industrial countries 3.9 percent. This should stimulate both foreign investment and foreign exports in their growing economies.[14] He observes: "While only 5.1 percent of the industrial countries' manufacturing output was sold in the developing countries in 1978, this share is projected to double by 1990, with exports to the developing countries accounting for 18 percent of the increment in output between 1978 and 1990."[15] The stake of developed nations in the prosperity and progress of the Third World is increasing because their own future is tied up with it.

In time members of the Third World will have to consider joining the group of trading nations because they cannot subsist on their own. Most such countries are either too small or have too poor a consumer sector to stimulate their own development on the basis of home demand. Such countries also do not produce the range of goods, minerals, and industrial equipment that they need to prosper in the late twentieth century. Oil and machinery often have to be purchased abroad, to say nothing of high technology goods for consumers and industry. If countries have to buy abroad, they also have to sell, and they come back into the system after a period of nationalist or ideological introversion as effective exporters of new commodities as well as new ideas.

Conclusion

It is too early to conclude that the Soviet Union, the United States, and many Third World nations can agree to join a trading world in international politics. As large and somewhat bureaucratic states the United States and the Soviet Union have the past disadvantage of an isolationist tradition, a large home market, and a wealth of natural resources. If they are not small states, relative to growing international interdependence and the challenge of high technology, they may have become "analytically small": they cannot compete effectively without buying and selling abroad. Lacking the stimulus of competition in foreign markets, they may become less productive societies and fall further behind their industrial competitors. This is particularly true of the Soviet Union, where enormous expenditures on national defense have not been accompanied by rapid industrial or agricultural growth. Investment is lagging in Russia and if it is not renewed, the entire apparatus on which Soviet power rests will become shaky and uncertain. Hungary and China have shown that innovation and change in economic decision making in a communist country is not impossible and that it does not dilute the leading role of the Party and may, conceivably (though the verdict is still not in) increase its popularity.

The United States has other disadvantages. As the leading power in world politics, it has the least incentive to change. It might slight or partly overlook the challenge to modernize or even to shed its basic industries and to find new equivalents for them. It is not surprising that an economy which has a chronic unemployment problem has not introduced a wide range of robots on its assembly lines. With a large and, in the past, an assured home market, United States entrepreneurs have only begun to innovate in the automobile and steel industries. Investment has lagged in part because financial managers have been content to maximize "discounted cash flow" and have not invested where the return down the line, minus inflation, would not equal present returns in the money market.[16] American business has acted to magnify present quarterly returns, not market share or returns in the long run. In an era of inflation, business could always maintain profit margins by increasing prices. But if competitors' prices stay low, this is no longer a viable option. Thus the urge to innovate and to invest becomes overpowering, and if the home American market is no longer guaranteed, then the only alternative is also to sell abroad. In this way, even the laggard United States is forced to consider greater reliance upon a trading strategy in world politics.

The Third World presents perhaps the greatest enigma. New states are normally nationalist, ideological, militarist, and chauvinist. They engage in war with one another as well as nibble at the fringes of major power garments. War among such states could bring a new world war, as wars among Balkan states and the tensions that they created led to World War I. Yet the mandates of the trading world require such states to forego a primarily military and territorial strategy and to devote themselves to trade, economic development, and peace. More than other nations they are faced with a choice between fighting and trading because they cannot afford to do both. It is by no means certain which course all or most of them will choose. But the startling success of Far Eastern nations with such a strategy shows what can be accomplished if ideological and military factors do not get in the way. It is difficult to imagine the Middle East as a zone of peace, but it is possible to think that Islamic countries may have fewer reasons to war among themselves in the future than they have in the past and that Israel can return to a de facto relation of peace with some of the moderate Arab states. It is not clear that this movement will promote an overall settlement between Israel and the Arabs because the Israeli-occupied West Bank and Gaza remain obstacles to any long-term accommodation. Elsewhere, Africa has faced agricultural shortages and has not been able to develop a surplus on which a real industry could be built. In Latin America right-wing governments and guerrilla movements have complicated development in Central America. Argentina and Brazil, returning from military-dominated regimes, hold out great hopes for future development, and the Caribbean has a chance to overcome its chronic recession by selling in the United States.

The Third World success with a trading strategy will depend partly on access to North American and European markets, and thus the policy of developed states becomes a factor of great importance. In the late nineteenth century, though faced with a decline in its rate of growth, Britain did not cordon off its home market to its developing country partners. They were allowed, progressively, to repay their debts by running a surplus with Britain. Many industrial countries today, pressed by unemployment and political restiveness, have been tempted to be less generous, and restraints have proliferated on Third World exports like textiles and steel. But debtors cannot repay their loans unless they can sell abroad. Such restraints only imperil the Western banking system and must, inevitably, be lifted or modified. In the longer term, the Third World and the industrial countries have overarching common interests in expanding the world economy and world trade. The West wants developing nations to expand so it can sell to them. The Third World wants the world market to expand so that it can follow a strategy of export-led growth. The development of new Third World industries having a comparative advantage in world trade will require investment funds from the developed world, which should be glad to provide them.[17] If such reciprocities are recognized on both sides, the Third World will be more tempted to join the trading system because the benefits could become more mutual than they have been in past years when industrial countries sold and bought in each others' markets and allowed the terms of trade for Third World goods to deteriorate. Even agriculture, as the Ivory Coast as well as the United States have shown, can yield important returns in world trade, and these returns may increase in the future. Thus, Third World nations may be tempted to sequester themselves from the international trading system, but there are overwhelming advantages to be gained from participating in it.

11

Toward the Future

The worst aspects of the Westphalian system with its emphasis on territoriality, sovereignty, and a spurious independence, are likely to be mitigated in the years ahead. That does not mean that nations will move all the way to the trading strategy. The contemporary knife-edge equipoise between the two systems cannot be sustained indefinitely, but even if it tips measurably toward the trading world, the military-political component will remain very significant.

No pure type is feasible in international politics because the success of one depends upon either balance or failure in the other. And as long as international politics is composed of particular states with independent powers of decision, the issue of military security will continue to be extremely important. There are different combinations of military and trading approaches: states can devote as little attention to defense as do Iceland or Austria, or as much as Korea, Germany, or France. They may choose a mid-position like that of Japan. They may decide to rely almost entirely on allies or to adopt armed neutrality like Sweden and Switzerland. Commerce with other nations may be all-important, as it is with the Japanese and certain small West European nations, like Luxembourg, Holland, and Belgium, or it may be a significant addition to the resources of the national market, as it would be in the case of India, China, and the United States. But whatever balance is chosen, a successful new trading posture could not offer military incentives to aggressive powers. Either nations will have to spend enough on defense to deter attack on their own, or they will have to associate with like-minded states to offer such resistance.

Factors Shaping the Balance Chosen

We have already seen that the comparative cost and benefit of force and trade will influence the balance between systems. These are in turn shaped by the degree of economic and military interdependence, the depth and scope of ideological conflicts between states, the openness of the international economy (as it responds to world growth or depression), the political mobilization of the populace, and the degree of social learning, internationally. If war were to be both simple and generally successful (as it has been at most times in the past), the trading system would not emerge at all. Fortunately, the growing military interdependence of nations makes such an outcome extremely unlikely. Even if there were a sudden renaissance in offensive military power, the trading system could remain in place if it conferred benefits disproportionate to those to be won militarily. Such an outcome could be fostered by social learning, which would accustom the members of the state system to behave in new ways.

Ideological factors have been very important in international history: religious, political, and economic differences have often caused long and disastrous wars. Only to the degree that conflicts, between Protestant and Catholic, liberal and conservative, Communist and liberal-democratic nations, could be contended peacefully did the system avoid the excesses of violence.

Economic and military interdependence restrains conflict in both positive and negative ways. Economic interdependence offers an alternative to force, and military interdependence suggests that force may not be successful. But habits of interdependence would not restrain antagonisms if trade were suddenly blocked between erstwhile commercial partners. Then some nations would seek to take by force what they had previously acquired through trade.

Toward the Future

An open international economy is prerequisite to a peaceful trading system.

One of the most important factors affecting the use of force has been the degree of political mobilization of the population. So long as political mobilization was limited, foreign invaders could rule conquered territory without disadvantage, as they did from the sixteenth to the nineteenth centuries. In the twentieth century it has taken the full apparatus of contemporary totalitarianism to subdue ethnic and nationalist tendencies in Eastern Europe, and even this has not been altogether successful. Overseas, foreigners have had difficulty controlling nationalist movements, as in different ways Vietnam, Afghanistan, and Lebanon demonstrate. The costs of foreign intervention rise under such circumstances. Paradoxically, such ethnic and political nationalism often contributes to the very ideological strife which undermines peaceful relations among states. Such disputes are particular in character and generally do not contribute to large scale assaults on the system.

Social learning has both advanced and retarded desirable adjustments in international politics. Each political generation operates upon its own interpretation of the past. Neville Chamberlain and his entourage believed they were saving humanity when they sought to avoid another futile war in 1939. Conversely, statesmen of the 1940s and 1950s saw the dangers of Munich on all sides and were ready to engage in wholesale intervention to prevent gains by the opponent. The surprising endurance of the Westphalian system was a tribute to the widespread inculcation and acceptance of nationalist and military values. Meanwhile political economists have finally begun to understand the long-term effects of protectionism upon commerce and international welfare. Having experienced the disasters of the 1930s, they do not wish to repeat them in the 1990s. And this essential social learning has helped to prevent new defaults and economic crises as well as permanent restraints on international trade.

The trend toward military-political or trading worlds, however, is not a reflection of habit or sheer inertia: it is affected by factors which make the cost of trade or that of force exhorbitant. In historical terms each system had opportunities, but the military-political world had overall dominance. It depended upon a strong and growing national state with the ability to conquer new territories as well as to gain support from its domestic population. The increasing deconsolidation of traditional states and the decline of national loyalty as they seek to serve such purposes gradually undermines the military-political system. The growing incompatibility between the political jurisdiction needed to achieve social purposes and its actual limited extent means that to prosper nations need to shift in the direction of new trading strategies.

The Process of Transformation

The push toward a trading system has to come from somewhere. Content to continue business as usual, nations do not often change their ways. In the past, some dramatic failure or crisis was necessary to force statesmen to rethink their positions. It might be military; it might be economic. Another superpower crisis could be the stimulus. In the Middle East and South Asia, the two giants have important client states locked in competition with one another. Israel is the enemy of Syria and the PLO; Pakistan rivals India over Kashmir. A new Middle Eastern or South Asian war could bring the superpowers face to face, with the initiative in the hands of smaller states. In the subcontinent America would "tilt toward" Pakistan and Russia toward India, but the two guarantors would need to keep in communication to prevent escalation of the stakes. In the Indo-Pakistan conflict these are automatically raised by the near eventuality of Pakistan's "Islamic bomb," paralleling India's "peaceful" atomic device of 1974. As in 1971, India might take action when a domestic crisis broke out in Karachi. This could raise the danger of a World War I outcome: with the two major states incapable of exerting enough leverage on their clients in its final stages. Unlike 1914, however, the two superpowers would still retain the ability to disengage and to cooperate between themselves. The "near-miss" of the Cuban missile crisis in 1962 greatly improved superpower relations in the short term, and successful crisis management would do so again. The heightened dangers of war could lead both Moscow and Washington to scale down their conflict, reduce spending on arms, and search for alternative and more cooperative modes of foreign policy.

Sudden economic reversals could have a similar effect. A toppling of the United States dollar and a sudden rush to move assets out of New York could press America toward a trading strategy. If her "invisible" balance of trade (capital movements, shipping, investment, and financial services) went into the red, she would have to gain a favorable balance in "visible" (merchandise) trade to make up the shortfall. This would depend upon private and governmental groups making decisions to earn a higher percentage of the gross national product through exports abroad. In the Soviet case, shortages of energy in the 1990s could be an occasion for recasting foreign policy. If the USSR had to buy a much larger percentage of oil from the Middle East, she would require funds to pay for them. The Soviet gold reserve and hard currency holdings are not unlimited. Her shipments of raw materials (even natural gas) would be unlikely to cover her needs in the long run. At some point Soviet planners will have to think in terms of industrial, as well as raw material, exports, and that raises the question: what can they sell abroad that others would want to buy? In this way Soviet industrial strategy could be gradually reshaped to serve a more sophisticated and cost-conscious public.

The change need not be a product of crisis. Unilateral moves sparking emulation might ultimately be more effective than response to sudden events.

Suppose the CIA leaked the following White House strategy memo:

> An analysis of the Russo-American struggle in recent years indicates that this would be an advantageous time for the United States to shift its long-term strategy toward the Soviet Union. In recession at home, 1980–82, the US desirably provoked the USSR into a new arms race, and this race has had considerable negative impact upon Soviet growth, investment, and in time it will reduce Russian civilian consumption as well. As America moves into a moderate growth cycle, however, the US cannot take full advantage

of the domestic and international plight of the Soviet Union. If US arms procurement continues at current rates we will face chronic deficits of over $200b. a year. This will either prevent interest rates from declining further or (if interest rates are allowed to fall) generate renewed inflation. For political reasons tax rates cannot be increased sufficiently to reduce fiscal pressure, and even if they could, the economy cannot stand a new drag on its forward growth. To finance large deficits, however, the government will have to compete with private entrepreneurs in the capital market. If the dollar falls on world markets, foreign investors will begin to take their money home, and US borrowing requirements will have to be met from an even smaller pool of funds, further increasing the pressure on interest rates.

US private investment will lag as a result, and American productivity, which gained greatly in the past several years, will decline once again. If inflation mounts, US exports will be restrained by higher prices, despite the decline in the dollar. If inflation is held under control by high interest rates, the dollar will rise again and exports receive no stimulus. In short, continued economic growth without inflation is not consistent with very high government deficits, deficits spurred by excessive defense spending.

In the period ahead, therefore, we do not want an arms race with the Soviet Union. Instead, we will put most pressure on Moscow by shifting our strategy at this point, reducing defense procurement, and redirecting capital to productivity gains, the export sector, and research and development in a variety of across the board high technology fields—such as, for example, the fifth generation computer.

The Soviet Union would be particularly vulnerable to such a strategy because it is now suffering from low growth, low investment, and is operating an antiquated industrial plant. Accordingly, the US should gear itself for a long-term competition in growth with the Soviet Union ("We will bury them" is our watchword), a competition which we will almost certainly win because the USSR, given its suspicious nature, will hesitate to reduce defense expenditure sufficiently to generate new economic growth.

An American shift to an economic growth strategy would have great impact in the USSR. Moscow would then have to decide whether it would seek to maximize its short-term military advantage (which the present balance would almost certainly prevent it from doing) or develop its economy and long-term mobilization base. Without exports to the West and Japan, it could not acquire needed technology and expertise and (like China during the Cultural Revolution) would fall further behind. Thus, a United States decision to increase economic growth through a strategy of investment and trade would strengthen the modernizers in Russia and perhaps ultimately shift resources away from defense. A unilateral initiative by the United States on its own behalf might even have greater effect than an attempt to work out a bilateral agreement to pursue such a strategy. In all of these ways—détente after a crisis, economic pressures, and unilateral moves—the United States and the Soviet Union might be encouraged to join the growing group of trading nations in world politics.

International and Domestic Outcomes

Two political forms of trading system can be imagined. One might grow from the existing blocs, with a continuance of alliances and bloc relationships. States could save money this way, because pooling defense burdens would reduce the cost for a single state. The continuance of the Warsaw Pact and the North Atlantic Treaty (and other Western alliances) would certainly contribute to political stability in Europe, even though it would probably prolong Soviet influence in Eastern Europe. In the much longer term, there would be the alternative possibility of a breakup of existing blocs and perhaps some reformulation of security ties. A Central and West European group might take over some of the functions hitherto performed by NATO. A withdrawal of American forces from the Continent would depend upon an equivalent withdrawal of Soviet forces—well into the Western districts of the USSR and a concomitant freeing of East European states. The latter might declare neutrality between the superpowers or decide to associate themselves with a new European entity. Though tensions might be reduced by such shifts, nations would come to rely more on themselves, and the individual defense burden of some countries might well increase. Several nations might then move to overt nuclear weapons programs to offer a partial substitute for past guarantees. These might be individual or combined in a single European group.

In either case the reversion to a growth and trading strategy would lessen the need to be armed to the teeth, and the increased trade between East and West would reduce exaggerated fear and hostility. It would not entirely dismantle political grievances, however, and rapprochement would await proof of the reality of trading intentions. This proof or demonstration would have to be greater in case blocs were demobilized.

If nuclear war can be ruled out, economic processes will progressively act to reshape the international world. Since the seventeenth century the consolidation of nation-states has, until fairly recently, pressed toward a growing homogeneity of objectives and means in international politics: sovereign states endowed with territory and population used their power to gain advantage over others. Despite ideological rifts and ethnic differences, the policy of states became ever more similar. International relations socialized nations and led most of them to pursue the same goals with the same means: territorial expansion.

But states did not manage to command their fates. Their ambitions failed in almost every case. Not only has the militarization of international relations become very expensive, it also has become increasingly futile. The great military powers had their time at center stage in world politics, but they had little staying power.[1] While the powers mesmerized by Louis XIV's solutions have locked themselves into military competition, those states less centrally involved in the power struggle have been able to devote themselves to economic and trading innovations. Increasingly, the latter group has come to surpass those that adhered to traditional strategies.

Economic and cultural processes have started to reshape the previous homogeneity of world politics. The logic of comparative advantage favors economic differentiation. Ethnic and political mobilization has brought national differentiation and has guaranteed that new units in international relations would be small and compact. Another trend in a similar direction is the growing efficiency of smaller plants in competition with larger ones. Smaller capital requirements mean that "mini-mills" have begun to capture a growing part of the American steel market. In textiles, shoes, machine tools, and chemicals, the trend toward smaller, more flexible production (without massive production runs for one standard item) has taken hold in a number of areas of the world.

In Prato, Italy, small specialty shops developed an aggressive alternative to the large textile firm. "In its place emerged a vast network of small shops, employing one to twenty workers (often members of a single extended family) who possessed an intimate knowledge of materials and machines."[2] These were coordinated through federations in which the modern version of a medieval merchant capitalist made sure that the latest trends in fashion were being served and brought specialty production from a series of small firms together in new fabrics, designs, and colors. Even in the automotive industry, differentiation provided by small component shops is becoming the rule as compared with long production runs for an absolutely standard unit, like the old Ford Model T. Internationally, General Motors' and Ford's attempt to build a uniform "world car" failed against sophisticated consumer taste which demanded product differentiation and a variety of engineering options. In these circumstances the structure of comparative advantage has become more complex and variable than in past ages. Economically vigorous small nations have kept ready to move from one product line or industry to another as international costs and tastes evolve.[3]

Two forms of national differentiation exist. One produces ideological and political differences; the other gives rise to economic differences. The first set leads to disparateness and rivalry between nations,[4] but they also make conquest very difficult. The second set offers complementarity on which trading reciprocity can be based. In the late twentieth century the issue is largely whether the benefits of economic differentiation are growing rapidly enough to offset the conflict inherent in political heterogeneity and discord. In Europe, East Asia, North and South America, a largely positive response can be given to this question. In the Middle East, South Asia, and parts of Northern and Southern Africa, the outcome is much more mixed. At the same time, even though political differences remain, they have not prevented participation in the general world economy, and even in the context of political rivalry, individual nations have been led to transform their positions through economic development.

In the domestic realm, as well as in international relations, the growth of trade and interdependence has progressively reshaped the structure of politics and government. Instead of sovereign independence and efficacy there has been the development of a mediative state. Governmental jurisdiction no longer coincides, if it ever did, with control over the essential elements of a national livelihood. A rapid and massive flow of funds into or out of a society will determine its interest rates, its rate of inflation, and influence its amount of unemployment. Such transnational flows—transactions in which one of the parties is *not* a government—are becoming increasingly characteristic of world economic relations.[5] Recession or high interest rates in another country will cause a trade imbalance at home, to be avoided only by economic contraction and the spread of recession from one nation to another. Thus domestic welfare with full employment can no longer be ensured by a single national government with the policy instruments at its command. National sovereignty and full employment policies are undercut by the unprecedented size and power of the international sector. Governments can control the flow of goods across their frontiers, but when they have tried to regulate capital flows, overseas dollar and Eurocurrency holdings have risen; new banking centers operating outside major regulatory environments have sprouted in the Middle East, the Bahamas, and Hong Kong. The pool of currencies outside their country of issue now mounts into the trillions of dollars.

One response to this largely uncontrolled flow of funds is to seek to increase the jurisdiction of political states. But no greater regional state, be it the European Community or an even more embracing instrumentality, will include the necessary territory. A world state would do so, but it cannot be established at this stage of history. Hence the policy of a smaller state, like the United States of America, depends for its success on cooperative arrangements with other nations. Policy is no longer governed by fiat; it is a matter of negotiation. The increase in world interdependence has led nations to rely on goods and raw materials produced by other societies. Sovereignty under these conditions no longer means supreme power unrestrained by law. The concepts of domain and property have themselves undergone a profound metamorphosis. Property, a legal concept, is no longer typified by land, which in years past, involved ownership of all associated rights from under the earth's crust to outer space. Property rights now come as much from governmental largesse as they do from physical assets and real estate.[6] As the state awards and takes away such rights in its licensing, pensionary, and franchise-awarding functions, property takes on a contingent character. Within society the ownership of "time-sharing" condominiums emphasizes the incomplete and impermanent nature of property. Between societies, the ability of giant corporations to negotiate with governments for access to capital and consumer markets on favorable terms may even approximate a kind of nineteenth-century "extraterritoriality." Foreign military bases may also have a kind of extranational status. Governments agree to such arrangements not because they like the implied or actual restriction on their powers but because of the benefits which accrue in practical economic or military terms. It is the reciprocal exchange of benefits within each other's territories that facilitates the adjustment process. Concrete stakes in the success of another society may be the best guarantee of long-term cooperation among states. Interpenetration, however, must be mutual to have a desirable restraining effect.

Despite the inability to control its fate, the modern state remains the primary unit of international politics. This does not mean it is not influenced by the multinational corporation, transnational flows between economies, and the growing autonomy of trading cities in certain countries. If cities and corporations prosper, countries can sometimes do well even when they contain parasitic urban areas and an inefficient agricultural sector. Sao Paulo, Pusan, Kaohsiung, Shanghai, Wuhan, Seoul, Milan, Bombay, Amsterdam, London, Lyons, New York, Boston, Los Angeles, and San Francisco serve as dynamos to power the countries in which they are embedded. Silicon Valley and the Route 128 informatics complex (now extending to New Hampshire) may have more influence on the ultimate competitiveness of North America than decisions made in Washington, D.C. International corporations like Philips, Shell, IBM, Nissan, Nestlé, Michelin, NatWest, Hong Kong and Shanghai Bank, Citicorp, and Exxon will help determine the economic futures of the countries in which they operate, but unlike state governments, they cannot be held fully accountable for their actions. Multinational corporations could never serve as the basis for a new system of international politics or for cooperation among peoples because they have no geographic jurisdiction. Under these conditions, the state remains as flawed but still the only reliable instrument of popular will; yet it cannot simply be a conveyor belt for popular wishes. Because many, perhaps most, of the desirable features of modern life depend upon what other countries do, one government cannot assure economic security or welfare for its citizens. It can only negotiate with these objectives in mind.

Popular dissatisfaction with this result has led to an increasing debility of the governing power in democratic societies. The nation has been reduced to a "mediative state," an instrument that balances the pressures of international life on the one hand with domestic life on the other. The government has to obey two masters but the electorate would wish that it were only one. Much greater public understanding of the dilemma that leaders face is required before the two can be reconciled.

It is possible that the "mediative state" will fail. It is the keystone of the arch and rests on the twin pillars of domestic claims and international intransigence. If they move further apart, the arch will collapse. Such an outcome would mean a return to medievalism, with ecumenical pressures undermining the domestic cohesion of the territorial state. The attempt to compose international differences would subvert domestic consensus, and chaos would once again return to the internal realm. International history would then have come full circle in one millenium. The delicate balance needed to sustain the intermediate position of the mediative state depends upon a greater enlightenment and refinement of popular knowledge and expectations.

President Jimmy Carter was right to speak of a persistent "malaise" in democratic societies. The malaise is in part a feeling of impotence and frustration, but it is borne by an inability to understand what is going on. In the late 1960s and early 1970s popular assumptions were discredited by the outcome in Vietnam and in the oil crisis. Leaders were no longer able to produce the results that electorates asked of them. The combined assault of "limits to growth," the buildup of pollution, and foreign policy frustration appeared to overwhelm any answers that leaders gave.

If policy makers failed to offer solutions, experts, academics, and savants were no better. The computer and the information revolution barraged the citizenry with undigested facts, discrediting existing social theories, prognoses, and policies. No one could outline a theory that explained the direction of events. Television news abetted this trend, inundating the watcher with "brute empiricism" and leaving him to sort out kaleidoscopic impressions and fabricate his own theories. A variety of quasi-religious or pseudo-scientific groups came forward to provide answers, but they usually conflicted with one or another demonstrable aspect of reality. Ronald Reagan's election and re-election were a partial tribute to the longing of the American electorate for someone who could provide a reassuring theory of government, economics, and foreign policy.

The problem, however, was that the continued emphasis upon arms spending, territorial confrontation, and preparing to fight a nuclear war under both Presidents Carter and Reagan conflicted with strategies of domestic growth, private investment, and low interest rates. Nations which focused primarily upon international and territorial competition often were unable to design a trading strategy of advancement and economic rejuvenation. From this standpoint both the United States and the Soviet Union—hypnotized by territory, space, and power—neglected the vital fourth dimension.

The mediative state also poses new and fundamental problems of domestic as well as international management. If governments lean in the direction of responding to international pressures, they will do so at some domestic cost. Only certain forms of internal polity may be capable of rapidly adjusting to changes in the international market, transformations of technology, and enhanced information. Decentralized societies may have greater difficulty than more centralized ones where some degree of social corporatism may already be in place.[7] Cooperation among business, labor, and government may need to be more advanced than it is at the moment in most democratic and industrial societies. The trend toward smaller size and flexible specialization may further such relationships.[8] A society based more on rational information and less on ideologies might also assist such an outcome. David Apter may be right that governments rule with a varying combination of coercion and information and that there is a feasible transfer between the two constituents of governance. If power and authority are no longer sufficient because the government has lost its ability to exact unquestioning obedience, greater confidence might be instilled through greater frankness about the problems society faces. Information that can be evaluated by people themselves can lead in the same direction as policies enforced by government. A nation which founds its fortunes on exports can explain the problems posed by international competition, and electorates can judge accordingly. Coercion is not the only way to run a society, and it is increasingly a less efficient way.

A mediative state leads increasingly to a "safeguard state," that is to a condition in which the government guards citizens against the worst eventualities that might befall but cannot protect them against sudden inflation or recession, shifts of capital or currency values. Full employment can no longer be guaranteed by any modern government operating in an open international economic system. Citizens have to take steps to acquire the training necessary to compete in an ever more technological world. They can no longer expect that the single firm in which they have worked will endure forever. This means, in some cases, that they will have to be prepared to find jobs in other areas of the country or perhaps even overseas, and this in turn places a premium upon knowledge, not only of one's own country but also of the outside world. In surprising measure, people in the Third World have already seized on these requirements and possibilities and sought employment and training in other nations.

Such solutions will not remedy economic dislocations unless there is an overarching context of world economic growth, particularly in the Third World, and this means much greater success with population control than has occurred up to now. World growth will augment the market for the products of North and South and give breathing space to infant and declining industries. It will also stimulate investment in both parts of the world. Such growth will be possible only if foreign trade burgeons rapidly, holding inflation in check. A further reduction in the barriers to world trade is needed to achieve this purpose.

The domestic society will be a less secure place in which to live in that it will furnish fewer of life's necessities. Important segments of the American, Western European, and Japanese populations will have to consider spending long periods of time in other countries, much as Greek, Turkish, Mexican, Haitian, East Asian, Indian, and Pakistani populations do now. For those with international expertise and enterprise, the results could be much more satisfactory than mundane domestic life.

At the international level the mediative state creates other perplexities. Unquestioning loyalties have been partly undercut by the deconsolidation of the state in traditional liberal-democratic societies in the past half-century or so. But the decline of loyalty to one center, the state, has not meant greater loyalty to international institutions. The International Monetary Fund and the United Nations are not objects of universal affection. The institutions of the European Community do not inspire general loyalty or confidence among Europeans. We have undercut the national level without strengthening the supranational one, and in so doing the level of social disorganization might have been increased in toto.

Yet, one should avoid premature conclusions in this respect. In the transition from the medieval to the modern period, the values of political men and women were progressively reshaped. Religious and ecumenical values increasingly gave way to the values of liberal humanism and then to those centered on the nation-state. The last has been questioned and partly transcended. In many countries, even in Eastern Europe, there is an abiding attachment to peace. There is also a renewing faith in constructive and productive economic engagement, not so much centered on large corporations as on small enterprises of individual entrepreneurship. Economic growth for societies and individual self-improvement once more seem possible. Ultimate success in such ventures, however, will depend on moving beyond the national state as the limit of economic and political horizons.

In the past, some of the unproductive hostility between

national states and ideologues was based upon skewed or mistaken information or images about opponents. In the seventeenth or eighteenth centuries one could fight wars and never come to know the antagonist. Wars did not involve citizen or subject participation to any great extent. They were specialized encounters between highly trained mercenaries. This is still possible today as conventional war has become so mechanized and technological that it keeps the combatants at arms length. War, thus, may become a self-generating endeavor. "Trading" relations, however, show a different visage of the foreigner. As well-regulated economic contracts are carried out in precise monetary terms, the image of the partner changed and usually improved.

This is not to say that familiarity always breeds respect; it may also breed contempt as it has done for many years between Jew and Arab, Sunni and Shi'ite, Hindu and Moslem. But even in these contexts the enemy exists after the most recent round of war, and preparations must either be made to fight another unproductive round or to find means of settlement. In short, one possible reason why the degeneration of the domestic state may not plunge us into a new form of political chaos is that information and knowledge could begin to substitute for coercion, internationally as well as nationally. Social learning can begin to moderate or dissipate hostilities based on traditional and unexamined animosity; it can produce results that avoid making the same social mistake over and over again. In time, it could even transcend war.

Is it possible then that the age of the territorial and military state is coming to a close, that the future resides in the small state? Not in formal terms. The United States and particularly the Soviet Union remain geographically large even if they are progressively becoming functionally small. Size is a relative concept, and it refers not only to the geographic extent of states but to the magnitude of the problems they seek to solve. Little England was for many years large in comparison to the tasks it undertook to accomplish. Large America is small compared with what it seeks to do in world politics. Dynamic qualities inhere in small cohesive nations, countries which are not so multifarious internally that they cannot reach agreement on social and international missions. In this respect Japan is a kind of Venice, and the Federal Republic of Germany a lineal descendant of the Hanseatic League. Trading states are beginning to emerge once again in world politics, and the erstwhile low politics of trade and growth is becoming high politics once again.

But if elements of similarity exist between the late twentieth and the late fourteenth centuries, there are important differences. Luxury goods are no longer the staple in trade, but necessities. Markets are open, and the convenient monopoly with which Venice and later Amsterdam regulated the spice trade is no longer available to contemporary small states. They have to beat the competition economically, not defeat them militarily, and thus the basic thrust of trade today is entirely different from what it was in the 1380s, the 1880s, and the 1930s.

In past epochs fundamental changes in historical trend were only revealed at the last minute. Afterward one could always look back and explain how the French Revolution or the First World War was inevitable and stemmed from a whole series of culminating events in the late eighteenth or nineteenth centuries. On the very eve of crisis, however, the trends were still unclear. So it may be today. It is possible that major changes in world history are already in process, but we do not recognize them. Further evidence and the benefits of hindsight will be required to understand what has been going on. In the past there was a continual transformation, as Walter Bagehot recognized, of the efficient to the ceremonial in British history.[9] In the English Constitution the Crown was originally the efficient element, or at least it was until the Glorious Revolution of 1688. Afterward Parliament held the reins of power and the king or queen became a ceremonial symbol, a figurehead. By some point in the nineteenth century strict party lines ensured that a Government would not be deposed as a result of failing to win a vote of confidence in Parliament. At that point, the Cabinet became efficient and Parliament, despite its magnificent oratory, merely ceremonial.

In the seventeenth century military expansion was not only the raison d'être of new consolidating monarchies, it was a defensive necessity. A state incapable of expansion might not hold its own in the religious war of the period. Equally in the eighteenth century, war and commerce were fused in the policy of mercantilism, and nations conquered new commodity-producing areas while driving competitors out of business, seizing their sugar islands or tea plantations. After the revolutionary and Napoleonic wars at the turn of the century, nations became less enamored of war as a means of social change and there was a period of general European peace, interrupted by a few particular conflicts, which lasted until the beginning of the twentieth century. During this period, and despite the improvements in military technology, nations held back from major war and under England's leadership and inspiration devoted themselves to the peaceful arts of industrialization and commerce. The first half of the twentieth century halted this nineteenth-century period of progress, but after 1945 commerce was extended to a wider network of nations and the benefits began to spread from the North and West to the East and South. Like those in the nineteenth century small wars and proxy wars continued apace, but a major conflict was avoided. While armaments and terrorism multiplied by factors of two or three, commerce expended by factors of ten or more. Japan emerged as the symbolic leader of the new trading world, exerting somewhat the same influence (though with a much more restrictive internal economic policy) that Britain had done in the Victorian era. Nations continued to mount large military forces, but the most awesome power located in strategic nuclear weapons was held in check and not used. Conventional battles, revenge expeditions, and assassination were plotted on all sides. But none of these degenerated into a world crisis as the Sarajevo assassination had done in 1914. Events like the killing of United States marines and French paratroopers in Lebanon transpired without calling for the same retribution as had occurred after the sinking of the battleship *Maine* in Havana harbor in 1898.

Aware of the catastrophic consequences that might befall, governments could now tolerate greater affronts to the national dignity without reprisal. In the Middle East, Afghanistan, South Asia, and on the borders of Vietnam, conventional or insurgent warfare would continue. But it was just possible that weapons of mass destruction had come to perform a ceremonial as well as an efficient function. They served as a warning and a deterrent, but like orb, scepter, crown, and mace, they symbolized a majestic power that could no longer be used for rational political ends. While this transformation was still in process, a multiplicity of trading arrangements between nations were gradually but inexorably changing the face of the world and of traditional international relations. An old world was beginning to be transformed into a new one.

Appendix

International Relationships

Individual and Collective Action (Public and Private Goods)

In international politics, nations engage in individual as well as collective action. They aim to gain private as well as public goods. Individual action (aimed at acquiring private goods) may be of two forms, mutually beneficial or one-sided (what one gains, the other loses). Collective action (aimed at gaining public goods) is also of two forms: where all collaborate and contribute to the good, and where some are free-riders on the largesse of others. Public goods are goods that, once created, can be enjoyed by all: clean air, clean water, an international payments regime and freedom from nuclear war are all public goods. Private goods result from action or agreement by individual states who are themselves the only beneficiaries from their creation. Two party trade agreements, exchanges of territory, and alliances are private goods for those who negotiate them.

The Military-Political and Trading Worlds

The military-political world arises either in games of constant-sum or in games of increasing-sum in which one party advantages himself (defects from a cooperative arrangement) at the expense

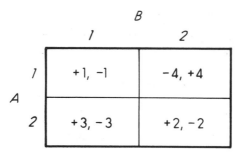

Figure 1

of the other. The military-political world is found in private goods where one-sided payoffs exist; it is found in public goods where one state becomes a free rider on goods provided by another. The trading world arises in increasing-sum games of either a collective or individual nature in which the parties do not defect or seek to take one-sided advantage.

The relationship of the players in international relations is of two possible sorts: it is either constant-sum (with zero-sum as a variant) or variable-sum in character.[1] Zero or constant-sum games are those of the military-political world. These games may or may not have an equilibrium (or saddlepoint).

Military-Political Relationships

Figures 1 and 2 are zero-sum games in that what one player wins, the other loses. Figure 1 has an equilibrium point (saddlepoint), but figure 2 does not. In figure 1 player A can guarantee an outcome of no less than +2, and player B can always avoid a loss of more than 2. Thus the A_2B_2 outcome satisfies both, relative to the other choices. Once A_2B_2 has been chosen, neither player can benefit by switching strategies. If A chooses strategy 2, B will not gain by playing strategy 1. If B chooses strategy 2, A will not improve his position by playing strategy 1. The result is therefore stable and does not depend upon what the other player does.

In games without saddlepoints, like that in figure 2, however,

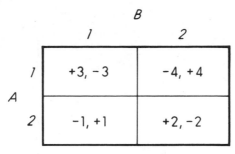

Figure 2

a player's choice of strategy will depend upon the opponent's choice. If A chooses strategy 2 (seeking to minimize his loses), B will be tempted to choose strategy 1 with an outcome of (−1, +1). But if B chooses strategy 1, A will also be tempted to choose strategy 1 with an outcome of (+3, −3). But this would lead B to choose strategy 2 with an outcome of (−4, +4); then A chooses strategy 2, and we repeat the process, with no stable result. It goes without saying that cooperation does not characterize such games. In figure 1, B must lose; in figure 2, either could lose.

Indeterminate Relationships = Mixed Motive Games

Figure 3 has no single stable outcome. If A played strategy 1, seeking to minimize losses, B would be tempted to play strategy 2, gaining the favorable (2, 4) payoff. If, however, B started with strategy 1, A would counter with strategy 2 leading to (4, 2). Either A_1B_2 or A_2B_1 would be stable, because neither party would

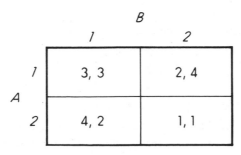

Figure 3

B

	1	2
1	3, 3	1, 4
2	4, 1	2, 2

A

Figure 4

want to risk strategy 2 in response to the other's strategy 2 and the inferior outcome (1, 1). Each party would like the other to gain the impression that she would certainly play strategy 2, but neither would want to become so committed to strategy 2 that she could not change at the last minute. The game in figure 3 never leads to the inferior outcome (A_2B_2) if the parties take successive turns. This game, dubbed "chicken" in conventional parlance, helps to explain why US-Soviet crisis management has generally been successful since 1945. The worst outcome for both is a clash (1, 1) and both would prefer to play strategy 1 to avoid it.[2] Thus "chicken" is less likely to lead to conflict in the real world than in the hypothetical world of simultaneous play.

Figure 4 has a saddlepoint at A_2B_2 (2, 2) even though a better mutual outcome (Pareto Optimality and also the Nash solution) can be achieved at A_1B_1 (3, 3). Seeking to minimize losses and also maximize gains, A will choose strategy 2. B will do the same thing. The result is stable. If A switched to strategy 1, B would remain at 2. If B switched to strategy 1, A would remain at 2. There is thus a dominant strategy and what A does, does not depend on B. At the same time, *if* both could move to A_1B_1 (without the one-sided outcomes of A_1B_2 and A_2B_1 intruding), *both* would be better off. The outcome of figure 4, often called the Prisoner's Dilemma, undercuts cooperative strategies in world politics. A and B may agree to play A_1B_1 but each is tempted to defect, and both play their second strategy, yielding (2, 2), an inferior outcome for both.

If states (players) could agree to stable cooperative play, they would move from the military-political world to the trading world, engaging in dependable exchange and keeping their agreements. Tariffs would remain low, and arms races would be curbed. But

234

how can such agreements be policed? Some game theorists contend that the Prisoner's Dilemma (figure 4) is the normal form of international interaction, and conflict and defection the normal result in anarchic international relations.[3] We know, on the other hand, that, faced with incentives to defect from an agreement, nations often honor their obligations and gain the benefits of mutual cooperation. When play is repetitive; when there is a small number of players; when players may meet and interact in other situations, agreements often can be kept.[4] When interdependence exists between parties on a range of issues, there is an overwhelming incentive to avoid Prisoner's Dilemma outcomes on one particular issue. In iterative play the strategies which players use also matter. Tit-for-tat strategies reward cooperation, punish defection, and help to buttress cooperative relationships, once achieved. If nations decide to enter and to abide by international regimes in trade, monetary relations, sea law and the oceans, they can often conform to a preexisting set of rules and expectations. Whether they will decide to enter such arrangements, and, Russia, to take one example, has consistently declined to do so, is partly determined by whether states are prepared to extend their involvement in the network of interdependence, giving up some of their autonomy in return for concrete benefits. Here social learning plays an important role and national policy can be inhibited by the precepts of the past or informed by those of the present.

Once established, the greater the range and depth of interdependent ties the more difficult it is for parties to break cooperative relationships in any given area. Such a termination would affect relations in other areas. Thus a connection between issues often facilitates agreement, since one party can concede in one issue in return for partner concessions in others.

The Prisoner's Dilemma matrix offers an incentive and payoff structure similar to that of the dilemma of collective goods. In the provision of collective goods—such as clean air or water, defense, police or welfare systems—some individuals are tempted to be Free Riders. As a result, so it is argued, there is an underprovision of collective goods in many industrial countries. Free riders wait for others to pay the initial costs of creating the collective good; afterward they can expect to benefit without paying any cost.

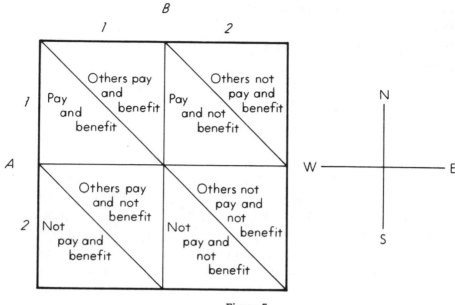

Figure 5

Governments overcome the dilemma of collective goods by enforcing payment of taxes for many such services. The temptation to be a free rider and to enjoy, say, defense, without paying the cost is similar to the incentive to defect from a cooperative arrangement. Each party, in deciding not to pay (defect) is assuming that others will pay, so that he may get the benefit of the (4, 1) payoff (A_2B_1) in figure 4. If each individual hoping to benefit from collective defense reasoned this way, the defense would not be provided.

Figure 5 illustrates the series of outcomes, with the individual A trying to achieve a southwest payoff box, and other individuals B a northeast box. Since an individual, however, does not have power over others' choices, he cannot simply opt for: *not pay and benefit,* while others *pay and not benefit.* If any substantial number of individuals reasoned in this fashion, the good would not be provided and outcomes 2, 1 and 1, 2 would not obtain, leaving only 1, 1 and 2, 2. In fact, free rider outcomes can only be based on the assumption that most of the members of the group providing the collective good act on motives different from those of the free riders, which cannot be true.[5] When A realizes that all act on the same motives, he will have incentives to stay in the

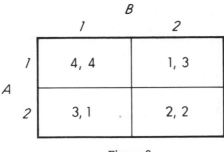

Figure 6

group and to pay in order to receive the benefits of the good. Thus, despite contentious disputes about "burdensharing" in NATO, there have been few free-riders, and the benefits have been generally more equitably shared than is often asserted.

Reciprocal, Trading Relationships

After a sequence of cooperative responses, two parties can build trust between themselves to the point where it can be assumed that their agreements will be carried out. Then the terms of the agreement become the issue. Both parties assume that agreement is necessary; the question is on whose terms.[6] Assuming that a bargain must be struck, the weaker party may be the stronger bargainer, for it cannot afford many, expensive concessions.[7] Here one has the reversal of "normal" military-political outcomes where the stronger wins, and agreement is not essential.

In figure 6 the premium on agreement is illustrated in the payoff for cooperative strategy 1 in both cases (4, 4). In this game, unlike Prisoner's Dilemma, one party does not do better by defecting if the other cooperates. The question, rather, is establishing a framework of "assurance" in which the cooperative results can be obtained.[8]

On a minimax basis A may choose his second strategy; in that way, regardless of what B plays, he will assure an outcome of 2. Reasoning similarly B will also play his second strategy,

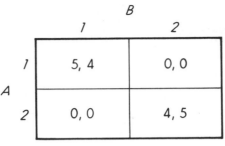

Figure 7

giving an outcome of (2, 2). But if A could be "assured" that B would respond in the same way, he would pick his first strategy, and the two together would derive the Pareto optimal and Nash outcome (4, 4) which is better for both. Picking strategy 1 in this case, the parties benefit from trust built up through previous negotiations. If sufficient trust did not exist initially to ensure the result, a tit-for-tat strategy on successive plays would powerfully reinforce cooperative incentives on both sides. The interesting difference between the "assurance" game and Prisoner's Dilemma is that in the former, agreement is essential to obtaining favorable outcomes. In much the same way, no party benefits in a chaotic trade war. It is necessary to have a trade and payments regime in place (by previous agreement) for high and mutual benefits to flow.

The premium on agreement is further reinforced in figure 7 where no gains occur unless both sides pick the same strategy. A few years ago, Richard Cooper illustrated the features of this "coordination" game in noting that the United States and France had different objectives for the international monetary regime in the 1970s.[9] The French typically wanted fixed exchange rates based on gold; the Americans, flexible exchange rates based on the dollar. But each side was prepared to drop its objections rather than fail to set up some form of exchange and payments regime. The Americans would take the French system for a mutual payoff of (4, 5) and the French would take the American system for a mutual payoff of (5, 4). But each side derived nothing (0, 0) from failure to agree on a regime. In figure 7 either strategies 1, 1 or 2, 2 provide such stable outcomes.

International Relationships

Historical Development

Since 1500 the internal capacity of the state has grown, but relative to the external challenges it faces, it has declined. In both economic and military terms states can no longer provide all their own needs. Also, agreements with one or two other nations have frequently been insufficient to cope with the problems of modern commerce, technology, finance, communications, and military security. Increasingly, collective action has been sought as a remedy. If noncontributors could not be excluded from the benefits of the collective (public) goods, however, those collective regimes were in jeopardy. Once several key states either could or would not support them, they were likely to fail.

Two remedies have been suggested. First, tit-for-tat strategies among potential participants elicit greater cooperation in support of provision of the good. Small groups, continuing relationships, and involvement in other issue-areas, facilitate cooperation. Second, inveterate Free-riders may be discouraged if they can be partly excluded from enjoyment of the good. Japan's participation in the American and Western market will become increasingly dependent on opening up her markets and modifying her commercial practices to allow others to sell there.

Long-term maximization strategies, however, may not be followed by all states. Some will defect from multilateral agreements or free ride on collective goods provided by others. The military political world still determines many important outcomes.

NOTES

Chapter 1

1. Quoted in Jonathan Rosenblum, *Problems in Deterrence Theory: A Case Study of the Superpower Crisis of October 24-25, 1973* (Ph.D. diss., Cornell University, 1983), p. 31.

2. Henry A. Kissinger, *Years of Upheaval* (Boston: Little Brown, 1982), p. 583.

3. Based on material derived from interviews, Israel, 1982.

4. Quoted in Walter L. Dorn, *Competition for Empire* (New York: Harper & Row, 1940), p. 370.

5. See R. Keohane, *After Hegemony* (Princeton: Princeton University Press, 1984), p. 199.

6. See the account in Kissinger, pp. 891-95, 939-45, 975-78.

7. Charles Tilly, ed., *The Formation of National States in Western Europe* (Princeton: Princeton University Press, 1975), p. 24.

Chapter 2

1. There has been an important difference between those who see homogeneity as desirable and those who find it disruptive in the international system because of different definitions of the term. Raymond Aron and Hedley Bull believe a homogeneous system, that is, one without ideological differences is more cohesive than a heterogeneous system. Kenneth Waltz contends that the state system is homogeneous, in that all states depend only on themselves. Peter Blau notes that "exchange" can only emerge in a social system when there is some differentiation in the functions performed by the parties, and therefore suggests that heterogeneity and social exchange can level power hierarchies and produce cooperation. Ideological heterogeneity (in Aron's sense) may be quite compatible with homogeneity (in Waltz's sense) for ideological disunity can be the stimulus to seek total independence. Raymond Aron, *Peace and War* (New York: Praeger, 1967), pp. 99-103; Hedley Bull, *The Anarchical Society* (New York: Columbia University Press, 1977), pp. 33-34, 317; Kenneth Waltz, *Theory of International Politics* (Reading, Mass: Addison-Wesley, 1979), pp. 93-97; Peter Blau, *Exchange and Power in Social Life* (New York: John Wiley & Sons, 1964), pp. 190-192.

2. See Peter Blau, *Exchange and Power in Social Life* (New York: John Wiley & Sons, 1964), pp. 106-12.

3. Blau, See chap. 4 and 5.

4. J. Herz, "Rise and Demise of the Territorial State" in *World Politics,* 9:4 (July 1957), pp. 473-93.

5. Edward Whiting Fox, *History in Geographic Perspective: The Other France* (New York: W.W. Norton, 1971), pp. 33-37, 55-71. In this path-breaking book, Fox calls this system "The Commercial Society."

6. R. G. Albion, *Rise of New York Port, 1815-1860* (New York: Charles Scribner's Sons, 1939), pp. 120-21.

7. See Michael Howard, *The Continental Commitment* (London: Maurice Temple Smith Ltd., 1972); Paul Kennedy, *Strategy and Diplomacy, 1870-1945* (London: Fontana Paperbacks, 1984), chap. 8, esp. p. 216.

Notes

8. See John Mearsheimer, *Conventional Deterrence* (Ithaca: Cornell University Press, 1983), chap. 7.

9. The efficacy of Soviet air attack on allied formations is evaluated in Joshua Epstein, *Measuring Military Power: The Soviet Air Threat to Europe* (Princeton: Princeton University Press, 1984).

10. See the data offered in Sir Frank Cooper, "The Management of Defence Expenditure" in *Defence and Consensus: The Domestic Aspects of Western Security*, pt. 1, Adelphi Paper No. 182, (London: Institute for Strategic Studies, 1983), pp. 53–55.

11. See Gordon Wright, *Ordeal of Total War 1939–1945* (New York: Harper & Row, 1968), chaps. 6 and 7, and pp. 119–21.

12. This discussion is further developed in chap. 6.

13. Karl Kaiser, "Transnational Relations as a Threat to Democratic Process" in R. Keohane and J. Nye, eds., *Transnational Relations and World Politics* (Cambridge, Mass.: Harvard University Press, 1972), pp. 356–70.

14. See Peter J. Katzenstein, *Corporatism and Change: Austria, Switzerland and the Politics of Industry* (Ithaca: Cornell University Press, 1984), pp. 245ff.

15. See Charles P. Kindleberger, *The World in Depression* (Berkeley: University of California Press, 1973), p. 292 and *Manias, Panics and Crashes* (New York: Basic Books, 1978), p. 4.

Chapter 3

1. In such a situation there can be no static stability because no state will be satisfied with a negative outcome. In a constant-sum game, on the other hand, static stability (with all states enjoying a positive position) is possible, but dynamic stability is not.

2. This view has been offered in Kenneth Waltz's *Theory of International Politics* (Reading, Mass.: Addison-Wesley, 1979), see esp. chap. 5.

3. See Hans J. Morgenthau, *Politics Among Nations* (New York: Alfred Knopf, 1973), chaps. 1 and 14.

4. A. F. K. Organski, *World Politics*, (New York: Alfred Knopf, 1968), chap. 12.

5. This is the central thesis of Geoffrey Blainey in *The Causes of War* (London: Macmillan, 1973), esp. chap. 8.

6. See John Harsanyi, "Game Theory and the Analysis of International Conflict" in J. N. Rosenau ed., *International Politics and Foreign Policy* (Glencoe: Free Press, 1969), chap. 34.

7. See appendix.

8. For each state, the desired outcomes range from C, C (best) to C, D (worst), with D, C and D, D between the two. In the absence of information and prior coordination, a player would choose D, which provides the highest minimum payoff, not C, which he can only choose if he is confident that the other player will also choose C (see figs. 5 and 6 in app.).

9. Robert Axelrod, *The Evolution of Cooperation* (New York: Basic Books, 1984).

10. See Morton Kaplan, *System and Process in International Politics* (New York: John Wiley & Sons, 1956), chap. 2.

11. This is the conclusion of Karl Deutsch and his colleagues in *Political Community and the North Atlantic Area* (Princeton: Princeton University Press, 1957).

12. See Stephen Rock, "Why Peace Breaks Out" (Ph.D. diss., Cornell University, 1985).

13. V. I. Lenin, *Imperialism, the Highest State of Capitalism* (New York: International Publishers, 1933).

14. Karl Kautsky pointed out that conflict in world politics would not necessarily be between nations but rather between international trusts. *The Class Struggle* (Erfurt Program), trans. W. E. Bohn (Chicago: C. H. Kerr, 1910), p. 81.

15. See Johan Galtung, "A Structural Theory of Imperialism" in *Journal of Peace Research* 8:1 (1971), p. 81.

16. Peter Evans, *Dependent Development* (Princeton: Princeton University Press, 1979).

17. It did, however, cause Joseph Schumpeter to regard late nineteenth-century European and Japanese capitalism as insufficiently developed because it contained "precapitalist" elements. See his *Imperialism and Social Classes* (New York: A. M. Kelley, 1951), pp. 100–25.

18. David Landes gives the following comparative figures for England and Germany:

Germany and United Kingdom Foreign Investment (as Percentage of Total Net Capital Formation in Current Prices)

Germany		United Kingdom	
Year	Percentage	Year	Percentage
1871/75–1881/85	14.1	1875–84	28.9
1881/85–1891/95	19.9	1885–94	51.2
1891/95–1901/5	9.7	1895–1904	20.7
1901/5–1911/13	5.7	1905–14	52.9

NOTE: "Technological Change and Development in Western Europe, 1750–1914" in H. J. Habakkuk and M. Postan, eds., *The Industrial Revolutions and After: Incomes, Population and Technological Change (1)* vol. 6, *The Cambridge Economic History of Europe* (Cambridge: Cambridge University Press, 1965), p. 558.

19. Charles Kindleberger, "Needed: World Monetary Leadership" in *The New York Times*, June 4, 1972, and Robert Gilpin, "Economic Interdependence and National Security in Historical Perspective" in K. Knorr and F. Trager, eds., *Economic Issues and National Security* (Lawrence, Kan.: The Regents Press of Kansas, 1977), p. 54.

20. See Robert Gilpin, "The Politics of Transnational Economic Relations" in R. Keohane and J. Nye, eds., *Transnational Relations and World Politics* (Cambridge, Mass.: Harvard University Press, 1972), pp. 55–63.

21. See Duncan Snidal, "The Limits of Hegemonic Stability Theory," *International Organization*, 39:4 (Autumn 1985).

22. Robert Keohane, *After Hegemony* (Princeton: Princeton University Press, 1984).

23. See Stephen Krasner, ed., *International Regimes*, A Special Issue of *International Organization*, 36:2 (Spring 1982).

24. See R. Keohane and J. Nye, *Power and Interdependence* (Boston: Little Brown, 1977), esp. pp. 23–29.

Chapter 4

1. This does not mean that other city-states or countries did not previously import goods from overseas. Venice relied upon the shores of the Black Sea for its food supplies. But Victorian England sacrificed existing food supplies at home in order to develop a more efficient division of labor in the international trading system.

2. See the interesting argument to this effect in Jane Jacobs, *Cities and the Wealth of Nations* (New York: Random House, 1984), chaps. 2 and 3.

3. Joseph Strayer, *On The Medieval Origins of the Modern State* (Princeton: Princeton University Press, 1970), chap. 1.

Notes

4. William Hardy McNeill, *The Shape of Modern History* (London: Oxford University Press, 1974), p. 123.

5. See Edward Whiting Fox, *History in Geographic Perspective: The Other France* (New York: W. W. Norton, 1971), chaps. 2 and 3.

6. This is one of the essential theses of Immanuel Wallerstein's work, *The Modern World System, I* (New York: Academic Press, 1974).

7. See Jan DeVries, *The Economy of Europe in an Age of Crisis, 1600-1750* (Cambridge: Cambridge University Press, 1976), p. 216.

8. See the discussion in Fernand Braudel, *Le Temps du Monde,* (Paris: Librairie Armand Colin, 1979), chaps. 4 and 5.

9. Ralph Davis, *The Rise of the Atlantic Economies* (Ithaca: Cornell University Press, 1973), p. 306.

10. Paul Kennedy, *The Rise and Fall of British Naval Mastery* (London: Allen Lane, 1976), p. 109.

Chapter 5

1. Robert Jervis provides an interesting catalogue of reasons why a Concert system can sometimes emerge from a balance of power system after hegemonic war ("From Balance to Concert: A Study of International Security Cooperation." Prepared for the 1984 Annual Meeting of the American Political Science Association).

2. See William L. Langer, *The Diplomacy of Imperialism* (New York: Alfred Knopf, 1950), chap. 3.

3. The nineteenth-century saw such trends in the large, but there were exceptions. The Spanish Empire broke up in the aftermath of the Napoleonic Wars, and the Turkish Empire grudgingly gave ground to new states in the Balkans during the course of the century.

4. The extent of the European peace movement is well recounted in Francis H. Hinsley, *Power and the Pursuit of Peace* (Cambridge: Cambridge University Press, 1963), chap. 7.

5. Some will agree with Ronald E. Robinson and John Gallagher that there was an "imperialism of free trade" in that Britain's industrial and commercial strength gave her great advantages in an open trading system. This may be true, but despite her increasing chain of strategic bases, Britain had no conscious imperialist and annexationist policy in the period 1830-70. See Paul Kennedy, *The Rise and Fall of British Naval Mastery* (London: Allen Lane, 1976), pp. 152-55, and William Roger Louis, ed., *Imperialism: The Robinson-Gallagher Controversy* (New York: New Viewpoints, 1976).

6. Arnold J. Toynbee, *A Study of History*, vol. 4 *The Breakdown of Civilizations* (London: Oxford University Press, 1939) p. 182. He writes: "This new British method of trade in staple commodities, and this economic requisite required in its turn the uninterrupted maintenance of World Peace. It is no exaggeration to say that the early nineteenth-century British pioneers of industrialism staked their daily bread, and the daily bread of future generations in Great Britain upon the quite unwarrantable expectation of a world order which was to be equally secure on the economic plane and on the political."

7. See Paul Kennedy, *Strategy and Diplomacy* (London: Fontana Paperbacks, 1984), chap. 1.

8. C. C. Eldridge, *England's Mission* (London: Macmillan, 1973),p. 37.

9. See Jean Jacques Rousseau, *Discourse on the Origins of Inequality among Men,* trans. Roger Masters (New York: St. Martin's, 1964), p. 145, and the useful gloss on Rousseau's ideas in Kenneth Waltz, *Man, the State, and War* (New York: Columbia University Press, 1959), chap. 6.

10. Karl Polanyi argues the same point for domestic economic stability. *The Great Transformation* (Boston: Beacon Press, 1957), pp. 192ff.

11. C. C. Eldridge, *England's Mission* (London: Macmillan, 1973), p. 248. Robinson and Gallagher point out that the carving up of Africa was due, in Victorian perceptions, as much to local pressures as to any strategic design. France and Germany may have had more forthrightly imperial motives than Britain. In Ronald Robinson and John Gallagher with Alice Denny, *Africa and the Victorians: The Official Mind of Imperialism,* 2nd ed. (London: Macmillan, 1981), p. 478.

12. Quoted in William L. Langer, *The Diplomacy of Imperialism* (New York: Alfred Knopf, 1951), p. 78.

13. For a provocative analysis of their political staying-power, see Arno J. Mayer, *The Persistence of the Old Regime* (New York: Pantheon Books, 1981), esp. chap. 3.

14. Felix Gilbert, *The End of the European Era, 1890 to the Present,* 2nd ed. (New York: W.W. Norton, 1979), pp. 184–85.

15. Hajo Holborn, *A History of Modern Germany, 1840–1945* (Princeton: Princeton University Press, 1969), p. 752.

Chapter 6

1. The effects of this syndrome are analyzed in A. George, D. Hall, and W. Simon, *The Limits of Coercive Diplomacy* (Boston: Little Brown, 1971).

2. See John Mearsheimer, *Conventional Deterrence* (Ithaca: Cornell University Press, 1983), chap. 6.

3. See William J. Perry, *The FY 1981 Department of Defense Program for Research, Development and Acquisition* 1 (Washington, D.C.: Government Printing Office, Feb. 1, 1980), pp. 10–15. If such a trend continued, it would progressively cancel the advantage that armor protection and mobility once gave to ground formations.

4. Halford Mackinder, "The Geographical Pivot of History" in *Geographical Journal,* 23: 4 (April 1904).

5. Nicholas J. Spykman, *The Geography of the Peace,* ed. Helen Nicholl (New York: Harcourt, Brace, 1944), pp. 43–44.

6. Robert DeGrasse, Jr., *Military Expansion: Economic Decline* (Armonk, New York: M. E. Sharpe, 1983), p. 47.

7. DeGrasse, p. 47.

8. Daniel Baugh, "British Strategy in the First World War in the Context of Four Centuries: Blue Water versus Continental Commitment." *Papers of the 6th Naval History Symposium,* Annapolis, 1985.

9. The Falkland and Grenada episodes do not contradict this view because they were short, victorious, and not too costly.

10. For a contrary view see Darryl Roberts, "Origins of War in the Periphery" (Ph.D. diss., Cornell University, 1984).

Chapter 7

1. It is true that the greatest imperial edifices were constructed after the start of the Industrial Revolution. It was precisely that revolution, however, which prepared the groundwork for their demise.

2. Paul Kennedy, *Strategy and Diplomacy 1870–1945* (London: Fontana Paperbacks 1984), pp. 95–96.

Notes

3. Michael Stewart, *The Age of Interdependence* (Cambridge, Mass.: MIT Press, 1984), p. 20.

4. John H. Dunning, *Studies in International Investment* (London: George Allen and Unwin, 1970), p. 1.

5. "International Investment Position of the United States at Year End" in *Survey of Current Business* (Washington, D.C.: Department of Commerce, June 1984).

6. Karl W. Deutsch and Alexander Eckstein, "National Industrialization and the Declining Share of the International Economic Sector, 1890–1959" in *World Politics*, 13 (January 1961), pp. 267–99.

7. *National Power and the Structure of Foreign Trade* (Berkeley: University of California Press, 1980), pp. 129–43.

8. Richard Rosecrance and Arthur Stein, "Interdependence: Myth or Reality" in *World Politics* (July 1973), pp. 7–9.

9. Kenneth Waltz, "The Myth of National Interdependence" in Charles Kindleberger, ed., *The International Corporation* (Cambridge, Mass.: MIT Press, 1970), p. 206.

10. Paul Kennedy, *The Rise and Fall of British Naval Mastery* (London: Allen Lane, 1976), pp. 187–88.

11. Nothing could be more misleading than to equate these interrelations with those of nineteenth-century imperialism. Then imperial dictates went in one direction—military, economic, and social. The metropole dominated the colony. Today, does North America become a colony when Chicanos and Hispanics move to it in increasing numbers or England a tributary of the West Indies? Does Chinese or Korean investment in the United States render it a peripheral member of the system? The point is that influence goes in both directions just as does investment and trade in manufactured goods.

12. See Ronald Muller, *The Revitalization of America* (New York: Simon and Schuster, 1980), chap. 6.

13. See Charles Sabel, *Work and Politics* (Cambridge: Cambridge University Press, 1982), chap. 5.

Chapter 8

1. Arthur Alexander, *Armor Development in the Soviet Union and the United States*, R–1860–NA (Santa Monica, Calif.: Rand Corporation, Sept. 1976), pp. 118, 126, 127.

2. For a new and powerful analysis of the Soviet air threat to Europe, see Joshua Epstein, *Measuring Military Power*, (Princeton: Princeton University Press, 1984), pp. 10–13 and app. C.

3. Sir Frank Cooper, The Management of Defence Expenditure" in *Defence and Concensus: The Domestic Aspects of Western Security, pt. 1*, Adelphi Paper No. 182, (London: Institute for Strategic Studies, 1983), pp. 53–55.

4. The phenomenon is usefully analyzed in Arthur Stein, *The Nation at War* (Baltimore: Johns Hopkins University Press, 1978).

5. Stein, p. 98.

6. See Robert Jervis, "Cooperation Under the Security Dilemma" in *World Politics* vol. 30 (January 1978), pp. 167–214.

Chapter 9

1. See Kenneth Waltz, *Man, the State, and War* (New York: Columbia University Press, 1959), chap. 6.

2. See William H. McNeill, *The Pursuit of Power* (Chicago: University of Chicago

Press, 1982), chaps. 9 and 10. *The Human Condition* (Princeton: Princeton University Press, 1980), p. 62.

3. See Mancur Olson, *The Rise and Decline of Nations* (New Haven: Yale University Press, 1982).

4. See Edward Vose Gulick, *Europe's Classical Balance of Power System* (Ithaca: Cornell University Press, 1955).

5. Ronald Rogowski, "Structure, Growth and Power: Three Rationalist Accounts" in *International Organization* (Autumn 1983), p. 725.

6. Rogowski, p. 728. Emphasis in the original.

7. Rogowski, p. 728.

8. This outcome is favorably viewed in Barry Buzan, "Economic Structure and International Security: The Limits of the Liberal Case" in *International Organization* (Autumn 1984).

9. See Charles P. Kindleberger, "Needed World Monetary Leadership" in *The New York Times*, June 4, 1972.

10. A view contrasting with the hegemonic stability theory is offered in R. Keohane, *After Hegemony* (Princeton: Princeton University Press, 1984).

11. See Richard Kimber, "Collective Action and the Fallacy of the Liberal Fallacy" in *World Politics* (January 1981), pp. 187–88.

12. See Rajni Kothari, *Footsteps into the Future* (New York: Free Press, 1975).

13. For contrasting views on the changing terms of trade for agricultural goods see Paul Bairoch, *Economic Development of the Third World Since 1900* (Berkeley: University of California Press, 1977), chap. 6; J. D. Gould, *Economic Growth in History* (London: Methuen, 1972), chap. 4; and R. Nurkse, *Patterns of Trade and Development* (Oxford: Blackwell, 1961).

14. See Ronald Muller, *Revitalizing America* (New York: Simon and Schuster, 1980), chap. 6.

15. See Bela Belassa, *The Newly Industrializing Countries in the World Economy* (New York: Pergamon Press, 1981), chap. 9.

16. Jean-François Revel. *How Democracies Perish* (Garden City: Doubleday, 1984), pp. 3–4.

17. Cited in Revel, p. 15.

18. See O. Spengler, *Der Untergang des Abendlandes*, vol 3, 15th–22nd, ed., trans. A. J. Toynbee, p. 153. Spengler writes: "A civilization (*Kultur*) is born at the moment when, out of the primitive psychic conditions of perpetually infantile (raw) humanity, a mighty soul awakes and extricates itself: a form out of the formless, a bounded and transitory existence out of the boundless and persistent. This soul comes to flower on the soil of a country with precise boundaries, to which it remains attached like a plant. Conversely a civilization dies if once this soul has realized the complete sum of its possibilities in the shape of peoples, languages, creeds, arts, states and sciences, and thereupon goes back into the primitive psyche from which it originally emerged."

19. John Steinbrunner, "Nuclear Decapitation," in *Foreign Policy* (Winter 1981–82), pp. 16–28.

20. See Sidney Drell, Philip Farley, and David Holloway, *The Reagan Strategic Defense Initiative: A Technical, Political, and Arms Control Assessment*. A Report of the Center for International Security and Arms Control (Stanford: Stanford University, 1984), sects. 1, 2, and 3.

21. Thomas C. Schelling, *The Strategy of Conflict* (London: Oxford University Press, 1975), p. 22.

22. Thomas C. Schelling, *Arms and Influence* (New Haven: Yale University Press, 1966), p. 37.

23. See Paul Bracken, *The Command and Control of Nuclear Forces* (New Haven: Yale University Press, 1983) pp. 224–237.

Notes

24. See Daniel Lang, *An Inquiry into the Nature of Enoughness* (New York: McGraw-Hill, 1965).

25. Such options have been the focus of United States doctrine at least since the time of Secretary of Defense Robert McNamara. Secretaries James Schlesinger, Harold Brown, and Caspar Weinberger have endorsed such formulations.

26. See particularly Theodore Sorenson, *Kennedy* (New York: Harper & Row, 1965), p. 705.

Chapter 10

1. Walther Kirchner, *History of Russia* (New York: Barnes and Noble Books, 1976), p. 5.

2. Clive Trebilcock, *The Industrialization of the Continental Powers, 1780–1914* (London: Longman, 1981), p. 232.

3. *The New York Times*, October 14, 1984, p. 3.

4. Quoted in Erik Hoffmann and Robbin Laird, *The Politics of Economic Modernization in the Soviet Union* (Ithaca: Cornell University Press, 1982), pp. 102–3.

5. Quoted in Hoffmann and Laird, p. 164.

6. David Apter, *The Politics of Modernization* (Chicago: University of Chicago Press, 1967), pp. 237–40.

7. See Barrington Moore, *Terror and Progress: USSR* (Cambridge, Mass.: Harvard University Press, 1954). For a comprehensive assessment of the effect of such trends see Jacob Bielasiak, "Political Change and Economic Development: A Study of Elite Composition in Eastern Europe" (Ph.D. diss., Cornell University, 1975).

8. Seweryn Bialer, *Stalin's Successors* (Cambridge: Cambridge University Press, 1980), p. 305.

9. One exponent of this view is Darryl Roberts in "Origins of War in the Periphery of the International System" (Ph.D. diss., Cornell University, 1984).

10. R. Barnet and R. Muller, *Global Reach: The Power of the Multinational Corporation,* (New York: Simon and Schuster, 1974), chaps. 5–7, and Richard Barnet, *The Lean Years* (New York: Simon and Schuster, 1980), chap. 9.

11. See Peter Evans, *Dependent Development* (Princeton: Princeton University Press, 1979), chap. 2.

12. See the account in W. Arthur Lewis, *The Evolution of the International Economic System* (Princeton: Princeton University Press, 1978).

13. Jane Jacobs rightly sees "import-replacing cities" as the fount of economic progress and growth. "Import replacement," however, may not be sufficient if it is not extended into an export drive. J. Jacobs, *Cities and the Wealth of Nations* (New York: Random House, 1984), chap. 2, and Bela Belassa, *The Newly Industrializing Countries in the World Economy* (New York: Pergamon Press, 1981), chap. 1.

14. Belassa, pp. 215–216.

15. Belassa, p. 226.

16. Robert H. Hayes and William J. Abernathy, "Managing Our Way to Economic Decline" in *Harvard Business Review* (July–August 1980), p. 67–78.

17. See Ronald Muller, *Revitalizing America* (New York: Simon and Schuster, 1980), chap. 6.

Notes

Chapter 11

1. See Robert Gilpin, *War and Change in World Politics* (Cambridge: Cambridge University Press, 1981), chap. 4.

2. Michael Piore and Charles Sabel, *The Second Industrial Divide* (New York: Basic Books, 1984), p. 214.

3. It is this flexible adaptation of "import-replacing cities" that Jane Jacobs sees as the dynamic element in contemporary industrialism. See her *Cities and the Wealth of Nations* (New York: Random House, 1984), chaps. 2 and 3.

4. This is what concerns Adam Watson and Hedley Bull. See their book, *The Expansion of International Society* (Oxford: The Clarendon Press, 1984), esp. chap. 28.

5. Robert Keohane and Joseph Nye were the first to note the effect of "transnationalism"—transactions in which one of the parties is *not* government—upon international politics. See their *Transnational Relations and World Politics* (Cambridge, Mass.: Harvard University Press, 1972), and *Power and Interdependence* (Boston: Little Brown, 1977). The latter represents one of the first efforts toward a dualistic theory of world politics.

6. See Charles A. Reich, "The New Property" in *Yale Law Journal* (April 1964), pp. 733–87.

7. See Peter Katzenstein, *Corporatism and Change* (Ithaca: Cornell University Press, 1984), esp. chap. 7.

8. See Piore and Sabel, pp. 13–18.

9. Walter Bagehot, *The English Constitution*, (Ithaca: Cornell University Press, 1966), p. 262.

Appendix

1. For an introduction to such concepts, see Melvin Dresher, *The Mathematics of Games of Strategy* (New York: Dover Publications, 1980), and Duncan Luce and Howard Raiffa, *Games and Decisions* (New York: John Wiley & Sons, 1957).

2. See Robert Jervis, "Bargaining and Bargaining Tactics" in J. R. Pennock and J. W. Chapman, eds., *Coercion* (Chicago: Aldine Atherton, 1972), pp. 272–88.

3. See John Harsanyi, "Game Theory and International Politics" in J. N. Rosenau, ed., *International Politics and Foreign Policy* (Glencoe: Free Press, 1969).

4. See Robert Axelrod, *The Evolution of Cooperation* (New York: Basic Books, 1984), J. Elster, *Ulysses and the Sirens* (Cambridge: Cambridge University Press, 1979), and Russell Hardin, *Collection Action* (Baltimore: Johns Hopkins University Press, 1982). Charles Lipson in "The Problem of Cooperation in Economic and Security Issues" [(American Political Science Association Paper, September 1984), pp. 8–9] lists the requirements for overcoming *PD* incentives as:

> 1. the actors' perceptions that they are interdependent and that their decisions are mutually contingent; 2. a timely capacity to monitor and react to each other's decisions; 3. a strong interest in the long haul; 4. moderate differences between the payoffs for cooperation and defection.

5. See Richard Kimber, "Collective Action and the Fallacy of the Liberal Fallacy" in *World Politics* (January 1981), p. 187. For a brilliant analysis of the provision of collective goods in the absence of a hegemonic power, see Duncan Snidal, "The Limits of Hegemonic Stability Theory," *International Organization*, 39:4(Autumn 1985).

Notes

6. See Howard Raiffa, *The Art and Science of Negotiation* (Cambridge, Mass.: The Belknap Press of Harvard University Press, 1984), chap. 1.

7. Thomas Schelling in *The Strategy of Conflict* [(Oxford: Oxford University Press, 1975), p. 22] writes: "in bargaining, weakness is often strength."

8. This is taken from Elster, p. 19.

9. Richard Cooper, "Prolegomena to the Choice of an International Monetary System" in *International Organization* (Winter 1975), pp. 63–97.

INDEX

Access to world resources in trading system, 23–25, 93–94, 98, 159; tariffs and, 39; *see also* Control

Afghanistan: Soviet Union and, 20, 34–35, 37, 119, 124, 127, 174, 183, 193; Western response to Soviet invasion of, 184

Africa: British holdings in nineteenth century, 92; Cold War and, 70; colonialism and nineteenth century, 95, 98; economic development and twentieth century, 209; nineteenth century, 88, 95; post-World War II, 137; poverty in twentieth century, 180; Soviet penetration of, 119; subdivision of, potential for, 15; superpowers and, 126; U.S. and twentieth century, 118

Alaska, Russian sale of (1867), 192

Alexander I, czar of Russia, 77

Alignment of twentieth-century nations, 127

Alliance networks, post-World War II, 115

American Civil War (1861–1865), 27, 96, 192, 200

American Revolutionary War (1775–1781), 82–84, 92, 94; effects of, 166

Amsterdam, in seventeenth century, 73

Anarchy: international state of nature and, 144; interstate relations and, 23, 235; in Medieval period, 77, 85

Antinuclear campaign, European, 118, 129

Appeasement, 19, 37, 62–63; World War II and German, 134

Apter, David, 224

Arab-Israeli politics, 20, 38, 209

Arab-Israeli War, 9, 33, 116, 133, 174

Arab oil countries, foreign investment in, 148–149

Arab oil embargo (1973–1974), 9–13, 21

Arabs, Yom Kippur War and, 4–5

Areal organization of international politics, 72, 77; *see also* Linear organization

Argentina: British trade with, in nineteenth century, 92; economy of, in twentieth century, 206, 209; foreign debt and twentieth century, 57, 179; income distribution in nineteenth century, 52–53

Arms control, military cost and, 158

Arms race, 117, 128–130, 158, 161–162, 171, 187, 189, 234

Aron, Raymond, 240

Asia: Cold War and, 70; industrial development and nineteenth century, 53; post-World War II, 137; subdivision of, potential for, 15; superpowers and, 126; *see also* East Asia, South Asia, Southeast Asia

Index

of, 61; Leninist view of, 50–53, 61, 140

Caribbean, 7, 209

Carter, President Jimmy, 222; administration of, 129

Catherine II (the Great), 7

Catholic Church, decay of medieval, 74

Catholicism, decline of ecumenical, 67, 77–78

Central America, Soviet aid to, 20; *see also* Latin America, Third World, *specific countries*

Central Europe: post-World War I, 102; Soviet Union and, 127; in twentieth century, 123; in World War II, 113

Chad, Libya, Sudan and, 133

Chamberlain, Prime Minister Neville, 112, 129, 213

Charlemagne, 23

Charles V, Holy Roman Emperor, 7

Charles XII, king of Sweden, 196

Chile, economy of, in twentieth century, 206

China: agricultural development of, in twentieth century, 181; British war with, in nineteenth century, 91; communism in, 114; Cultural Revolution and, 217; defense capability of, in twentieth century, 120; economy of, in twentieth century, 52, 197, 199, 208, 211; Japan and twentieth century, 108, 123, 144, 159; "loss of," 70, 114, 118; in nineteenth century, 99; nuclear capability of, 134; post-World War II, 154; Tibet, occupation of (1950), by, 119; trading system and, 17; Vietnam and, 133; Western influence on, in twentieth century, 186; world GNP and twentieth century, 121–122; Yalta conference and, 119

Chinese-British agreement on Hong Kong, 199

Chinese-Soviet relations, 34, 134, 185, 195

City-states: Renaissance, 72; role of, 169; in sixteenth and seventeenth century, 73; trade and, 242

Colbert, Jean Baptiste, 29

Cold War, 45, 131, 136

Collective action, international politics and, 231

Collective goods, 235–236, 239

Colonialism: Marxist view of, 51; nineteenth century and, 98–99; post-World War II, 138; in twentieth century, 95–96, 127

Command economy, 173–175; *see also* McNeill, William H.

Communications, role of, in trade world, 142, 194

Communism, 114, 162, 182; Chinese, 114; economic growth and, 208; European, 36, 173; war inspired by, 33

Conrad, Joseph, 188

Constant-sum game, 48, 231–232, 241; *see also* Zero-sum game

Containment, 114, 116

Control, 23–25, 39, 93–94, 98, 159

Conventional war, *see* War, conventional

Cooper, Richard, 238

Cooperation among nations, *ix, xi,* 13–14, 26, 46, 49; stability theory and, 57; *see also* Interdependence

"Coordination" game, 238

Corporations, role of, future, 221; *see also* Multinational corporations

Credibility and post-World War II defense, 114, 116

Crimean War (1853–1856), 34, 89–90, 95, 131, 135, 170

Cuban Missile Crisis (1962), 116, 185, 189, 214

Czechoslovakia: post-World War I, 103; Soviet Union and, 35, 49, 116, 183–184; World War II and, 112–113

da Gama, Vasco, 72

Debtors, international, 57

"Decline of the West" theory, 183–184

Decolonialization: Leninist view, 50; post-World War II, 137

Index

Index

Index

Index

10–12, 21, 148–149; prices of, Arab oil embargo and, 73–74; supply of, 11–13

Oil-producing regions, 13

Organization for Economic Cooperation and Development (OECD), 142

Organization of Petroleum Exporting Countries (OPEC), 9–12, 82, 121; Arab foreign investments and, 149

Orwell, George, 14, 171

Pakistan: atomic weapons and, 192, 214; post-World War II, 192

Pakistan-India War, 33, 122–123, 133, 214

Palestine Liberation Organization, 11, 204

Pan-Islamic movement, 168, 192, 204–205

Papacy, 74, 77–80

Pareto Optimality, 234, 238

Paris Peace Conference (1919), 68, 104–105, 126

Peace: as a means of national advancement, 9; movement, 132; theories for achieving international, 100; trade and strategy for, post-World War II, 139–140; in twentieth century, 165, 168–169

Peace of Paris (1783), 82

Peace of Utrecht (1713), 80–82

Peace of Westphalia (1648), 8, 41–42, 78–81

Pearl Harbor, attack on (1941), 108, 111

Persian Gulf, xi, 113; countries of, economic growth of, in twentieth century, 205; oil fields in, 11; Soviet potential for taking over, 193; wars of, in twentieth century, 122

Peru, sixteenth-century Spanish conquest of, 72

Peter I (the Great), 77

Phillip II, king of Spain, 28

Pitt, William, 83

Pitt, William the Elder, 7

PLO, see Palestine Liberation Organization

Poland: post-World War I, 102; Soviet Union and, 35, 193; World War I and, 196; World War II and, 112–113, 159

Political mobilization, and the use of force, 212–213

Population growth: in developing countries, 151; interdependence and, 25

Portugal: in fourteenth century, 72; military-political system and, 160; in seventeenth century, 7, 73

Portuguese Empire, 126

Power, xi, 6; as cause of war, 44–45; distribution of, 45; in dualistic theory, 62; in mercantile world, 7; in realistic theory, 44–45; territorial system and, 16; trading world and, 25; see also Balance of power

Prisoner's Dilemma, 40, 46, 234–235, 237–238

"Project Independence," 9

Property, current status of, 220–221

Protectionism, 213

Protestant Reformation, 8, 26, 74, 118

Prussia, 37, 85, 96; in eighteenth century, 29; industrialization of, 140; in nineteenth century, 8, 26, 87, 118

Prussia-Germany, 91

Punjab, agricultural development and, 181

Reagan, President Ronald: administration of, 129; election of, 223; Grenada and, 202; Soviet pipeline and, 184

Realistic theory of international politics 44–49, 55, 60–61

Rearmament, 117–118, 128–130, 132, 135, 193; of U.S., 201; Western, 184

Recession: international trading system and, 220; in twentieth century, 156, 177

Religious struggles, 80, 85; prospects for, in twentieth century, 205

Index

Index